A Broken Heart Still Beats

A
BROKEN
After
HEART
Your Child
STILL
Dies
BEATS

EDITED BY

ANNE McCRACKEN

AND

MARY SEMEL

INFORMATION & EDUCATIONAL SERVICES

Hazelden
Center City, Minnesota 55012-0176

1-800-328-0094 (Toll Free U.S., Canada, and the Virgin Islands)
1-651-257-1331 (Fax)
www.hazelden.org

Library of Congress Cataloging-in-Publication Data

A broken heart still beats : after your child dies / [edited by]
    Anne McCracken, Mary Semel.
        p.   cm.
    ISBN 1-56838-201-4 (hardcover)
    1. Grief.   2. Bereavement—Psychological aspects.   3. Children—Death—
Psychological aspects.   4. Brothers and sisters—Death—Psychological aspects.
    5. Loss (Psychology)   I. McCracken, Anne, 1948–   . II. Semel, Mary, 1944–   .
BF575.G7B74 1998
155.9′37—dc21
                                                                                98-28450
                                                                                CIP

01 00 99 98   6 5 4 3 2 1

Book design by Will H. Powers
Typesetting by Stanton Publication Services, Inc.
Cover design by David Spohn

IN MEMORY OF

our son Alexander Ward Semel
and young friends
Erik Horne Morstein and Dusty Klein

MS

and
Jake Tyson McCracken
our little Peter Pan

AM

Contents

Chapter 11: Time Moves Differently Now
PAGE 251

Chapter 12: The Legacy of Loss
PAGE 261

INTRODUCTORY NOTES

Acknowledgments

1. Thunderstruck

Stan Rice, "Look!" and "Déjà Vu Again" from *Singing Yet: New and Selected Poems* (New York: Alfred A. Knopf, 1992). © 1992 by Stan Rice. Reprinted with the permission of the author. Raymond Carver, excerpt from "A Small, Good Thing" from *Where I'm Calling From: New and Selected Stories* (Boston: Atlantic Monthly Press, 1988). © 1986, 1987, 1988 by Raymond Carver. Reprinted with the permission of Grove/Atlantic, Inc. Stephen Dixon, excerpt from *Interstate*. © 1995 by Stephen Dixon. Reprinted with the permission of Henry Holt and Company, Inc. and Witherspoon Associates. Robb Forman Dew, excerpt from *Fortunate Lives*. © 1992 by Robb Forman Dew. Reprinted with the permission of William Morrow & Company, Inc. Michael S. Harper, "We Assume: On the Death of Our Son, Reuben Masai Harper" from *Images of Kin: New and Selected Poems*. Originally published in *Quarterly Review of Literature*. © 1970 by Michael S. Harper. Reprinted with the permission of the author and the University of Illinois Press. Reynolds Price, excerpt from *The Promise of Rest*. © 1995 by Reynolds Price. Reprinted with the permission of Scribner, a division of Simon & Schuster. Bharati Mukherjee, excerpt from "The Management of Grief" from *The Middleman and Other Stories,* as it appears in *The Best American Short Stories 1989,* edited by Margaret Atwood with Shannon Ravenel. © 1988 by Bharati Mukherjee. Reprinted with the permission of Grove/Atlantic, Inc. Jane Kenyon, "The Sandy Hole" from *Otherwise: New and Selected Poems*. © 1996 by the Estate of Jane Kenyon. Reprinted with the permission of Graywolf Press, Saint Paul, Minnesota. Bret Lott, excerpt from *Reed's Beach*. © 1993 by Bret Lott. Reprinted with the permission of Pocket Books, a division of Simon & Schuster. Walter Pavlich, "On the Life and Death of Stan Laurel's Son" from *Manoa,* as it appears in *The Pushcart Prize XV: Best of the Small Presses,* edited by Bill Henderson. Reprinted with the permission of the author. Naguib Mahfouz, excerpt from *Palace Walk,* translated by William Maynard Hutchins and Olive E. Kenny. © 1990 by the American University in Cairo Press. Reprinted with the permission of Doubleday, a division of Bantam Doubleday Dell Publishing Group, Inc.

2. What Kind of Universe Is This Anyway?

Raymond P. Scheindlin, translator, excerpt from *The Book of Job*. © 1998 by Raymond P. Scheindlin. Reprinted with the permission of W. W. Norton & Company, Inc. Fyodor Dostoevsky, excerpt from *The Brothers Karamazov*. A Norton Critical Edition, edited by Ralph E. Matlaw, translated by Constance Garnett, revised by Ralph E. Matlaw. Translation © 1976 by W. W. Norton & Company, Inc. Reprinted with the permission of W. W. Norton & Company, Inc. John Irving, excerpt from *The World According to Garp*. © 1978 by Garp Enterprises Ltd. Reprinted with the permission of Dutton, a division of Penguin Putnam Inc., and the author c/o The Turnbull Agency, Inc. Albert Camus, excerpt

___

from *The Plague*, translated by Stuart Gilbert. © 1948 by Stuart Gilbert. Reprinted with the permission of Alfred A. Knopf, Inc. Peter De Vries, excerpt from *The Blood of the Lamb* (Boston: Little, Brown and Company, 1961). © 1961 by Peter De Vries. Reprinted with the permission of the Estate of Peter De Vries and the Watkins/Loomis Agency, Inc. Frank Deford, excerpt from *Alex: The Life of a Child* (New York: Viking Penguin, 1983). © 1983 by Frank Deford. Reprinted with the permission of Sterling Lord Literistic, Inc. Mary Ann Taylor-Hall, excerpt from *Come and Go, Molly Snow*. © 1995 by Mary Ann Taylor-Hall. Reprinted with the permission of W. W. Norton & Company, Inc.

3. A Storm in the Heart: Pain and Despair

Ann K. Finkbeiner, excerpt from *After the Death of a Child: Living with Loss Through the Years.* © 1995 by Ann K. Finkbeiner. Reprinted with the permission of The Free Press, a division of Simon & Schuster. Gordon Livingston, excerpt from *Only Spring: On Mourning the Death of My Son,* with a foreword by Mark Helprin. © 1995 by Gordon Livingston, M.D. Reprinted with the permission of HarperCollins Publishers, Inc. Jan Kochanowski, "Lament 1" from *Laments,* translated by Stanislaw Baranczak and Seamus Heaney. Translation © 1996 by Stanislaw Baranczak and Seamus Heaney. Reprinted with the permission of Farrar, Straus & Giroux, Inc. Nicholas Wolterstorff, excerpt from *Lament for a Son*. © 1987 by the Wm. B. Eerdmans Publishing Co. Reprinted with the permission of the Wm. B. Eerdmans Publishing Co. Paula Trachtman, excerpt from "An Absence of Amy" from *Out of Season: An Anthology of Work by and about Young People Who Died,* edited by Paula Trachtman (Amagansett, N.Y.: The Amagansett Press, 1983). Reprinted with the permission of the author and The Amagansett Press. Jane Kenyon, "Now Where?" from *Otherwise: New and Selected Poems.* © 1996 by the Estate of Jane Kenyon. Reprinted with the permission of Graywolf Press, Saint Paul, Minnesota. Tom Crider, excerpt from *Give Sorrow Words: A Father's Passage through Grief.* © 1996 by Tom Crider. Reprinted with the permission of Algonquin Books of Chapel Hill, a division of Workman Publishing. Eric Clapton, "Tears in Heaven." Words and music by Eric Clapton and Will Jennings. © 1992 by E. C. Music Ltd. and Blue Sky Rider Songs. All rights for E. C. Music Ltd. Administered by Unichappell Music Inc. International copyright secured. All rights reserved. Reprinted with the permission of the Hal Leonard Corporation. C. S. Lewis, excerpt from *A Grief Observed.* © 1961 by C. S. Lewis Pte. Ltd. Reprinted with the permission of Curtis Brown, London. J. D. McClatchy, excerpt from "Fog Tropes" from *The Rest of the Way* (New York: Alfred A. Knopf, 1990), as it appears in *Poets for Life: Seventy-Six Poets Respond to AIDS,* edited by Michael Klein. © 1990 by J. D. McClatchy. Reprinted with the permission of the author. Rita Dove, "Demeter Mourning" from *Mother Love: Poems.* © 1995 by Rita Dove. Reprinted with the permission of W. W. Norton & Company, Inc. Anne Morrow Lindbergh, excerpt from *Hour of Gold, Hour of Lead: Diaries and Letters of Anne Morrow Lindbergh 1929–1932.* © 1973 by Anne Morrow Lindbergh. Reprinted with the permission of Harcourt Brace & Company. Stéphane Mallarmé, excerpt from *A Tomb for Anatole,* translated by Paul Auster (San Francisco: North Point Press, 1983). © 1983 by Paul Auster. Reprinted with the permission of the Carol Mann Agency. John Tittensor, excerpt from *Year One: A Record* (Fitzroy, Australia: McPhee Gribble Publishers, 1986). © 1985 by John Tittensor. Reprinted with the permission of the author. Jim Simmerman, "Child's Grave, Hale County, Alabama" from *Once Out of Nature* (Sparks, Md.: The Galileo Press, 1989), as it appears in *The Bread Loaf Anthology of Contemporary American Poetry,* edited by Robert Pack, Sydney Lea, and Jay Parini. Reprinted with the permission of the author. Russell Banks, excerpt from *The Sweet*

Hereafter. © 1991 by Russell Banks. Reprinted with the permission of HarperCollins Publishers, Inc. and the Ellen Levine Literary Agency, Inc. Fyodor Dostoevsky, excerpt from *The Brothers Karamazov.* A Norton Critical Edition, edited by Ralph E. Matlaw, translated by Constance Garnett, revised by Ralph E. Matlaw. Translation © 1976 by W. W. Norton & Company, Inc. Reprinted with the permission of W. W. Norton & Company, Inc. W. H. Auden, "Musée des Beaux Arts" from *W. H. Auden: Collected Poems,* edited by Edward Mendelson, as it appears in *The Norton Anthology of Poetry,* 4th ed., edited by Margaret Ferguson, Mary Jo Salter, and Jon Stallworthy. © 1940, renewed 1968 by W. H. Auden. Reprinted with the permission of Random House, Inc.

4. A Storm in the Heart: Anger and Guilt

Anne Tyler, excerpt from *The Accidental Tourist.* © 1985 by Anne Tyler Modarressi. Reprinted with the permission of Alfred A. Knopf, Inc. C. J. Hribal, excerpt from "The Clouds in Memphis" from *TriQuarterly* (spring/summer 1995). © 1995 by C. J. Hribal. Reprinted with the permission of the author. Susan Cohen, excerpt from "Rage Makes Me Strong" from *Time* (July 29, 1996). Reprinted with the permission of the author. John Walsh with Susan Schindehette, excerpt from *Tears of Rage: From Grieving Father to Crusader for Justice, the Untold Story of the Adam Walsh Case.* © 1997 by John Walsh. Reprinted with the permission of Pocket Books, a division of Simon & Schuster. Robert Harling, excerpt from *Steel Magnolias.* © 1988 by Robert Harling. The reprinting of *Steel Magnolias* included in this volume is reprinted by permission of the author and Dramatists Play Service, Inc. The stock and amateur stage performance rights in this play are controlled exclusively by Dramatists Play Service, Inc., 440 Park Avenue South, New York, N.Y. 10016. No professional or nonprofessional production of the play may be given without obtaining, in advance, the written permission of the Dramatists Play Service, Inc., and paying the requisite fee. Inquiries regarding all other rights should be addressed to Chuck Googe, Esq., c/o Paul, Weiss, Rifkind, Wharton & Garrison, 1285 Avenue of the Americas, New York, N.Y. 10019. Stephen B. Oates, excerpt from *William Faulkner: The Man and the Artist.* © 1987 by Stephen B. Oates. Reprinted with the permission of HarperCollins Publishers, Inc. Christopher Hitchens, excerpt from "Young Men and War" from *Vanity Fair* (February 1997). © 1997 by Christopher Hitchens. Reprinted with the permission of the author. George McGovern, excerpt from *Terry: My Daughter's Life-and-Death Struggle with Alcoholism.* © 1996 by George McGovern. Reprinted with the permission of Villard Books, a division of Random House, Inc. John Edgar Wideman, excerpt from "Welcome" from *The Stories of John Edgar Wideman.* © 1992 by John Edgar Wideman. Reprinted with the permission of Pantheon Books, a division of Random House, Inc. Barbara Lazear Ascher, excerpt from *Landscape Without Gravity: A Memoir of Grief* (New York: Penguin Books, 1994). © 1992 by Barbara Lazear Ascher. Reprinted with the permission of the author. Ann K. Finkbeiner, excerpt from *After the Death of a Child: Living with Loss Through the Years.* © 1995 by Ann K. Finkbeiner. Reprinted with the permission of The Free Press, a division of Simon & Schuster. Frances Gunther, excerpt from "A Word From Frances" from *Death Be Not Proud: A Memoir* by John Gunther. © 1949 by John Gunther, renewed 1976 by Jane Perry Gunther. Reprinted with the permission of HarperCollins Publishers, Inc. Judith Guest, excerpt from *Ordinary People.* © 1976 by Judith Guest. Reprinted with the permission of Viking Penguin, a division of Penguin Putnam Inc., and the Patricia Karlan Agency. Anne Rivers Siddons, excerpt from *Outer Banks.* © 1991 by Anne Rivers Siddons. Reprinted with the permission of HarperCollins Publishers, Inc.

5. Parents, Lost in the Storm Together

Lynn Darling, excerpt from "For Better and Worse" from *Esquire* (May 1996). Reprinted with the permission of Sterling Lord Literistic, Inc. Anne Rivers Siddons, excerpt from *Outer Banks.* © 1991 by Anne Rivers Siddons. Reprinted with the permission of HarperCollins Publishers, Inc. Nicholas Wolterstorff, excerpt from *Lament for a Son.* © 1987 by the Wm. B. Eerdmans Publishing Co. Reprinted with the permission of the Wm. B. Eerdmans Publishing Co. Gwendolyn Parker, excerpt from *These Same Long Bones.* © 1994 by Gwendolyn Parker. Reprinted with the permission of Houghton Mifflin Company. All rights reserved. Anne Morrow Lindbergh, excerpt from *Hour of Gold, Hour of Lead: Diaries and Letters of Anne Morrow Lindbergh 1929–1932.* © 1973 by Anne Morrow Lindbergh. Reprinted with the permission of Harcourt Brace & Company. Ian McEwan, excerpt from *The Child in Time* (Boston: Houghton Mifflin Company, 1987). © 1987 by Ian McEwan. Reprinted with the permission of Georges Borchardt, Inc. on behalf of the author. Robert Frost, "Home Burial" from *The Poetry of Robert Frost: The Collected Poems, Complete and Unabridged,* edited by Edward Connery Lathem. Copyright 1942, © 1958 by Robert Frost, © 1967, 1970 by Lesley Frost Ballantine, Copyright 1930, 1939, © 1969 by Henry Holt and Company, Inc., © 1997 by Edward Connery Lathem. Reprinted with the permission of Henry Holt and Company, Inc. Richard Ford, excerpt from *The Sportswriter.* © 1996 by Richard Ford. Reprinted with the permission of Alfred A. Knopf, Inc. Patricia Neal, excerpt from *As I Am: An Autobiography.* © 1988 by Patricia Neal. Reprinted with the permission of Simon & Schuster. Stan Rice, "Singing Death" from *Singing Yet: New and Selected Poems* (New York: Alfred A. Knopf, 1992). © 1992 by Stan Rice. Reprinted with the permission of the author. Antonya Nelson, excerpt from "Mud Season" from *Prairie Schooner* (1989). © 1989 by Antonya Nelson. Reprinted with the permission of the author. Elizabeth Glaser and Laura Palmer, excerpt from *In the Absence of Angels.* © 1991 by Elizabeth Glaser. Reprinted with the permission of The Putnam Publishing Group. John Irving, excerpt from *The World According to Garp.* © 1978 by Garp Enterprises Ltd. Reprinted with the permission of Dutton, a division of Penguin Putnam Inc., and the author c/o The Turnbull Agency, Inc. Robb Forman Dew, excerpt from *Fortunate Lives.* © 1992 by Robb Forman Dew. Reprinted with the permission of William Morrow & Company, Inc.

6. Sisters and Brothers Grieve Too

Jill Ker Conway, excerpt from *The Road from Coorain.* © 1989 by Jill Ker Conway. Reprinted with the permission of Alfred A. Knopf, Inc. Wallace Stegner, excerpt from *The Big Rock Candy Mountain.* © 1938, 1940, 1942, and 1943 by Wallace Stegner. Reprinted with the permission of Doubleday, a division of Bantam Doubleday Dell Publishing Group, Inc. Patricia Neal, excerpt from *As I Am: An Autobiography.* © 1988 by Patricia Neal. Reprinted with the permission of Simon & Schuster. Jacquelyn Mitchard, excerpt from *The Deep End of the Ocean.* © 1996 by Jacquelyn Mitchard. Reprinted with the permission of Viking Penguin, a division of Penguin Putnam Inc. Ursula Hegi, excerpt from *Floating in My Mother's Palm.* © 1990 by Ursula Hegi. Reprinted with the permission of Simon & Schuster. Stephen Dixon, excerpt from *Interstate.* © 1995 by Stephen Dixon. Reprinted with the permission of Henry Holt and Company, Inc. and Witherspoon Associates. Debra Spark, excerpt from "Last Things" from *Ploughshares* (fall 1994). © 1994 by Debra Spark. Reprinted with the permission of the author. Sapphire, "where jimi is" from *American Dreams* (New York: Vintage Books, 1996). Originally published New York: High Risk Books/Serpent's Tail, 1994. Reprinted with the permission of the Charlotte Sheedy Literary Agency, Inc. Laura Wexler, excerpt from "I'm Still Here" (previously unpublished). Reprinted with the permission of the author. Maxine Kumin, "Man of Many L's" from *Our Ground Time Here Will Be Brief* (New York: Viking Penguin, 1982). © 1982 by Maxine Kumin. Reprinted with the permission of the author. David Mason, "A Motion We Cannot See" from *The Country I Remember: Poems* (Brownsville, Oreg.: Story Line Press, 1996). Originally published in *The American Scholar* (spring 1996). © 1996 by David Mason. Reprinted with the permission of the author. Richard Hoffman, excerpt from *Half the House: A Memoir.* © 1995 by Richard Hoffman. Reprinted with the permission of Harcourt Brace & Company.

7. Especially Bad Days
Nicholas Wolterstorff, excerpt from *Lament For a Son.* © 1987 by the Wm. B. Eerdmans Publishing Co. Reprinted with the permission of the Wm. B. Eerdmans Publishing Co. Gwendolyn Parker, excerpt from *These Same Long Bones.* © 1994 by Gwendolyn Parker. Reprinted with the permission of Houghton Mifflin Company. All rights reserved. Stan Rice, "First Xmas after DaughterDeath, 1972" from *Singing Yet: New and Selected Poems* (New York: Alfred A. Knopf, 1992). © 1992 by Stan Rice. Reprinted with the permission of the author. John Edgar Wideman, excerpt from "Welcome" from *The Stories of John Edgar Wideman.* © 1992 by John Edgar Wideman. Reprinted with the permission of Pantheon Books, a division of Random House, Inc. Richard Ford, excerpt from *The Sportswriter.* © 1996 by Richard Ford. Reprinted with the permission of Alfred A. Knopf, Inc.

8. Complicated Loss
John Conrad Sr., "John Conrad Jr. (1979–1993)" from *Journal of Child Neurology* 1995, 10:270, as it appears in *The Book of Eulogies: A Collection of Memorial Tributes, Poetry, Essays, and Letters of Condolence,* edited by Phyllis Theroux (New York: Scribner, 1997). Reprinted with the permission of Decker Periodicals and the author. Daniel Spurr, excerpt from *Steered by the Falling Stars: A Father's Journey* (Camden, Maine: Ragged Mountain Press, 1992). © 1992 by Daniel Spurr. Reprinted with the permission of the author. Dan Chaon, excerpt from "Fitting Ends" from *Fitting Ends and Other Stories* (Evanston, Ill.: TriQuarterly Books/Northwestern University Press, 1995). First published in *TriQuarterly.* © 1995 by Dan Chaon. Reprinted with the permission of Northwestern University Press and the author. All rights reserved. George McGovern, excerpt from *Terry: My Daughter's Life-and-Death Struggle with Alcoholism.* © 1996 by George McGovern. Reprinted with the permission of Villard Books, a division of Random House, Inc. Nina Bawden, excerpt from *In My Own Time: Almost an Autobiography.* © 1994 by Nina Bawden. Reprinted with the permission of Clarion Books/Houghton Mifflin Company and Curtis Brown, Ltd. All rights reserved. Gordon Livingston, excerpt from *Only Spring: On Mourning the Death of My Son,* with a foreword by Mark Helprin. © 1995 by Gordon Livingston, M.D. Reprinted with the permission of HarperCollins Publishers, Inc. Jennifer Egan, excerpt from *The Invisible Circus.* © 1995 by Jennifer Egan. Reprinted with the permission of Doubleday, a division of Bantam Doubleday Dell Publishing Group, Inc. and Pan Books, a division of Macmillan Publishers, Ltd. Robert Lowell, "Robert Frost" from *History,* as it appears in *Selected Poems.* © 1973 by Robert Lowell. Reprinted with the permission of Farrar, Straus & Giroux, Inc. Mark Doty, "Bill's Story" from *My Alexandria* (Champaign, Ill.: University of Illinois Press, 1993), as it appears in *Poets for Life: Seventy-Six Poets Respond to AIDS,* edited by Michael Klein (New York: Crown Publishers, 1989). © 1993 by Mark Doty. Reprinted with the permission of the author and the University of Illinois Press. Marcie Hershman, excerpt from *Safe in America.* © 1995 by Marcie Hershman. Reprinted with the permission of HarperCollins Publishers, Inc. Abraham Verghese, excerpt from *My Own Country: A Doctor's Story*

of a Town and Its People in the Age of AIDS. © 1994 by Abraham Verghese. Reprinted with the permission of Simon & Schuster. Rick Barrett, excerpt from "Running Shoes" from *Best American Gay Fiction 1996,* edited by Brian Bouldrey (Boston: Little, Brown and Company, 1996). Reprinted with the permission of the author.

9. We Feel Like Aliens in the World

C. S. Lewis, excerpt from *A Grief Observed.* © 1961 by C. S. Lewis Pte. Ltd. Reprinted with the permission of Curtis Brown, London. C. J. Hribal, excerpt from "The Clouds in Memphis" from *TriQuarterly* (spring/summer 1995). © 1995 by C. J. Hribal. Reprinted with the permission of the author. Sue Grafton, excerpt from *"K" Is for Killer.* © 1994 by Sue Grafton. Reprinted with the permission of Henry Holt and Company, Inc. and the Aaron M. Priest Literary Agency, Inc. Russell Banks, excerpt from *The Sweet Hereafter.* © 1991 by Russell Banks. Reprinted with the permission of HarperCollins Publishers, Inc. and the Ellen Levine Literary Agency, Inc. Shelly Wagner, "Andrew and Thomas" from *The Andrew Poems.* © 1994 by Shelly Wagner, Texas Tech University Press. Reprinted with the permission of Texas Tech University Press. Anne Tyler, excerpt from *The Accidental Tourist.* © 1985 by Anne Tyler Modarressi. Reprinted with the permission of Alfred A. Knopf, Inc. William Styron, excerpt from *Sophie's Choice.* © 1979 by William Styron. Reprinted with the permission of Random House, Inc. John Tittensor, excerpt from *Year One: A Record* (Fitzroy, Australia: McPhee Gribble Publishers, 1986). © 1985 by John Tittensor. Reprinted with the permission of the author. Tom Crider, excerpt from *Give Sorrow Words: A Father's Passage through Grief.* © 1996 by Tom Crider. Reprinted with the permission of Algonquin Books of Chapel Hill, a division of Workman Publishing. Rev. William Sloane Coffin, excerpt from "Alex's Death" from *The Book of Eulogies: A Collection of Memorial Tributes, Poetry, Essays, and Letters of Condolence,* edited by Phyllis Theroux (New York: Scribner, 1997). Reprinted with the permission of the author. Bret Lott, excerpt from *Reed's Beach.* © 1993 by Bret Lott. Reprinted with the permission of Pocket Books, a division of Simon & Schuster. Antonya Nelson, excerpt from "Mud Season" from *Prairie Schooner* (1989). © 1989 by Antonya Nelson. Reprinted with the permission of the author. Mary Ann Taylor-Hall, excerpt from *Come and Go, Molly Snow.* © 1995 by Mary Ann Taylor-Hall. Reprinted with the permission of W. W. Norton & Company, Inc. Stephen Dobyns, "Spider Web" from *Cemetery Nights,* as it appears in *The Bread Loaf Anthology of Contemporary American Poetry,* edited by Robert Pack, Sydney Lea, and Jay Parini. © 1987 by Stephen Dobyns. Reprinted with the permission the author and Viking Penguin, a division of Penguin Putnam Inc. Judith Guest, excerpt from *Ordinary People.* © 1976 by Judith Guest. Reprinted with the permission of Viking Penguin, a division of Penguin Putnam Inc., and the Patricia Karlan Agency.

10. A Fire in the Mind: Memories, Dreams, Fantasies

William Stafford, "For a Lost Child" and "Going On" from *Passwords: A Program of Words* (New York: HarperCollins Publishers, 1991). © 1991 by William Stafford. Reprinted with the permission of the Estate of William Stafford. Randall Jarrell, "The Lost Children" from *The Complete Poems,* as it appears in *Selected Poems,* edited by William H. Pritchard. © 1969 by Mrs. Randall Jarrell. Reprinted with the permission of Farrar, Straus & Giroux, Inc. Anne Tyler, excerpt from *The Accidental Tourist.* © 1985 by Anne Tyler Modarressi. Reprinted with the permission of Alfred A. Knopf, Inc. Shelly Wagner, "Faded" from *The Andrew Poems.* © 1994 by Shelly Wagner, Texas Tech University Press. Reprinted with the permission of Texas Tech University Press. Norman Maclean, excerpt from *Young Men and Fire.* © 1992 by The University of Chicago. Reprinted with the permission of The University of Chicago

Press. Robb Forman Dew, excerpt from *Fortunate Lives*. © 1992 by Robb Forman Dew. Reprinted with the permission of William Morrow & Company, Inc. Jill Ker Conway, excerpt from *The Road from Coorain*. © 1989 by Jill Ker Conway. Reprinted with the permission of Alfred A. Knopf, Inc. Laura Kalpakian, excerpt from "The Battle of Manila" from *Dark Continent and Other Stories* (New York: Viking Press, 1989). © 1989 by Laura Kalpakian. Reprinted with the permission of the author. Cynthia Ozick, excerpt from *The Shawl*. © 1980, 1983 by Cynthia Ozick. Reprinted with the permission of Alfred A. Knopf, Inc. Anne Morrow Lindbergh, excerpt from *Hour of Gold, Hour of Lead: Diaries and Letters of Anne Morrow Lindbergh 1929–1932*. © 1973 by Anne Morrow Lindbergh. Reprinted with the permission of Harcourt Brace & Company. Mark Twain, excerpt from *Papa: An Intimate Biography of Mark Twain* by Susy Clemens, edited by Charles Neider (New York: Doubleday, 1985).© 1985 by Charles Neider. Reprinted with the permission of Charles Neider. Richard Hoffman, excerpt from *Half the House: A Memoir*. © 1995 by Richard Hoffman. Reprinted with the permission of Harcourt Brace & Company.

11. Time Moves Differently Now

Sydney Lea, excerpt from "After Labor Day" from *No Sign*, as it appears in *The Bread Loaf Anthology of Contemporary American Poetry*, edited by Robert Pack, Sydney Lea, and Jay Parini. © 1987 by Sydney Lea. Reprinted with the permission of the author and The University of Georgia Press. John Edgar Wideman, excerpt from "Welcome" from *The Stories of John Edgar Wideman*. © 1992 by John Edgar Wideman. Reprinted with the permission of Pantheon Books, a division of Random House, Inc. Norman Maclean, excerpt from *Young Men and Fire*. © 1992 by The University of Chicago. Reprinted with the permission of The University of Chicago Press. John Irving, excerpt from *The World According to Garp*. © 1978 by Garp Enterprises Ltd. Reprinted with the permission of Dutton, a division of Penguin Putnam Inc., and the author c/o The Turnbull Agency, Inc. Kenneth Rexroth, translator, "The Mother of the Commander Michitsuna" from *One Hundred Poems from the Japanese*. © New Directions Publishing Corp. Reprinted with the permission of the New Directions Publishing Corp. All rights reserved. Judith Guest, excerpt from *Ordinary People*. © 1976 by Judith Guest. Reprinted with the permission of Viking Penguin, a division of Penguin Putnam Inc., and the Patricia Karlan Agency. W. D. Ehrhart, ". . . the light that cannot fade . . ." from *The Outer Banks & Other Poems* (Easthampton, Mass.: Adastra Press, 1984), as it appears in *Out of Sesason: An Anthology of Work by and about Young People Who Died*, edited by Paula Trachtman (Amagansett, N.Y.: The Amagansett Press, 1983). Reprinted with the permission of the author. Thomas Wolfe, excerpt from "The Lost Boy" from *The Hills Beyond* (New York: Harper & Brothers, 1941), as it appears in *Literature: Structure, Sound, and Sense*, edited by Laurence Perrine. © 1964. Reprinted with the permission of Paul Gitlin, Administrator, C.T.A. of the Estate of Thomas Wolfe.

12. The Legacy of Loss

Shelly Wagner, "Your Questions" from *The Andrew Poems*. © 1994 by Shelly Wagner, Texas Tech University Press. Reprinted with the permission of Texas Tech University Press. Lucille Clifton, "For deLawd" from *Good Woman: Poems and a Memoir 1969–1980*. © 1987 by Lucille Clifton. Reprinted with the permission of BOA Editions, Ltd., 260 East Ave., Rochester NY 14604. Robert Frost, "Never Again Would Birds' Song Be the Same" from *The Poetry of Robert Frost: The Collected Poems, Complete and Unabridged*, edited by Edward Connery Lathem. Copyright 1942, © 1958 by Robert Frost, © 1967, 1970 by Lesley Frost Ballantine, Copyright 1930, 1939, © 1969 by Henry Holt and Company, Inc., © 1997 by

Edward Connery Lathem. Reprinted with the permission of Henry Holt and Company, Inc. John Tittensor, excerpt from *Year One: A Record* (Fitzroy, Australia: McPhee Gribble Publishers, 1986). © 1985 by John Tittensor. Reprinted with the permission of the author. Anna Quindlen, excerpt from "Life After Death" from the *New York Times* (May 4, 1994). © 1994 by the New York Times Co. Reprinted with the permission of the New York Times Co. Edna St. Vincent Millay, "Read history: thus learn how small a space" from *Collected Poems*, edited by Norma Millay. © 1954, 1982 by Norma Millay Ellis. Reprinted with the permission of Elizabeth Barnett, literary executor. All rights reserved. Tom Crider, excerpt from *Give Sorrow Words: A Father's Passage through Grief.* © 1996 by Tom Crider. Reprinted with the permission of Algonquin Books of Chapel Hill, a division of Workman Publishing. Katy Butler, excerpt from "Around the Network." This article first appeared in *The Family Therapy Networker* (May/June 1995). Reprinted with the permission of *The Family Therapy Networker*. Rita Dove, "Lamentations" from *Mother Love: Poems.* © 1995 by Rita Dove. Reprinted with the permission of W. W. Norton & Company, Inc. Frances Gunther, excerpt from "A Word From Frances" from *Death Be Not Proud: A Memoir* by John Gunther. © 1949 by John Gunther, renewed 1976 by Jane Perry Gunther. Reprinted with the permission of HarperCollins Publishers, Inc. Peter De Vries, excerpt from *The Blood of the Lamb* (Boston: Little, Brown and Company, 1961). © 1961 by Peter De Vries. Reprinted with the permission of the Estate of Peter De Vries and the Watkins/Loomis Agency, Inc. Homer, excerpt from *The Iliad of Homer*, translated by Richmond Lattimore. © 1951 by The University of Chicago, renewed 1979 by Richmond Lattimore. Reprinted with the permission of The University of Chicago Press. Norman Maclean, excerpt from *Young Men and Fire.* © 1992 by The University of Chicago. Reprinted with the permission of The University of Chicago Press. WilliamStafford, "Consolations" and "Yes" from *Passwords: A Program of Words* (New York: HarperCollins Publishers, 1991). © 1991 by William Stafford. Reprinted with the permission of the Estate of William Stafford.

Introduction

When Mary and I met, we had two things in common: we had lost our sons and we had lost our way. Over and over we'd wandered the trails of sadness, anger, and guilt, hoping to come upon a new vista or fork that would lead us . . . who knows where, but somewhere different. Like Peter Matthiessen, explaining his own search for answers in *The Snow Leopard*, we too "only knew that at the bottom of each breath there was a hollow place that needed to be filled."

Readers, both of us, we first tried grief self-help books—and indeed, one or two can be ice water for the thirsty, especially early in mourning. But we were beyond that. We needed more sustenance than inspiration. Memoirs too proved limiting. Some are quite wonderful; we've taken excerpts from them. But ultimately, they're about one family, one child, one death. Our questions were bigger than that.

So, independently, we turned to literature. And specifically to writers who had hiked this territory before us, explored it thoroughly, and come back with nuggets of gold. It was one thing to find comfort in other bereaved parents who now shared a common vocabulary. It was quite another to read the thoughts of true wordsmiths, writers by trade. Eschewing the clichés of grief, they purposely wrestled with words to *say* something, something that often went beyond or contradicted easy thinking. We learned from them. Sometimes their observations were so on target it took our breath away. We finally had words for what we were experiencing—the right words.

And without intending to, we had started a book. A book we wish had been on the shelves when we needed it. We'd read general grief anthologies, and they had proved helpful. But losing a child is different from losing a parent, spouse, or lover. So while those anthologies were travel guides for the country we were plodding through, they were not for the specific canyons in which we found ourselves trapped.

In contrast, our book focuses exclusively on mourning the death of a child or sibling. Many of our writers have lost their own children. William Shakespeare, Isabel Allende, Fyodor Dostoevsky, and Anne Morrow Lindbergh come to mind. It also turns out that numerous writers, although untouched by this loss themselves, have chosen to tackle the subject that brings parents to their knees. Writers like Anne Tyler, Reynolds Price, Russell Banks, and Stephen Dixon are just a few.

In addition, Mary and I introduce many of the chapters with reflections of our own. Neither of us dares claim Albert Camus or Archibald MacLeish as peers. But as grieving mothers—one a psychiatric social worker, the other a former journalist—we too had something to say. Reluctant experts, we knew this pain as well as anyone.

So if a poem or passage spoke to our hearts, we included it. If it was bitter, dark, and despairing, we did not shy away. We trusted our own experiences. We wanted inspiration; we wanted permission to hope. But we *craved* validation of our feelings. We hope that this book, with its full choir of voices, offers all of that.

Mary and I have come to believe that comfort, such as it is, derives from recognizing that others before us, many others, have felt this very pain, struggled with the same questions, and reluctantly given up the lives they too had counted on. In this sense, misery does love company. It's not that we'd wish this pain on anyone, not Winston Churchill or Samuel Clemens, who both lost daughters; or Robert Frost, who, incredibly, lost *four* of his six children. However, we do welcome the painful truth that they were once as devastated as we, and yet found the courage to stay productive in this world. That Robert Frost got out of bed every morning, let alone wrote notable poetry, is nothing short of inspiring. And it's this kind of inspiration— inspiration by example—that proved most healing for us.

Grief books usually offer *one* authoritative voice, often that of a therapist, minister, or rabbi. This book offers dozens of voices, which echoed our own despair and anger. We were grateful to hear others express, and express so well, their feelings of alienation, and their guilt for being alive when their children aren't. They confirmed for us that mourning is indeed a solitary business, even between spouses. And they reminded us of the magnificence of mankind—though grievously sad, we can still enjoy a sunset.

Like young children who lie awake in their beds at night, fearful of the silence, Mary and I had started off feeling alone. But just as children draw comfort from their tape players, filling their bedrooms with sound, we found comfort in the voices of other writers. The darkness still enveloped us, but we now had company. Good company. And if they could make it through the night, so could we.

ANNE McCRACKEN, 1998

A Broken Heart Still Beats

1

Thunderstruck

The forty-year-old woman squeezed the last suitcase into her car trunk, got into the driver's seat, and reached back to check her son's seat belt. Her mother, their grandmother, kissed her good-bye, then the children, and waved to them until the car disappeared. Hardly a mile down the road, Jake, almost six, was already half shouting, half singing "Chicken Lips and Lizard Hips" as a young man in a heavy pickup truck blacked out at the wheel. His truck hurtled across the center line and hit the car. Forty minutes later, Jake was dead, his mother was in surgery, and his sister, Hollis, two and a half, was sitting in her grandmother's lap, asking, "Gam, where are they?"

I am that mother. Eight hours of surgery. My heart mocked me; I did not die.

"The children? Are they all right?" I later pleaded. My husband fed me the truth, like bitter quinine to a malaria patient. It might kill me, but it had to be given.

My heart mocked me; I did not die. And I did not care.

ANNE

These days I try to keep as busy as I can. Although Allie constantly hovers in my thoughts, I don't often replay the accident in my mind. Then sometimes, for no reason I can discern, a mental switch is flicked, and image after image reels through my head like a home movie. Only this is a horror movie.

The phone rings. A friend tells me she's heard that Allie has had an accident. She thinks he's okay, but the car is not. Peter and I drive madly up Greenspring Avenue. Our son is in trouble. We have to go to him.

An orange barricade blocks Old Court Road. A fire truck emerges. I think, *This looks serious.*

Beyond the barricade, there is a crowd and a lot of vehicles. We get out of the car and people in uniforms approach.

"Your son is deceased."

Deceased? I don't understand. What does this mean? Deceased?

I gather myself. I have to get to Allie. I have to be with my son.

They try to restrain me, but I insist.

The blue car is wrapped around a tree. Under a tarp, two slender bodies stretch side by side. My sweet son lies, lips parted innocently, as if he were asleep, except his face has a mottled pallor and blood oozes from his nose. My precious child, my love, my heart. I touch a freckle on his finger.

Many times in the next weeks I return to that tree—the place where Allie left us. Shards of broken glass lie around. My life is shattered too. Shell shocked, I pick up fragments here and there, trying to find some that fit together, then I let them drop. How can I patch a life when my heart is smashed?

MARY

HOW DO WE HEAR THIS AND LIVE?

MARK TWAIN

After finishing an around-the-world speaking tour, Samuel Clemens (Mark Twain) was in England, standing in his dining room, "thinking of nothing in particular," when he was handed a cablegram. It read: "Susy [his twenty-four-year-old daughter, still in America] was peacefully released to-day." Almost ten years later, he still marveled.

from *The Autobiography of Mark Twain*

It is one of the mysteries of our nature that a man, all unprepared, can receive a thunder-stroke like that and live. There is but one reasonable explanation of it. The intellect is stunned by the shock and but gropingly gathers the meaning of the words. The power to realize their full import is mercifully wanting. The mind has a dumb sense of vast loss—that is all. It will take mind and memory months and possibly years to gather together the details and thus learn and know the whole extent of the loss. A man's house burns down. The smoking wreckage represents only a ruined home that was dear through years of use and pleasant associations. By and by, as the days and weeks go on, first he misses this, then that, then the other thing. And when he casts about for it he finds that it was in that house. Always it is an *essential*—there was but one of its kind. It cannot be replaced.

Thirteen years after Susy's death from meningitis and five and a half after his wife, Livy, died, Clemens was at home when his twenty-nine-year-old daughter Jean died from an epileptic convulsion and heart failure while in her bath.

from "The Death of Jean," in *Harper's Monthly Magazine*, January 1911

About three in the morning, while wandering about the house in the deep silences, as one does in times like these, when there is a dumb sense that something has been lost that will never be found again, yet must be sought, if only for the employment the useless seeking gives, I came upon Jean's dog in the hall down-stairs, and noted that he did not spring to greet me, according to his hospitable habit, but came slow and sorrowfully; also I remembered that he had not visited Jean's apartment since the tragedy. Poor fellow, did he know? I think so. . . .

Christmas Night.—This afternoon they took her away from her room. As soon as I might, I went down to the library, and there she lay, in her coffin, dressed in exactly the same clothes she wore when she stood at the other end of the same room on the 6th of October last, as Clara's chief bridesmaid. Her face was radiant with happy excitement then; it was the same face now, with the dignity of death and the peace of God upon it.

They told me the first mourner to come was the dog. He came uninvited, and stood up on his hind legs and rested his fore paws upon the trestle, and took a last long look at the face that was so dear to him, then went his way as silently as he had come. *He knows.*

STAN RICE

The poet's daughter Michele died shortly before her sixth birthday from a rare form of leukemia. Two years later her mother, Anne Rice, turning to words with her own grief, wrote Inteview with the Vampire *in which she created the beautiful child vampire Claudia in Michele's image.*

from *Singing Yet: New and Selected Poems*

Look!

Look! she is dead: no cover can cover her: look,
her hands are dead just as her face is dead: all of her is dead:
where is the soul? she looked no lighter on the pillow when it went.
My eyes fill with water that falls from under my sunglasses:

when the bells ring: even the oxygen grieves:
surely this is not what she was meant for:
look! a shaft of light pierces the dustball: just that effortlessly

she went.

Déjà Vu Again

Love went riding in a hearse
With me behind her in the flower car.
We stopped beside a hole where she
Was put by men who could not see.
I did not know we had just come there to rehearse.
It burns before me like a tree
Aflame with treeness, clear and whole.
I wish my thoughts could see their fill
Of that invisibility.
They never will. I see and see and see the film
Of the cadillac in which Love rode
With me behind her in the flower car,
Dressed fit to kill.

RAYMOND CARVER

In this Carver short story, which Robert Altman adapted for his movie
Short Cuts, *eight-year-old Scotty is walking to school with another boy,
intent on finding out what his friend will be giving him later that afternoon at his birthday party. Preoccupied, Scotty steps off the curb without
looking and is hit by a car. He dies several days later at the hospital. Here
Scotty's parents, Ann and Howard, are just beginning to take it all in.*

from "A Small, Good Thing," in *Where I'm Calling From: New and Selected Stories*

The doctor walked them to the hospital's front door. People were entering and
leaving the hospital. It was eleven o'clock in the morning. Ann was aware of
how slowly, almost reluctantly, she moved her feet. It seemed to her that
Dr. Francis was making them leave when she felt they should stay, when it
would be more the right thing to do to stay. She gazed out into the parking lot
and then turned around and looked back at the front of the hospital. She began shaking her head. "No, no," she said. "I can't leave him here, no." She

heard herself say that and thought how unfair it was that the only words that came out were the sort of words used on TV shows where people were stunned by violent or sudden deaths. She wanted her words to be her own. . . .

At home, she sat on the sofa with her hands in her coat pockets. Howard closed the door to the child's room. He got the coffee-maker going and then he found an empty box. He had thought to pick up some of the child's things that were scattered around the living room. But instead he sat down beside her on the sofa, pushed the box to one side, and leaned forward, arms between his knees. He began to weep. She pulled his head over into her lap and patted his shoulder. "He's gone," she said. She kept patting his shoulder. Over his sobs, she could hear the coffee-maker hissing in the kitchen. "There, there," she said tenderly. "Howard, he's gone. He's gone and now we'll have to get used to that. To being alone."

In a little while, Howard got up and began moving aimlessly around the room with the box, not putting anything into it, but collecting some things together on the floor at one end of the sofa. She continued to sit with her hands in her coat pockets. Howard put the box down and brought coffee into the living room. Later, Ann made calls to relatives. After each call had been placed and the party had answered, Ann would blurt out a few words and cry for a minute. Then she would quietly explain, in a measured voice, what had happened and tell them about arrangements. Howard took the box out to the garage, where he saw the child's bicycle. He dropped the box and sat down on the pavement beside the bicycle. He took hold of the bicycle awkwardly so that it leaned against his chest. He held it, the rubber pedal sticking into his chest. He gave the wheel a turn.

STEPHEN DIXON

Not a bereaved father himself, Dixon has told interviewers that the novel Interstate *was his way of addressing the fear of losing his own children in our increasingly violent world. The narrator in this excerpt, a father, is in shock. His young daughter Julie, less than an hour before, had been murdered in a random drive-by killing on the interstate, and he's at the hospital thinking out loud to his other young daughter, trying to bargain away the tragedy.*

from *Interstate*

"But do you really know what this all means?" [the father asks his surviving daughter] "With Julie I do." "It means that the worst possible thing that could ever happen, happened. No, it would've been worse if you had died too. And worse yet if Mommy had been in the car with us and she had died with the two of you. It wouldn't have been worse if I had died with all of you. That would have been better. Then I wouldn't know anything that happened, as I now do. It would, in fact, be better, if Julie died, that nobody died with her but me. Of course. But better yet, absolutely best of all, if somebody had to die in that car, though I don't know why anyone would, that only I had, that's true too. If only that had been the case. If only that could be made to be the case. How do we go about doing that? It would be bad for you all but not as bad as just Julie dying. Now that's a tragedy. So in moments like this, can't we all just crack up, or each to his own? Anyway," to the doctor, "what happened is just about the worst thing that could ever possibly happen, don't you agree with me?" "I'm sorry, sir, what? I didn't quite catch all that or realize till late that you were talking to me."

WE BEGIN TO FEEL THE WEIGHT OF OUR LOSS

RALPH WALDO EMERSON

At age five, Emerson's namesake son and constant companion, Waldo, died suddenly from scarlet fever. Ninety years later, when Anne Morrow Lindbergh was mourning the loss of her own son, she wrote in her journal, "Emerson on his deathbed saying, 'That beautiful boy.' Heart-breaking. I hope it is true."

from *Emerson: The Mind on Fire* by Robert D. Richardson Jr.

Nine-year-old Louisa May Alcott came to the door next morning to ask how Waldo was. Years later she remembered how "his father came to me, so worn with watching and changed by sorrow that I was startled and could only stammer out my message. "Child, he is dead" was the answer. "That was my first glimpse of a great grief," Alcott recalled.

Emerson wrote four short letters to friends and family the night Waldo died and he wrote six or seven more the next day. He was reduced to a stuttering and helpless repetition. "Farewell and farewell," "my darling my darling," "my boy, my boy is gone." To [his friend] Margaret Fuller he wrote, "Shall I ever dare to love anything again?"...

... Over time he wrote the long elegy "Threnody," one of the great elegies in English and a poem in which Emerson rivals the Milton whose "Lycidas" he had known by heart for so long. Emerson felt anger and shock and bitterness. He did not believe in a conventional afterlife. He was bereft alike of his son and of the usual consolation. . . .

Six months after Waldo's death, Emerson wrote to a well-wisher in Baltimore . . . that "the powers of the soul are commensurate with its needs." If there is affirmation in the first half of that sentence, there is a world of pain in the last word. Emerson's capacity for expression gave him the capacity to mourn. "The South wind brings / Life, sunshine and desire," he says at the beginning of "Threnody":

> But over the dead he has no power,
> The lost, the lost he cannot restore;
> And, looking over the hills, I mourn
> The darling who shall not return.

from "Threnody" by Ralph Waldo Emerson, in *The Portable Emerson*,
edited by Carl Bode and Malcolm Cowley

> Now Love and Pride, alas! in vain,
> Up and down their glances strain.
> The painted sled stands where it stood;
> The kennel by the corded wood;
> His gathered sticks to stanch the wall
> Of the snow-tower, when snow should fall;
> The ominous hole he dug in the sand,
> And childhood's castles built or planned;
>
> .   .   .   .
>
> But the deep-eyed boy is gone.
>
> .   .   .   .
>
> Was there no star that could be sent,
> No watcher in the firmament,
> No angel from the countless host
> That loiters round the crystal coast,
> Could stoop to heal that only child,
> Nature's sweet marvel undefiled,
> And keep the blossom of the earth,

Which all her harvests were not worth?

·   ·   ·   ·   ·   ·   ·   ·   ·   ·   ·

Covetous death bereaved us all,
To aggrandize one funeral.
The eager fate which carried thee
Took the largest part of me:
For this losing is true dying;
This is lordly man's down-lying,
This his slow but sure reclining,
Star by star his world resigning.

ROBB FORMAN DEW

In this sequel to Dew's American Book Award–winning novel, Dale
Loves Sophie to Death, *local basketball star Owen Croft, "preoccupied
at seventeen," rear-ends Martin's small blue car at thirty-five miles an
hour. In the front seats, Martin and his older son, David, are unharmed.
But the backseat, with twelve-year-old Toby in it, is crushed. Soon after
Toby's death, Owen and his parents ask Martin and his wife, Dinah, if
they may come by.*

from Fortunate Lives

Initially Dinah had wept and paced the house, pressing her fists against the
door of Toby's room and sliding downward in a crumpled heap as she let
herself understand the fact that whenever she opened that door Toby would
not ever be there again. And she had turned to Martin and embraced him,
as he had bent over her there, but she had never surrendered to him any bit
of her particular sorrow, nor had she accepted any of his. She had enclosed
herself in a monosyllabic grief, clearly mustering great energy even to respond to their youngest child, Sarah, or to David, who was so stunned by
the enormity of the catastrophe that he scarcely felt any emotion at all.

The evening they sat in the living room waiting for the Crofts, Martin
looked over at Dinah and put her behavior down to anger. He envied her for
it; he was filled only with a terrible lassitude and hopelessness.

Dinah sat silently on the couch with an alarmingly open expression on
her face, her eyes too wide, her mouth stretched taut at the corners. Watching her, Martin felt an absurd but keen expectation that she would reveal

something heretofore kept secret at the very core of herself, something that would resolve and dissipate the dreadfulness of what had happened to them.

When Judith Croft had come into the room, she had stopped short at the sight of Dinah and then stepped forward again with one hand stretching toward her. Martin had intercepted Judith with a slight hug. Martin and Dinah had known the Crofts for over fifteen years; they had served on school boards together, exchanged dinner invitations, and been dinner guests at the same houses. Martin automatically drew Judith toward him in an affirmation of their mutual sorrow and their long connection.

"I don't know . . ." Judith had begun, "I don't know how this could happen. I don't know why . . . and Owen . . . Owen doesn't know why. . . ." She was a small woman with an intense face. Her chin was slightly too square, and she had small, deep-set, but very brilliant blue eyes. Martin had always thought of her as a wiry, durable person—humorless and resilient. But that evening she had suddenly seemed gaunt and stringy and so abrupt in all her movements that it was as though she were about to fly apart. Her son loomed between his parents, taller than either of them and mute with misery. Martin found himself standing with his arm around Judith staring carefully at Owen, who waited with his father in the doorway, not meeting Martin's glance.

Owen was probably considered handsome, Martin thought, although he was awkwardly lanky, and his ears were large and stood too far away from his head. But he had beautiful, thickly lashed green eyes and blond hair, and he gave a strong impression of artlessness and even vulnerability. Martin was confused as he studied him. He had been thinking of Owen as the boy who had so carelessly, so recklessly, driven his car straight ahead into traffic that had stopped inconveniently, instantly killing Toby. And although he had seen Owen Croft around town over all the years since Owen was first able to ride his bike at about age six, Martin had imagined him as dark and sullen and sulky. Surly and spoiled, a doctor's son with too much money, too little caution.

"Could we sit down, Martin?" Larry finally said, still stranded at the door with Owen. And they had come into the room and settled on the chairs, but no one spoke until Owen turned to Dinah. His voice was strained and husky.

"I know there's nothing I can say that will change anything," he said, and he looked to Dinah for a signal, but she had her attention fixed on him only marginally, which made Martin cringe for him in spite of himself. Owen bent forward in his chair with the urgency of what he needed to say. "I was just driving *home*. . . ." It was an appeal. He was only going home; he was not rushing to any place particularly desirable. "I'd just gotten off from practice, and I was late. . . . The sun was in my eyes and I didn't *see*. . . ." His face suddenly tensed in an effort to fight tears, his mouth crumpled inward at the corners, and still Dinah simply gazed back at him, abstracted. "I didn't *see*. . . ." He couldn't go on with what he was saying until he looked down at his hands and took a long breath. "I don't even remember thinking about it. . . ." Finally he couldn't go on at all, but just bent his head to his hands. The adults were frozen where they sat, with Owen's words hanging over them.

Judith had begun to cry then, and she reached out her open hands in an appeal to Dinah. "Oh, *Dinah*! What do we do now? What do you want us to do? What can we do?"

For the first time since the accident, Dinah's attention seemed to become engaged. She blinked at Judith and her mouth quivered. "What can we do?" She spoke as though she were repeating a phrase in a foreign language whose meaning wasn't entirely clear to her. "Well . . . I don't know." She sat back in her chair, giving way to exhaustion all at once, her face becoming less taut, her eyelids drooping. "Well . . ."—and she gestured outward with one hand—"we just go on, I guess." And Judith leaned her head against the back of her own chair and closed her eyes while tears ran down her face.

Larry Croft looked from Dinah to Martin, but he didn't speak for a moment. "Owen's talked to the police, of course. We don't know what charges . . ."

But Dinah held her hand up to negate what he was saying, what she was hearing. She rose from her chair in oddly uncoordinated slow motion and turned away from all of them, making her way slowly off down the hall, her arms extended slightly, palms outward as though she were moving in the dark.

Larry got up, and Martin rose with him, although Judith continued to sit with her eyes closed in silent weeping. Owen had straightened up, but he was teary and he didn't look at anyone. They were all helpless in the silent room, and Martin realized that that was what Dinah had understood almost at once when she had heard about Toby's death—the pointlessness of all their overwhelming sorrow.

MICHAEL S. HARPER

The poet honors family members in this award-winning collection, but nowhere more than in this poem.

from *Images of Kin: New and Selected Poems*

We Assume: On the Death of Our Son, Reuben Masai Harper

We assume
that in 28 hours,
lived in a collapsible isolette,
you learned to accept pure oxygen
as the natural sky;
the scant shallow breaths
that filled those hours
cannot, did not make you fly—
but dreams were there
like crooked palmprints on
the twin-thick windows of the nursery—
in the glands of your mother.

We assume
the sterile hands
drank chemicals in and out
from lungs opaque with mucus,
pumped your stomach,
eeked the bicarbonate in
crooked, green-winged veins,
out in a plastic mask;

A woman who'd lost her first son
consoled us with an angel gone ahead
to pray for our family—
gone into that sky
seeking oxygen,
gone into autopsy,
a fine brown powdered sugar,
a disposable cremation:

We assume
you did not know we loved you.

REYNOLDS PRICE

With The Promise of Rest, *the last of a trilogy begun in 1975, novelist Price brings Wade Mayfield home to North Carolina to die. Wade, Hutch and Ann's estranged thirty-two-year-old son, is in the late stages of AIDS. At the end, when Wade is skeletal, blind, and drifting in and out of lucidity, his New York friend Jimmy Boat comes to help out.*

from *The Promise of Rest*

In death what was left of Wade Mayfield seemed the absolute proof that life is a power that fills real space with its mass and force. The cooling bones and hair and skin were hardly enough for a ten-year-old boy harrowed to death, much less a grown man whose shape had contained ten billion memories of life lived and stored. . . . Though Boat had shut the eyes before calling Hutch and Ann, they'd opened slightly. Through the long dark lashes, the enormous pupils had set at an angle like the angle in portraits whose eyes can follow you round a room. But they showed no threat now and made no plea.

Ann reached out and carefully shut them again. . . .

Though Ann and Hutch and Boat were silently sending out the last of their care and the start of their grief like a final healing or at least a balm, the abandoned body was already past such negligible wants. In Boat's word, the substance of what had been a life—a life with serious weight and reach, and with numerous thousand unmet hopes—had plainly *passed.*

After the funeral, Hutch, with help from eight-year-old Raven—in all likelihood Wade's own child—scatters Wade's ashes in a favorite boyhood spot by a stream in the woods. Ann isn't up to it.

[Hutch] said to Raven "You still want to help me?"

"Yes, just say the word." The boy's face lit again with the solemn force it had in the chapel yesterday, not a ritual funeral look but the image of innocent awe at the final mystery left.

Hutch said "Reach in then, take a good handful and spread it on the water."

Careful as a good young priest, Raven performed the gesture like something he'd learned years back and brought to effortless ease today.

The tan ashes lay on top of the water for an instant, then sifted downward and on with the stream.

Raven kept his eyes on their course. "Let me do one more."

Hutch waited with the urn while the boy spread a second handful.

In a quick shaft of light, the ashes spread on the surface—rainbowed for a moment in their startling colors of tan, white, ochre, blues and purples. The bits of bone cast circles around them that rode out of sight.

But Raven stood where he'd stopped and watched them, his dusty right hand held out from his side.

Hutch had crouched through that. Now he stood, walking slowly upstream to scatter the rest. If he'd been thrown forward, dead of grief and regret in the dirt any instant here, he'd have felt no surprise. But his blood beat on, he stayed upright, and the ashes were gone even sooner than he'd guessed. He was left with the urn and a weight of loss—iron desolation—like none he'd ever borne till today. For half a minute again he thought he'd pitch to the ground. His heart contracted like a terrified fist and slammed at his ribs. . . .

Raven had followed three steps behind Hutch; he'd also watched the last of the ashes rest on the water and then sift inward. When they'd sunk and Hutch had swung round to face the boy—thinking any instant he must beg for help—Raven went on watching the creek as if the world harbored no threats stronger than pine trees and gangster jays. Then the boy said "Your Wade can enjoy himself from now on."

VICTOR HUGO

In 1843, Hugo was in a cafe when he read in a newspaper of his favorite daughter's death. His mistress, Juliette Drouet, was there with him and later wrote in her journal, "Never, as long as I live, shall I forget the indescribable expression of despair upon his noble features. A moment back I had seen him smiling and happy, and now, in the space of a second, without the slightest transition, he seemed as though thunderstruck. His poor lips were white; his magnificent eyes were staring in front of him. His face and his hair were wet with tears. His poor hand was pressed to his heart as though to keep it from bursting from his breast."

His daughter Leopoldine and her husband had drowned in a sailing accident on the Seine. Newly married, they were buried in the same coffin. Later, Hugo poured his grief into writing Les Contemplations, *a* volume of poems that he divided into "Autrefois" and "Aujourd'hui," the moment of his daughter's death being the mark between yesterday and to-day. He found relief above all in working on a new novel, which became Les Misérables.

from *The Poems of Victor Hugo*

On the Death of His Daughter
Oh! je fus comme fou dans le premier moment

Oh, I was wild like a madman at first,
Three days I wept bitter tears and accurst;
O those whom God of your hope hath bereft!
Fathers and mothers like me lonely left!
Have ye felt what I felt, and known it all?
And longed to dash your heads on the wall?
Have ye been like me in open revolt,
And defied the Hand that had hurled the bolt?
I could not believe at all in the thing:
I gazed, and I gazed, for a light to spring.
Does God permit such misfortunes, nor care
That our souls be filled with utter despair?
It seemed as the whole were a frightful dream,
She could not have left me thus like a gleam;
Ha! That is her laughter in the next room!
Oh no, she cannot be dead in the tomb.
There shall she enter—come here by this door,
And her step shall be music to me as before.

Oh, how oft have I said,—silence,—she speaks,
Hold,—'tis her hand on the key, and it creaks;
Wait—she comes! I must hear—leave me—go out,
For she *is* in this mansion, somewhere, without doubt.

Three years later, Juliette's own daughter Claire, whom Hugo had unofficially adopted, died. In this stanza from "Claire," hard truth was all he could summon.

from "Claire," in *Les Contemplations*

What then? Yours too, yours that in her turn
Has followed mine: deep-hearted mother, though you yet may leave
The door wide open for her fond return,
This stone, half buried in the grass, is still a grave.

B H A R A T I   M U K H E R J E E

Mukherjee wrote this short story after coauthoring The Sorrow and the
Terror, *a nonfiction book about the June 1985 terrorist bombing off the
coast of Ireland of an Air India Boeing 747 on its way from Toronto and
Montreal to Delhi. All 329 passengers and crew members were killed,
more than 90 percent of them Canadian citizens, mostly women and children on their way to India to visit relatives. In this excerpt, the woman
speaking has lost her entire family only days before in the bombing. She
cannot understand her own calm. "Not peace, just a deadening quiet."
Here she and her Canadian next-door neighbor Kusum, whose daughter
and husband were killed, are in Ireland, staring at the piece of the sky
where their lives changed forever.*

from "The Management of Grief," in *The Best American Short Stories 1989,*
edited by Margaret Atwood with Shannon Ravenel

Four days later, I find Kusum squatting on a rock overlooking a bay in
Ireland. It isn't a big rock, but it juts sharply out over water. This is as close
as we'll ever get to them. June breezes balloon out her sari and unpin her
knee-length hair. She has the bewildered look of a sea creature whom the
tides have stranded.

It's been one hundred hours since Kusum came stumbling and screaming across my lawn. Waiting around the hospital, we've heard many stories.
The police, the diplomats, they tell us things thinking that we're strong, that
knowledge is helpful to the grieving, and maybe it is. Some, I know, prefer
ignorance, or their own versions. The plane broke into two, they say. Un-
consciousness was instantaneous. No one suffered. My boys must have just
finished their breakfasts. They loved eating on planes, they loved the small-
ness of plates, knives, and forks. Last year they saved their airline salt and
pepper shakers. Half an hour more and they would have made it to
Heathrow.

Kusum says that we can't escape our fate. She says that all those people—
our husbands, my boys, her girl with the nightingale voice, all those Hindus,

Christians, Sikhs, Muslims, Parsis, and atheists on that plane—were fated to die together off this beautiful bay. She learned this from a swami in Toronto.

I have my Valium.

Six of us "relatives"—two widows and four widowers—chose to spend the day today by the waters instead of sitting in a hospital room and scanning photographs of the dead. That's what they call us now: relatives. I've looked through twenty-seven photos in two days. They're very kind to us, the Irish are very understanding. Sometimes understanding means freeing a tourist bus for this trip to the bay, so we can pretend to spy our loved ones through the glassiness of waves or in sun-speckled cloud shapes.

I could die here, too, and be content.

HERMAN MELVILLE

Herman Melville wrote Moby Dick, *the story of Captain Ahab's monomaniacal search for the white whale who severed his leg, in 1851. Ahab learns he is finally closing in on the leviathan when his ship, the* Pequod, *meets the* Rachel, *another American whaling vessel. The* Rachel's *Captain Gardiner, a distraught father, begs Ahab to postpone his search to help him look for a whale-boat that has disappeared, dragged off by a white whale, with Gardiner's twelve-year-old son on board. It is significant that Ahab's last chance to preserve his humanity involves the loss of a child.*

Rachel, *the ship's name, comes from the biblical verse Jeremiah 31:15:*

> *A voice is heard in Ramah,*
> *mourning and great weeping,*
> *Rachel weeping for her children*
> *and refusing to be comforted,*
> *because her children are no more.*

Melville weaves this hauntingly beautiful verse into his telling of the final episode of Moby Dick.

Ironically, Melville himself was to lose both of his sons. In 1867, eighteen-year-old Malcolm Melville was found dead in bed from a gunshot wound to the head after a dispute with his father over his curfew. Whether his death was a suicide or accident is not clear. Stanwix Melville died in California in 1886, estranged from his family.

from *Moby Dick*

It seemed that somewhat late on the afternoon of the day previous, while three of the stranger's boats were engaged with a shoal of whales, which had led them some four or five miles from the ship; and while they were yet in swift chase to windward, the white hump and head of Moby Dick had suddenly loomed up out of the blue water, not very far to leeward; whereupon, the fourth rigged boat—a reserved one—had been instantly lowered in chase. After a keen sail before the wind, this fourth boat —the swiftest keeled of all—seemed to have succeeded in fastening—at least, as well as the man at the mast-head could tell anything about it. In the distance he saw the diminished dotted boat; and then a swift gleam of bubbling white water; and after that nothing more; whence it was concluded that the stricken whale must have indefinitely run away with his pursuers, as often happens. There was some apprehension, but no positive alarm, as yet. The recall signals were placed in the rigging; darkness came on; and forced to pick up her three far to windward boats—ere going in quest of the fourth one in the precisely opposite direction—the ship had not only been necessitated to leave that boat to its fate till near midnight, but, for the time, to increase her distance from it. But the rest of her crew being at last safe aboard, she crowded all sail—stunsail on stunsail—after the missing boat; kindling a fire in her try-pots for a beacon; and every other man aloft on the look-out. But though when she had thus sailed a sufficient distance to gain the presumed place of the absent ones when last seen; though she then paused to lower her spare boats to pull all around her; and not finding anything, had again dashed on; again paused, and lowered her boats; and though she had thus continued doing till day light; yet not the least glimpse of the missing keel had been seen.

The story told, the stranger Captain immediately went on to reveal his object in boarding the Pequod. He desired that ship to unite with his own in the search; by sailing over the sea some four or five miles apart, on parallel lines, and so sweeping a double horizon. . . .

"My boy, my own boy is among them. For God's sake—I beg, I conjure"—here exclaimed the stranger Captain to Ahab, who thus far had icily received his petition. "For eight-and-forty hours let me charter your ship— I will gladly pay for it, and roundly pay for it—if there be no other way—for eight-and-forty hours only—only that—you must, oh, you must, and you *shall* do this thing." . . .

"I will not go," said the stranger, "till you say *aye* to me. Do to me as you would have me do to you in the like case. For *you* too have a boy, Captain Ahab—though but a child, and nestling safely at home now—a child of your old age too—Yes, yes, you relent; I see it—run, run, men, now, and stand by to square in the yards."

"Avast," cried Ahab—"touch not a rope-yarn;" then in a voice that prolongingly moulded every word—"Captain Gardiner, I will not do it. Even now I lose time. Good bye, good bye. God bless ye, man, and may I forgive myself, but I must go." . . .

Soon the two ships diverged their wakes; and long as the strange vessel was in view, she was seen to yaw hither and thither at every dark spot, however small, on the sea. This way and that her yards were swung round; starboard and larboard, she continued to tack; now she beat against a head sea; and again it pushed her before it; while all the while, her masts and yards were thickly clustered with men, as three tall cherry trees, when the boys are cherrying among the boughs.

But by her still halting course and winding, wo[e]ful way, you plainly saw that this ship that so wept with spray, still remained without comfort. She was Rachel, weeping for her children, because they were not.

PEOPLE WATCH US,
BUT THERE'S SO MUCH THEY DON'T SEE

JANE KENYON

This poem was in Kenyon's last collection, completed as she was dying of leukemia in 1995.

from Otherwise: New and Selected Poems

The Sandy Hole

The infant's coffin no bigger than a flightbag. . . .
The young father steps backward from the sandy hole,
eyes wide and dry, his hand over his mouth.
No one dares to come near him, even to touch his sleeve.

BRET LOTT

In his novel Reed's Beach, *Lott touches on how exposed newly grieving parents feel, their grief laid out for all to see. We're unused to such public scrutiny. From the moment Hugh gets the call that his only child, seven-year-old Michael, has been struck by a car, people start watching him, "gauging their reactions and movements by his own." He understands*

their good intentions, but he wants none of it. He does not want to share
his sorrow. The more private he keeps his wound, Hugh knows, the harder
it will be to heal. It doesn't matter.

from Reed's Beach

They watched him and his wife, and even without looking at them, he could
feel their eyes boring into him while the pastor of the church Laura's [Hugh's
wife's] parents attended spoke from a lectern at the front of a bright and
shining new chapel at Monmouth Memorial Gardens. Somehow things had
been taken care of, decisions made, plot and casket and in-ground memorial plaque schemes settled upon, the three days since he had kissed his son's
forehead an unraveling movement of darkness and foreign places, until, finally, they had settled here, a casket of glimmering mahogany and brass before them, heaped around and before it monumental sprays of flowers, while
words tumbled down at him from a man he did not know about the nature
of God and the grace of children. . . .

But the blackest moments, those moments when he knew he stood on
the edge of a chasm, a bottomless abyss into which he was not certain he had
fallen yet or were about to, came to him in the midst of the ceremony, in-
dicting moments when he knew himself to be the spectator: the moments
when, in the hospital, everyone's moves, even his own, had seemed too large;
the moments when he had seen himself staring at sheets of paper on the desk
at the Memorial Gardens office, his signature somehow appearing at the
bottom of eight or nine sheets of paper; and the moment when, in the
middle of the eulogy, he had glanced away from the casket, looked down at
his right hand, and found his fingers intertwined with his wife's, her sobs
barely audible, the knuckles of both their hands white, bloodless. He, too,
was a spectator, only holding on. . . .

They had made the choice to leave it closed the afternoon before, when
they had brought down to the funeral home the clothing he would need,
Hugh the one to enter their son's room for the search through his closet,
Laura even then unwilling to enter the room. His wife stood just outside
the room, mouth closed tight, eyes wide open and on him, while he had
gone through his son's dresser, looked for a pair of socks, a pair of underwear, a belt. For an instant, the time it took to burrow for the right pair of
socks in a drawer of clothing hopelessly strewn in the manner only a boy
could bring off, he believed this might have been any other foray into his
child's possessions.

Then it hit him, the fact of this mission, and he stood, socks and T-shirt and underwear in hand, and surveyed the room . . . the closest he could ever hope to bringing back his son. . . .

Later, [after] they had driven to the funeral home to leave the clothing . . . there had come a call from the home, the faceless director informing them their son was ready. . . .

The director opened the door for them, ushered them in with a small sweep of his hand, and they followed him down the oak-paneled hallway. . . .

The director stopped at the double doors at the end of the hall, leaned toward them, and pushed them both open. The doors stayed in place, and he put his hands behind his back, disappeared.

It was his son, and the oak-paneled walls pressed at his shoulders, emptied his lungs. . . .

He reached in, touched at his son's forehead, felt the cool of it, tasted on his own lips yet again the cool of his son's skin when he had been inside the hospital room. Then he touched at the tear in the shirt where the pocket had pulled away.

This was Michael.

Then Laura reached in as well, and suddenly he saw that she had something in her hand, a cloth, and as it unfurled from her hand, draped itself across their son's chest, and as she tucked its edges into the satin crevasses on the far side of their son, he saw that it was Michael's old blanket, the one he'd had since he was in the bassinet. . . . Michael had slept with it until after he had turned six, the blanket useless as a blanket long before that. . . .

"Where was that?" he whispered to Laura, and reached his own hand, tucked the lower edges into the satin, the frayed bottom edge of the blanket reaching just below his son's waist.

She did not answer, and he was sorry he'd asked as soon as the words had left him: She had known where it was, had had the presence of mind enough to find it, and had brought it here. That was all that mattered.

And his son was covered by the blanket.

It was a gesture, he knew, just as the blanket in the last days before they had hidden it away had been merely gesture for Michael, thin companion for sleep. But Michael had needed the blanket, had known until it had not reappeared after a washday that sleep would be impossible without its company; this gesture, the laying on of the blanket, was one they two needed, an instant they now owned, infused with value, because it was their own gesture, no one else's. . . .

Then, in a move even more astounding than a blanket appearing from nowhere, he watched as his wife reached above and across their son, touched the open half-lid, her fingers gripping tight the edge of glossy wood, and started the lid down.

Then his hands were with hers, and in a gesture larger and truer than any he would ever know, the two of them pulled down the lid, set it gently and easily into place. . . .

They all watched as Hugh and Laura made their way from the chapel and into the waiting limousine for the quarter-mile ride to the plot, and watched them take their seats at the graveside. They watched as Laura, in yet another gesture, but one hollow and senseless, he believed, after what they had finished last night, dropped a single white rose onto the casket once it had been lowered into the ground, and they watched Hugh himself then drop a handful of dirt after her in yet another gesture. They watched all of this, and yet that secret, the clothes their son wore, the blanket over him, the pulling closed of the casket themselves, kept the proceedings as private as any act that could ever take place between husband and wife, as private as what they had done to conceive him.

They had all seen nothing, Hugh knew, only grief's gestures, sorrow's affectations: True grief, he saw with the last glimpse of his son in the oak-paneled room, was a secret that defied divulging. There was no way to know it unless it had been bestowed upon you, no way to pass it on once it had arrived.

WALTER PAVLICH

Pavlich points out how little we know of other's grief in this poem about funnyman Stan Laurel. The "thin one" of the Laurel and Hardy comedy team so popular on the screen in the 1920s and 1930s, Laurel lost his son Stanley, born two months prematurely, at nine days old.

from *The Pushcart Prize XV: Best of the Small Presses*, edited by Bill Henderson

On the Life and Death of Stan Laurel's Son

For nine days, two Stanleys, one funny,
one drowning, brain capsizing in its own blood,
lungs miscarrying air
from one breath to the next, a tenant
shut in its dissembling body,
incubator too much like a show room.

Stan's tired of crying on screen.
Off, that's all he can do. The night-nurse
steals his exhausted handkerchief, hides it
under her sleeve on her wrist-pulse.
Someday these tears might be worth something.

Stan Jr. dies without one chuckle
to smooth out its face, and is burned
into a little pile his father
pretends he keeps in a clear candy jar.
Every morning for luck Stan rubs
a fingerprint on the glass

cold as a spoon, his son
neutral inside. Then off to the laughter
works where he invents the same smile
each day, and that way of walking,
as if the ground were a ledge, and he's strolling
alone, three steps off the earth.

MARGARET MITCHELL

*In her sprawling 1937 Pulitzer Prize–winning novel, Mitchell shows us
private grief that must look deranged to any but the bereaved parent.
Rhett Butler has given his five-year-old daughter Bonnie a pony and allowed her to jump over a low bar. Every bit as high-spirited as her mother,
Scarlett O'Hara, Bonnie begs him for a higher bar, a foot and a half from
the ground, and Rhett relents. Bonnie falls and dies. Days later, Rhett still
refuses to let Bonnie be buried and tells Scarlett he'll kill her if she inter-
feres. In a panic, Scarlett's beloved Mammy, a former slave turned ser-
vant, goes to the Butlers' friend Melanie for help. "Miss Melly, Mist' Rhett
done—done los' his mine. He woan let us put Lil Miss away."*

from *Gone with the Wind*

"Miss Melly, Ah tell you eve'ything. Ah oughtn' tell nobody, but you is our
fambly an' you is de onlies' one Ah kin tell. Ah tell you eve'ything. You
knows whut a sto' he set by dat chile. Ah ain' never seed no man, black or
w'ite, set sech a sto' by any chile. Look lak he go plumb crazy w'en Doctah

Meade say her neck broke. He grab his gun an' he run right out an' shoot dat po' pony an', fo' Gawd, Ah think he gwine shoot hisseff. . . .

". . . Den he tuck her ter de unnertaker's hisseff an' he bring her back an' he put her in her baid in his room. An' w'en Miss Scarlett say she b'long in de pahlor in de coffin, Ah thought Mist' Rhett gwine hit her. An' he say, right cole lak: 'She b'long in mah room.' An' he tuhn ter me an' he say: 'Mammy, you se dat she stay right hyah tell Ah gits back.' Den he light outer de house on de hawse an' he wuz gone tell 'bout sundown. W'en he come t'arin' home, Ah seed dat he'd been drinkin' an' drinkin' heavy, but he wuz cahyin' it well's usual. He fling inter de house an' not even speak ter Miss Scarlett or Miss Pitty or any of de ladies as wuz callin', but he fly up de steps an' th'ow open de do' of his room an' den he yell for me. W'en Ah comes runnin' as fas' as Ah kin, he wuz stan'in' by de baid an' it wuz so dahk in de room Ah couldn' sceercely see him, kase de shutters wuz done drawed.

"An' he say ter me, right fierce lak: 'Open dem shutters. It's dahk in hyah.' An' Ah fling dem open an' he look at me an', fo' Gawd, Miss Melly, mah knees 'bout give way, kase he look so strange. Den he say: Bring lights. Bring lots of lights. An' keep dem buhnin'. An' doan draw no shades an' no shutters. Doan you know Miss Bonnie's 'fraid of de dahk?"

Melanie's horror struck eyes met Mammy's and Mammy nodded ominously.

WE BEGIN TO REALIZE HOW LONG THE PAIN WILL THROB

NAGUIB MAHFOUZ

Naguib Mahfouz received the Nobel Prize for literature in 1988. In his Palace Walk, *the first in* The Cairo Trilogy, *three young men go to the shop of al-Sayyid Ahmad Abd al-Jawad to inform him that his oldest son, Fahmy, has been killed. Earlier that day, British soldiers had suddenly opened fire on a peaceful crowd demonstrating for Egypt's independence. The father responds with the same shock and disbelief as Samuel Clemens. But he knows he has a lifetime to devote to his sorrow.*

from *Palace Walk,* translated by William Maynard Hutchins and Olive E. Kenny

Although there was an unmistakable look of belief and dismay in his eyes, the father rejected the news, shouting, "Fahmy?"

"He fell a martyr in the demonstration today."

The boy on his right said, "A noble patriot and sterling martyr was conveyed to a world of pious souls."

Their words fell on ears deafened by misery. His lips were sealed and his eyes gazed blankly and vacantly. They were all silent for a time. Even Jamil al-Hamzawi [his shop employee] was frozen to the spot where he stood beneath the shelves, looking dazed and staring at his employer with sorrowful eyes. Finally the young man murmured, "His loss has deeply saddened us, but we have no choice but to submit to God's decree with the patient endurance of Believers, of whom you, sir, are one."

"They are offering you their condolences," al-Sayyid Ahmad realized. "Doesn't this young man know that I excel in offering condolences in circumstances like these? What meaning do they have for an afflicted heart? None! How could words put out the fire? . . . How can I believe that Fahmy is really dead? How can you believe that Fahmy, who requested your approval just hours ago, when you were short with him—Fahmy, who was full of health, good spirits, hope, and happiness when we left home this morning—is dead? Dead! I'll never see him again at home or anywhere else on the face of the earth? How can I have a home without him? How can I be a father if he's gone? What has become of all the hopes attached to him? The only hope left is patience. . . . Patience? Oh. . . . Do you feel the searing pain? This really is pain. You were mistaken previously when you occasionally claimed to be in pain. No, before today you've never known pain. This is pain. . . ."

. . . Then they all departed. He leaned his head on his hand and closed his eyes. He heard the voice of Jamil al-Hamzawi offering his condolences in a sobbing voice, but he seemed distressed by kind words. He could not bear to stay here. He left his seat and moved slowly out of the store, walking with heavy steps. He had to get over his bewilderment. He did not even know how to feel sad. He wanted to be all alone, but where? The house would turn into an inferno in a minute or two. His friends would rally round him, leaving him no opportunity to think. When would he ponder the loss he had undergone? When would he have a chance to get away from everyone? That seemed a long way off, but it would no doubt come. It was the most consolation he could hope for at present. Yes, a time would come when he would be all alone and could devote himself to his sorrow with all his soul. Then he would scrutinize Fahmy's life in light of the past, present, and future, all the stages from childhood to the prime of his youth, the hopes he had aroused and the memories he had left behind, giving free rein to tears so he could totally exhaust them.

ELLA GERTRUDE CLANTON THOMAS

Thomas was a privileged Southern woman who wrote about the toppling of her world in the Civil War and its aftermath. "I have seen poverty staring me in the face when I expected Sherman in Augusta," she wrote in her journal, edited by her great-granddaughter Virginia Ingraham Burr. But fourteen years later, it was tragedy that stared hard.

from The Secret Eye: The Journal of Ella Gertrude Clanton Thomas, 1848–1889, edited by Virginia Ingraham Burr

November 16, 1879

Clanton is dead! Oh my God how strange it sounds. Clanton my bright, beautiful boy. Where, oh where is he? I saw him die. I saw him after he was dead, but oh darling I want to see you *now, now.* . . . I stood by his grave last Sunday morning for the first time since he was buried. I went by myself. I wished no one with me. I walked on and on until I entered the gate and then standing by the violet covered grave of my child I felt farther from him than I have done since he died. What! Clanton, my bright boy who could (altho only seven years old, a few weeks before) ride on horseback or drive a buggy. Clanton who had so much life, so much vigor, *he* buried there underneath all that earth. Oh, no, no! My God it is enough to make one cry out in utter despair.

ISABEL ALLENDE

Chilean writer Allende was celebrating the publication of one of her novels at a party in Barcelona when she heard that her daughter was in a hospital in Madrid. She got there in time to hear twenty-seven-year-old Paula say, "I love you too, Mama" just before going into a coma. Sitting, waiting by Paula's bed, Allende jotted her thoughts on yellow pads. Her daughter, it turned out, suffered from a rarely fatal metabolic disorder, porphyria, but a doctor's misdiagnosis precipitated irreversible brain damage. "After they told me [that], I went on writing because I could not stop. I could not let anger destroy me," said Allende. A year later Paula, still unconscious, died in her mother's arms. The jottings became a memoir.

from Paula, translated by Margaret Sayers Peden

A month ago, at this very hour, I was a different woman. I have a photograph from that day. I am at a party launching the publication in Spain of my most recent novel. I am wearing a silver necklace and bracelets and an aubergine-colored dress. My nails are manicured and my smile confident. I am a century younger than I am today. I don't know that woman; in four weeks, sorrow has transformed me.

2

What Kind of Universe Is This Anyway?

When Alexander was killed, my feeling that there was any sense or order in the universe was destroyed. Not only did I have searing, agonizing pain inside of me, but the plug was pulled on the force of gravity. I was free-falling into chaos.

I had no faith in divine benevolence to begin with: there is just too much wanton suffering for me to believe everything works out for the good. But I trusted in laws of nature or chance to keep me and my children safe: healthy children grow up, good parents are rewarded, and normal people have normal lives. Children bury parents, not the reverse. You don't question whether you believe in gravity; you just assume that your feet will hit the floor when you get up in the morning and your coffee cup will stay on the table. And you also assume that if you follow the rules, your healthy, exuberant sixteen-year-old son will be home for dinner.

I ranted and raved at a God I didn't believe in. How could He allow the most wonderful boy in the world, who was full of life yesterday, to be dead today? I loved Alexander so much and tried so hard to be a good mother. How could He let this happen to me? What was the point of me investing my heart and soul—not to mention time, energy, and money—into nursing, diapering, bathing, educating, and molding this child if he was to die at sixteen? What kind of monster could play such a cruel joke?

There are old, sick people waiting to die, there are unhappy people for whom life is a burden, there are parents who abuse and neglect children, there are children who cause their parents nothing but grief. Why do they live while my happy, handsome son, who had the world at his beckoning, lies in his grave and I am destroyed?

My outraged soul screamed for answers to these questions even as I knew they would never come. The same is true for all the other bereaved parents I have ever met or read about, from Job on. Some eventually find peace in the faith that there is purpose beyond human understanding; others, like Anne and me, make do with random chance, a roll of the dice—an explanation that is less satisfying, but more compatible with reality as we know it.

Years have passed and the questioning does not consume me as it used to, but the questions remain. Still, when I pick up the morning paper and read about a tragedy that has befallen an innocent child and its suffering parents, I am haunted by the question, "What kind of universe is this anyway?"

MARY

When your child dies, you wail, *Why?* "That question mark," as writer Peter De Vries saw it, "twisted like a fishhook in the human heart." This *why* has an answer, at least for me, but not one you're ready for in early grief. So you keep ignoring the obvious; you keep searching for *an explanation*. And truthfully, not really that so much as comfort. Any comfort will do.

Such searching inevitably takes grieving parents to God's door where some will open it and cry out for help. Others will furiously kick it and shout obscenities. And others still, citing God's powerlessness to avert suffering, will bypass it. "The only excuse for God," reasoned French writer Stendhal, "is that he does not exist."

I threw myself in with Stendhal. Jake's death nudged me off the fence of agnosticism on which I'd sat unconcerned for twenty years. It made me realize I was an atheist—confirmed, but not angry. Some friends were incredulous that now, especially, I would reject the solace of religion.

But where was the comfort? Unlike the jailhouse convert, hopeful of early release, I had nothing to bargain for here. The worst had happened. Jake was dead. What would I ask? Please let me be less sad? Please help me accept this better? God and I had been introduced years before, but I never followed up. We had no relationship. I might as well pick out a stranger on the street, fall sobbing into his arms, and expect healing consolation. Besides, new relationships take energy, and grieving sucks up what energy there is.

So I didn't turn to God; I didn't berate Him. He just didn't figure in. The only higher being in my life was some vestige of a punitive Zeus-like god who still shows up occasionally. A master marionettist, he seems to hold my family on long strings and make us dance at his whim. I see him as often distracted. He doesn't notice right away when we're doing all right. But when he does, he gives our strings a whack and sends us crashing into one another. Years later, even in good times, superstition compels us to warn each other, "Hush, *he* will hear you."

But that's just black humor. I have no real quarrel with any god. Instead,

I've come to see Jake's death in very simple terms: bad luck. And believe me, there's nothing comforting in that territory. It's just a dark place of sadness and fear. When you view life this pragmatically, there's no place to hide.

Friends would try to comfort me by saying, "Anne, nothing worse can ever happen." But yes, it can; they, and I, know better. My daughter and husband can be killed too. There's nothing statistically fair about bad luck. Just read the newspaper for a week if you need that driven home.

So early on, the only satisfactory answer to *Why?*—and the even more self-centered *Why me?*—became *Why not?* How could I have thought that tragedy was reserved only for others? That I was somehow special? Happiness and I had enjoyed a long run. I knew that. I just wasn't special anymore.

No, the question that pierces my heart is not *Why me?* but *Why Jake?* Just a month shy of six. *Why Jake?* That's harder. That's much, much harder.

ANNE

OUR QUESTIONS REVERBERATE THROUGH HISTORY

JOB

Written in the fourth or fifth century B.C., the biblical book of Job is a poem based on a story that can be traced as far back as 2000 B.C. It has been described as "the great poem of moral outrage." Job is a man of integrity, who fears God and lives righteously. He has a large family and great wealth. God bets Satan that Job's faith is unshakable, and to test this, He permits Satan to kill Job's children, destroy his home, and cover him with terrible boils. Job's friends come to comfort him, but antagonize him instead by saying he must have done something evil to warrant his suffering since God is just. Voicing the agony of all bereaved parents, Job protests his innocence to his friends and to God. God, who is referred to as Yahweh in this translation, answers Job with questions. Is Job not aware that He is the all-powerful creator of everything? Although God eventually restores Job's family and wealth in an epilogue to the poem, the God of Job is a God of brutal force, impervious to man's concern for justice. It is this remote, impenetrable God that many parents rail at in their grief.

from *The Book of Job*, translated by Raymond P. Scheindlin

[Job:]

3:25   One thing I feared, and it befell,
      and what I dreaded came to me.
   No peace had I, nor calm, not rest;
      but torment came.

9:20   I may be righteous, but my mouth convicts me;
      innocent, yet it makes me seem corrupt.
   I *am* good.
   I do not know myself.
   I hate my life.
   It is all one; and so I say,
   "The good and the guilty He destroys alike."
   If some scourge brings sudden death,
      He mocks the guiltless for their melting hearts;
   some land falls under a tyrant's sway—
      He veils its judges' faces;
   if not He, then who?

30:20   I cry to You—no answer;
      I stand—You stare at me,
   You harden Yourself to me,
      spurn me with Your mighty hand.
   You lift me up and mount me on a wind,
      dissolve my cunning,
   and I know that You will send me back to death,
      to the house awaiting every living creature.
   But why this violence to a pile of rubble?
      In his disaster is there some salvation?

30:25   Did I not weep for the hapless?
      Did my soul not grieve for the poor?
   Yes—
   I hoped for good, got only wrong;
      I hoped for light, got only darkness.
   My insides seethe and never stop,
      I face days of suffering,
   I go about in sunless gloom.

In assembly I stand up and wail,
changed to a jackal's brother,
    fellow to the ostrich.
30:30 My skin has blackened on my body,
    my bones are charred with fever.
My lyre has gone to mourning,
    my pipe to the sound of sobs.

38:1 Yahweh answered Job from the storm:

Who dares speak darkly words with no sense?

Cinch your waist like a fighter.
I will put questions, and you will inform me:
Where were you when I founded the earth?
Speak, if you have any wisdom:
Who set its measurements, if you know,
    laid out the building lot, stretching the plumb line?
Where was the ground where He sank its foundations?
Who was setting the cornerstone
when the morning stars were all singing.
    when the gods were all shouting, triumphant?

40:6 Yahweh answered Job from the storm:

Cinch your waist like a fighter.
    I will put questions, and you will inform me.
Would you really annul my judgment,
    make me out to be guilty, and put yourself in the right?
Is your arm as mighty as God's?
    Does your voice thunder like His?
40:10 Just dress up in majesty, greatness!
    Try wearing splendor and glory!
Snort rage in every direction!
    Seek out the proud, bring him down!
Seek out the proud man, subdue him,
    crush cruel men where they stand,
hide them together in dirt,

bind them in the Hidden Place:
Then even I would concede to you,
  when your right hand had gained you a triumph.

SOPHOCLES

Writing Antigone *in the fourth century* B.C., *Sophocles decries the capriciousness of fate through a messenger's announcement of the suicide of Haimon, the son of Creon, King of Thebes.*

from *Antigone*, translated by Dudley Fitts and Robert Fitzgerald

MESSENGER:

Men of the line of Kadmos, you who live
Near Amphion's citadel:
                    I cannot say
Of any condition of human life "This is fixed,
This is clearly good, or bad." Fate raises up,
And Fate casts down the happy and unhappy alike:
No man can foretell his Fate.
                    Take the case of Creon:
Creon was happy once, as I count happiness:
Victorious in battle, sole governor of the land,
Fortunate father of children nobly born.
And now it has all gone from him! Who can say
That a man is still alive when his life's joy fails?
He is a walking dead man. Grant him rich,
Let him live like a king in his great house:
If his pleasure is gone, I would not give
So much as the shadow of smoke for all he owns.

EPICTETUS

Epictetus, a freed slave of Greek origin, taught Stoic philosophy in Rome and Greece in the end of the first and beginning of the second centuries A.D. *All that is known of his personal life is that he married late in life "to help bring up a child who would otherwise have been left to die."*

from *The Discourses of Epictetus*, translated by Robin Hard, edited by Christopher Gill

You too should remind yourself that what you love is mortal, that what you love is not your own. It is granted to you for the present while, and not irrevocably, nor for ever, but like a fig or a bunch of grapes in the appointed season; and if you long for it in the winter, you are a fool. So, if you long for your son or friend when he is not granted to you, know that you are longing for a fig in winter. For as winter is to a fig, so is every state of affairs that arises from the order of things in relation to what is destroyed in accordance with that state of affairs. Henceforth, when you take delight in anything, bring to mind the contrary impression. What harm is there while you are kissing your child to say softly, "Tomorrow you will die"?

CHARLES LAMB

Charles Lamb was an English poet who wrote in the early nineteenth century.

from "On an Infant Dying as Soon as Born," in *In the Midst of Winter: Selections from the Literature of Mourning*, edited by Mary Jane Moffat

A flow'ret crushed in the bud,
A nameless piece of Babyhood,
Was in her cradle-coffin lying;
Extinct, with scarce the sense of dying
So soon to exchange the imprisoning womb
For darker closets of the tomb!
. . . .
Riddle of destiny, who can show
What thy short visit meant, or know
What thy errand here below?

FYODOR DOSTOEVSKY

Fyodor Dostoevsky's life was riddled with untimely deaths. His mother died when he was sixteen, his father was murdered when he was eighteen, and his first wife died after only seven years of marriage.

In 1868 Sonya, Dostoevsky's first child, died of pneumonia at three months old. He wrote, "But where is Sonya? Where is the little one for whom I declare in all honesty that I would rather have chosen a martyr's death in order to bring her back to life?" Ten years later his three-year-old son Alexey, his fourth child, died of epilepsy. Immediately afterwards,

Dostoevsky began writing The Brothers Karamazov, *his last and greatest work. In it, Ivan Karamazov explains to his brother Alyosha why he cannot accept the doctrine of original sin (suffering exists to atone for the sins of the fathers) because it does not justify the suffering of innocent children. Volumes have been written interpreting and analyzing Dostoevsky's work and its impact on philosophy and literature. But anyone who has lost a child will recognize the agony and moral outrage of a bereaved parent in the following passage.*

from The Brothers Karamazov, translated by Constance Garnett,
edited by Ralph E. Matlaw

But then there are the children, and what am I to do about them? That's a question I can't answer. For the hundredth time I repeat, there are numbers of questions, but I've only taken the children, because in their case what I mean is so unanswerably clear. Listen! If all must suffer to pay for the eternal harmony, what have children to do with it, tell me, please? It's beyond all comprehension why they should suffer, and why they should pay for the harmony. Why should they, too, furnish material to enrich the soil for the harmony of the future? I understand solidarity in sin among men. I understand solidarity in retribution, too; but there can be no such solidarity in sin with children. And if it is really true that they must share responsibility for all their fathers' crimes, such a truth is not of this world and is beyond my comprehension. Some jester will say, perhaps, that the child would have grown up and have sinned, but you see he didn't grow up, he was torn to pieces by the dogs, at eight years old. Oh, Alyosha, I am not blaspheming! I understand, of course, what an upheaval of the universe it will be, when everything in heaven and earth blends in one hymn of praise and everything that lives and has lived cries aloud: "Thou art just, O Lord, for Thy ways are revealed." When the mother embraces the fiend who threw her child to the dogs, and all three cry aloud with tears, "Thou art just, O Lord!" then, of course, the crown of knowledge will be reached and all will be made clear. But what pulls me up here is that I can't accept that harmony. And while I am on earth, I make haste to take my own measures. You see, Alyosha, perhaps it really may happen that if I live to that moment, or rise again to see it, I, too, perhaps, may cry aloud with the rest, looking at the mother embracing the child's torturer, "Thou art just, O Lord!" but I don't want to cry aloud then. While there is still time, I hasten to protect myself and so I renounce the higher harmony altogether. It's not worth the tears of that one tortured child who beat itself on the breast with its little fist and prayed in its stinking outhouse, with its unexpiated tears to "dear, kind God"! It's not worth it, because those tears are unatoned for. They must be atoned for, or there can be no harmony. But how? How are you going to atone for them? Is it possible? By their being avenged? But what do I care for avenging them? What do I care for a hell for oppressors? What good can hell do, since those children have already been tortured? And what becomes of harmony, if there is hell? I want to forgive. I want to embrace. I don't want more suffering. And if the sufferings of children go to swell the sum of sufferings which was necessary to pay for truth, then I protest that the truth is not worth such a price. I don't want the mother to embrace the oppressor who threw her son to the dogs! She dare not forgive him! Let her forgive him for herself, if she will, let her forgive the torturer for the immeasurable suffering of her mother's heart. But the sufferings of her tortured child she has no right to forgive; she dare not forgive the torturer, even if the child were to forgive him! And if that is so, if they dare not forgive, what becomes of harmony? Is there in the whole world a being who would have the right to forgive and could forgive? I don't want harmony. From love for humanity I don't want it. I would rather be left with the unavenged suffering. I would rather remain with my unavenged suffering and unsatisfied indignation, *even if I were wrong*. Besides, too high a price is asked for harmony; it's beyond our means to pay so much to enter on it. And so I hasten to give back my entrance ticket.

MARK TWAIN

To his close friend Rev. Joseph Twitchell, Clemens pours out his heart in a letter from London in 1897, five months after his daughter Susy died (see p. 4). While Clemens frantically checked telegrams and booked a return steamer from England, "Uncle Joe" had been at Susy's Connecticut bedside while she died. A heartbroken but grateful father, Clemens wrote to his friend, "I would have chosen you out of all the world to take my place at Susy's side and Livy's in those black hours."

from *The Selected Letters of Mark Twain*, edited by Charles Neider

Do I want you to write to me? Indeed I do. . . . The others break my heart but you will not. You have a something divine in you that is not in other men. You have the touch that heals, not lacerates. And you know the secret places of our hearts. You know our life—the outside of it—as the others do—and the inside of it—which they do not. You have seen our whole voyage.

You have seen us go to sea, a cloud of sail, and the flag at the peak. And you see us now, chartless, adrift—derelicts, battered, water-logged, our sails a ruck of rags, our pride gone. For it is gone. And there is nothing in its place. The vanity of life was all we had, and there is no more vanity left in us. We are even ashamed of that we had, ashamed that we trusted the promises of life and builded high—to come to this!

I did not know that Susy was a part of us. I did *not* know that she could go away. I did not know that she could go away and take our lives with her, yet leave our dull bodies behind. And I did not know what she was. To me she was but treasure in the bank, the amount known, the need to look at it daily, handle it, weigh it, count it, *realize* it, not necessary. And now that I would do it, it is too late. They tell me it is not there, has vanished away in a night, the bank is broken, my fortune is gone, I am a pauper. How am I to comprehend this? How am I to *have* it? Why am I robbed, and who is benefited?

AND WE CONTINUE TO SEARCH FOR EXPLANATIONS

WILLIAM MAXWELL

For many years, William Maxwell was fiction editor for The New Yorker, *as well as an author of novels and short stories. For him, writing was a way to "tap into the healing power of memory" which enabled him to cope with the "most shattering event of his life: the death of his beloved mother when he was ten."*

from *So Long, See You Tomorrow*

It seemed like a mistake. And mistakes ought to be rectified, only this one couldn't be. Between the way things used to be and the way they were now was a void that couldn't be crossed. I had to find an explanation other than the real one, which was that we were no more immune to misfortune than anybody else, and the idea that kept recurring to me . . . was that I had inadvertently walked through a door that I shouldn't have gone through and couldn't get back to the place I hadn't meant to leave. Actually, it was the other way round: I hadn't gone anywhere and nothing was changed, so far as the roof over our heads was concerned, it was just that she was in the cemetery.

JOHN IRVING

This excerpt from John Irving's novel occurs during a stormy period in Garp's marriage. He and his two sons drive home in the dark. Garp entertains the boys by drifting the car into the driveway at high speed, not realizing that Helen, his wife, is parked there in another car with her lover. In this bizarre crash, Duncan, the older boy, loses an eye, and Walt, their younger son, is killed instantly. After the accident, an endearing family story about the way Walt confused the word undertow *for "Under Toad" takes on symbolic meaning. For Garp and his family, the Under Toad (*tod *is the German word for death) becomes the symbol for "the forces that disrupt human life and sometimes destroy it."*

from *The World According to Garp*

Duncan began talking about Walt and the undertow—a famous family story. For as far back as Duncan could remember, the Garps had gone every summer to Dog's Head Harbor, New Hampshire, where the miles of beach in front of Jenny Fields' estate were ravaged by a fearful undertow. When Walt was old enough to venture near the water, Duncan said to him—as Helen and Garp had, for years, said to Duncan—"Watch out for the undertow." Walt retreated, respectfully. And for three summers Walt was warned about the undertow. Duncan recalled all the phrases.

"The undertow is bad today."

"The undertow is strong today."

"The undertow is *wicked* today." *Wicked* was a big word in New Hampshire—not just for the undertow.

And for years Walt watched out for it. From the first, when he asked what *it* could do to you, he had only been told that it could pull you out to sea. It could suck you under and drown you and drag you away.

It was Walt's fourth summer at Dog's Head Harbor, Duncan remembered, when Garp and Helen and Duncan observed Walt watching the sea. He stood ankle-deep in the foam from the surf and peered into the waves, without taking a step, for the longest time. The family went down to the water's edge to have a word with him.

"What are you doing, Walt?" Helen asked.

"What are you looking for, dummy?" Duncan asked him.

"I'm trying to see the Under Toad," Walt said.

"The what?" said Garp.

"The Under Toad," Walt said. "I'm trying to *see* it. How *big* is it?"

And Garp and Helen and Duncan held their breath; they realized that all these years Walt had been dreading a giant *toad,* lurking offshore, waiting to suck him under and drag him out to sea. The terrible Under Toad.

Garp tried to imagine it with him. Would it ever surface? Did it ever float? Or was it always down under, slimy and bloated and ever-watchful for ankles its coated tongue could snare? The vile Under Toad.

Between Helen and Garp, the Under Toad became their code phrase for anxiety. Long after the monster was clarified for Walt ("Under*tow,* dummy, not Under Toad!" Duncan had howled), Garp and Helen evoked the beast as a way of referring to their own sense of danger. When the traffic was heavy, when the road was icy—when depression had moved in overnight—they said to each other, "The Under Toad is strong today."

"Remember," Duncan asked on the plane, "how Walt asked if it was green or brown?"

Both Garp and Duncan laughed. But it was neither green nor brown, Garp thought. It was me. It was Helen. It was the color of bad weather. It was the size of an automobile.

DWIGHT D. EISENHOWER

Eisenhower adored his firstborn child, Doud Dwight, nicknamed "Icky." When Ike was stationed at Fort Meade, Icky was a mascot for the soldiers. In 1921, four-year-old Icky died of scarlet fever, leaving his parents grief-stricken. Mamie once said, "It was as if a shining light had gone out of Ike's life. Throughout all the years that followed, the memory of those bleak days was a deep inner pain, that never seemed to diminish much." Ike sent Mamie flowers every year on Icky's birthday. Thirty-five years later, Ike wrote the following in a letter of consolation to his brother Edgar when Edgar's forty-year-old son Jack died.

from *The Papers of Dwight David Eisenhower: The Presidency: The Middle Way XVII,* edited by Louis Galambos and Daun van Ee

It is, of course, difficult to understand why so often the oldsters go on and on into the eighties and nineties, while the younger, more vigorous men are cut down in their youth. There is no way to explain it except that it is one of the accidents of living. It happens with the trees and the birds and everything that grows. No individual can have any possible explanation, and therefore it is one of those things which must be accepted and absorbed into the philosophy that a man develops as he goes along.

In spite of all this . . . I know that it is hard for you to take. Yet you owe it to those still around you—your wife, your daughter and your grand-children—to provide an example that is not characterized by pessimism, cynicism and defeat.

This sounds like preaching—and possibly it is. My justification is that I lost a son of my own many years ago—the only one we then had. To this date it is not an easy thing to deal with when it comes fresh to my memory, but it is something that I had to learn to accept or to go crazy.

ALBERT CAMUS

In an address in 1948 at a Dominican monastery, philosopher and Nobel Prize–winning writer Albert Camus told the priests, "I share with you the same revulsion from evil. But I do not share your hope, and I continue to struggle against this universe in which children suffer and die." In his novel The Plague, *Camus has Father Paneloux and Dr. Rieux (clearly Camus's own voice) struggle with this metaphysical problem when a devastating plague strikes the city of Oran. Initially, Father Paneloux preaches to the people that "this plague came from God for the punishment of their sins" and "works for [their] good and points [their] path." In contrast, "suffering" has taught Dr. Rieux to wonder whether "since the order of the world is shaped by death, mightn't it be better for God if we refuse to believe in Him and struggle with all our might against death, without raising our eyes toward the heaven where He sits in silence?" Echoing Dostoevsky's character Ivan Karamazov (see p. 35), Father Paneloux's faith is finally challenged when he witnesses a child dying an excruciating death from the plague.*

from The Plague, translated by Stuart Gilbert

[Father Paneloux, after witnessing the child's death:] "That sort of thing is revolting because it passes our human understanding. But perhaps we should love what we cannot understand." . . .

[Dr. Rieux:] "No, Father. I've a different idea of love. And until my dying day I shall refuse to love a scheme of things in which children are put to torture."

Subsequently, when Father Paneloux preaches another sermon, his message changes dramatically. Dr. Rieux is in the congregation, his attention wandering.

His interest quickened when, in a more emphatic tone, the preacher said that there were some things we could grasp as touching God, and others we could not. There was no doubt as to the existence of good and evil and, as a rule, it was easy to see the difference between them. The difficulty began when we looked into the nature of evil, and among things evil he included human suffering. Thus we had apparently needful pain, and apparently needless pain; we had Don Juan cast into hell, and a child's death. For while it is right that a libertine should be struck down, we see no reason for a child's suffering. And, truth to tell, nothing was more important on earth than a child's suffering, the horror it inspires in us, and the reasons we must find to account for it. In other manifestations of life, God made things easy for us and, thus far, our religion had no merit. But in this respect He put us, so to speak, with our backs to the wall. . . . He, Father Paneloux, refused to have recourse to simple devices enabling him to scale that wall. Thus he might easily have assured them that the child's sufferings would be compensated for by an eternity of bliss awaiting him. But how could he give that assurance when, to tell the truth, he knew nothing about it? For who would dare to assert that eternal happiness can compensate for a single moment's human suffering? He who asserted that would not be a true Christian, a follower of the Master who knew all the pangs of suffering in his body and soul. No, he, Father Paneloux, would keep faith with that great symbol of all suffering, the tortured body on the Cross; would stand fast, his back to the wall, and face honestly the terrible problem of a child's agony. And he would boldly say to those who listened to his words today: "My brothers, a time of testing has come for us all. We must believe everything or deny everything. And who among you, I ask, would dare deny everything?"

PETER DE VRIES

A novel based on the suffering and death from leukemia of De Vries's youngest daughter, The Blood of the Lamb *follows Don Wanderhope's search for meaning after his only child, twelve-year-old Carol, also dies from leukemia. The first excerpt takes place before Carol dies. Wanderhope has befriended Stein, who has a daughter on the same children's cancer ward. Stein is a firm atheist, as Wanderhope had come to be. Now "on the brink of his child's grave," Wanderhope is trying to recover the faith he lost after his brother died many years before.*

from *The Blood of the Lamb*

As I neared the main lounge I heard voices raised in argument.

"These people who want to tell God how to run the universe," a man with a brick-red neck was saying, "they remind me of those people with five shares in some corporation who take up the entire stockholders' meeting telling the directors how to run their business."

I might have guessed who the object of the dressing down would be. Stein stood cornered behind the telephone booth, a carton of coffee in one hand and a smile on his face, obviously enjoying himself enormously. This was what he liked, proof of idiocy among the Positive Thinkers.

"I suppose you're going to tell me next I never met a payroll," he said, throwing me only the faintest sign of greeting so as not to interrupt the debate. Several visitors, mostly parents in various stages of vigil and disheshevelment, listened or chimed in.

"You ought to be ashamed," a woman in an Easter bonnet told Stein. "Your race gave us our religion. It's a good thing the ancient prophets weren't like you or we wouldn't have any." Stein drank from his carton and waited; she had not yet delivered herself into his hands. "From ancient polytheism, the belief in lots of gods," the woman continued a little more eruditely, "the Hebrew nation led us on to the idea that there is only one."

"Which is just a step from the truth," said Stein, and dropped his carton into a wastebasket.

The woman began to show anger, squirming a bit on her leather chair. "We with our finite . . ."

"What baffles me is the comfort people find in the idea that somebody dealt this mess. Blind and meaningless chance seems to me so much more congenial—or at least less horrible. Prove to me that there is a God and I will really begin to despair."

"It comes down to submitting to a wisdom greater than ours," said the man who had been attempting to focus the problem in terms of a stockholders' meeting. "A plan of which we can no more grasp the whole than a leaf can the forest of which it is a rustling part, or a grain of sand the seashore. What do you think when you look up at the stars at night?"

"I don't. I have enough to occupy me here."

"The Lord giveth and the Lord taketh away. What do you think of that?"

"I think it's a hell of a way to run a railroad."

"You ought to be ashamed!" the woman repeated with a further rise in spirit, not noticing a four-year-old patient watching the argument from a tricycle in the doorway. "Have you ever read your Bible?"

I nearly laughed. Where did she think he had got his pessimism? On what had he nurtured his despair if not on "Vanity of vanities," "All flesh is grass," "My tears have been my meat day and night," and "Is there no balm in Gilead: is there no physician there?"

Stein left his persecutors to join me in the hall, sending little Johnny Heard off on his tricycle with a pat on the head. We stood a moment comparing notes. Rachel [Stein's daughter] was in for the very same thing as Carol, after all these months of solid remission on Methotrexate and the 6-MP still to go. We sought out the girls in the recreation room, where they were getting on beautifully together. They didn't want any part of us. "How about a drink?" Stein proposed.

In my present need Stein might seem the last company I ought to seek. Yet in another sense he was precisely what I wanted at my side, the Devil's advocate off whom to bounce my speculations, the rock against which to hurl my yearnings and my thoughts, to test and prove them truly, an office that mealy-mouthed piety could not have performed. He was the goalkeeper past whom I must get my puck.

Much later, Carol has died, and Wanderhope, in cleaning out his daughter's bedroom, comes upon a tape she surreptitiously made and left for him.

"I want you to know that everything is all right, Daddy. I mean you mustn't worry, really. You've helped me a lot—more than you can imagine. I was digging around in the cabinet part at the bottom of the bookshelves for something to read that you would like. I mean, not something from your favorite books of poetry and all, but something of your own. What did I come across but that issue of the magazine put out by your alma mater, with the piece in it about your philosophy of life. Do you remember it? I might as well say that I know what's going on. What you wrote gives me courage to face whatever there is that's coming, so what could be more appropriate than to read it for you now? Remember when you explained it to me? Obviously, I don't understand it all, but I think I get the drift:

"I believe that man must learn to live without those consolations called religious, which his own intelligence must by now have told him belong to the childhood of the race. Philosophy can really give us nothing permanent to believe either; it is too rich in answers, each canceling out the rest. The quest for Meaning is foredoomed. Human life 'means' nothing. But that is not to say that it is not worth living. What does a Debussy *Arabesque* 'mean,' or a rainbow or a rose? A man delights in all of these, knowing himself to be no more—a wisp of music and a haze of dreams dissolving against the sun. Man has only his own two feet to stand on, his own human trinity to see him through: Reason, Courage, and Grace. And the first plus the second equals the third."

I reached the couch at last, on which I lay for some hours as though I had been clubbed, not quite to death. I wished that pound of gristle in my breast would stop its beating, as once in the course of that night I think it nearly did. The time between the last evening songs of the birds and their first cries at daybreak was a span of night without contents, blackness as stark as the lights left burning among the parlor furniture. Sometime towards its close I went to my bedroom, where from a bureau drawer I drew a small cruciform trinket on a chain. I went outside, walking down the slope of back lawn to the privet hedge, over which I hurled it as far as I could into the trees beyond. They were the sacred wood where we had so often walked, looking for the first snowdrops, listening for peepers, and in the clearings of which we had freed from drifts of dead leaves the tender heads of early violets.

I looked up through the cold air. All the stars were out. That pit of jewels, heaven, gave no answer. Among them would always be a wraith saying, "Can't I stay up a little longer?" I hear that voice in the city streets or on country roads, with my nose in a mug of cocoa, walking in the rain or standing in falling snow. "Pick one [snowflake] out and follow it to the ground."

How I hate this world. I would like to tear it apart with my own two hands if I could. I would like to dismantle the universe star by star, like a treeful of rotten fruit. Nor do I believe in progress. A vermin-eaten saint scratching his filth in the hope of heaven is better off than you damned in clean linen. Progress doubles our tenure in a vale of tears. Man is a mistake, to be corrected only by his abolition, which he gives promise of seeing to himself. Oh, let him pass, and leave the earth to the flowers that carpet the earth wherever he explodes his triumphs. Man is inconsolable, thanks to that eternal "Why?" when there is no Why, that question mark twisted like a fishhook in the human heart. "Let there be light," we cry, and only the dawn breaks. . . .

Sometime later, there was a footstep on the path and a knock on the door. It was Omar Howard, come to say good morning and to ask if I had found the Egyptian scarab ring of Carol's, which I had promised him. I had indeed, and, pressing it into his hand, received in return a volume I might find of interest — *Zen: The Answer?*

I sat paging through it for a few minutes after he had gone, sampling what would be perused at more leisure later. ". . . detached attachment . . . roll with nature . . . embrace her facts so as not to be crushed by them . . . swim with the . . ." And of course the Chinese original of that invisible wall-motto in the hospital corridor: "No fuss." On the jacket was a picture of the author, seen trimming a gardenia bush, his hobby. I boarded a train to California, in one or another of whose hanging gardens the wise man dwelt, and, bearding him there, asked whether there were any order of wisdom by which the sight of flowers being demolished could be readily borne. "Watch," I said, and tore from a branch the most perfect of his blossoms and mangled it into the dirt with my heel. Then I tore another, then another, watching studiously his expression as I ground the white blooms underfoot . . .

DAVID MORRELL

Morrell is best known for creating the character of Rambo, the hero of books and movies. He also wrote Fireflies, *a blend of fact and fantasy about the death of his fifteen-year-old son Matthew from cancer.*

from *Fireflies*

When you lose a child (and you truly loved that child and weren't just an indifferent caretaker or that scum of existence, a brutalizer), you search for some meaning, some justification, anything to ease your agony. You think about God and whether He exists and what kind of God would allow something so heinous as Matthew's death. You think about ultimates, about the point of existence and whether there's an afterlife and what it would be like. Would Matthew be waiting when his father, mother, and sister died? Would he be the same?

You question everything. You grasp at anything. To make sense of what seems to have no sense. To find meaning in what you despair might be the ultimate meaning: nothingness. You seek in all places, all cultures. You search in all philosophies and faiths.

Reincarnation? Plato believed in it. For that matter, a full half of the world's present population believes in it. In the East. As the theory goes, we struggle through various stages of existence, not always human, sometimes animal or even plant, rising until we've perfected our spirit sufficiently to abandon material existence and join forever in bliss with God.

A complicated but comforting belief. Because there's a point to life, a pay-off. Certainly it's easier to accept than the notion that God tortures us here on earth to punish us for our sins so we'll be happy with Him in Heaven. In that case, how do we explain the death of an infant, who couldn't possibly have sinned? Or the death of a fifteen-year-old boy, who by all accounts was remarkable and never harmed anyone?

Later in the book, Morrell writes:

I'm starting to believe in God and an afterlife. *Because I need to. Because I so desperately want to see my son again.* Believing in God gives me a hope. Can faith be far behind?

FRANK DEFORD

Sportswriter and National Public Radio and television commentator Frank Deford wrote Alex, *a memoir of his daughter, who died of cystic fibrosis at the age of eight.*

from Alex: The Life of a Child

I am not a nihilist or a sourpuss now that Alex is dead. I still laugh and love, marvel at the wonders of humanity and praise God for His. Neither, though, am I any wiser or stronger—and certainly no better—for what I went through. People assume you must be better for the experience, but I don't see why that must follow.

Neither must you necessarily abandon your faith. However, you do lose something every bit as important, for when your child dies, you yourself are robbed of that childish sanity that makes it tolerable to accept growing old. I don't see the incongruity of life so well anymore, because my child dying is the ultimate incongruity. A capricious world is much easier to deal with than the disordered one I have been forced to inhabit.

I do find one solace. Now that it is Alex who is dead (and not me), I really don't worry anymore about my own death. Oh sure, when the plane bumps about I gasp and grab the armrest and pray fervently that it will not plunge thirty-seven thousand feet and leave me in a number of charred little bits and pieces. I would not care for that at all. I'm not fey. But if you have an adorable little girl, and she up and dies, then a number of rules seem changed, including those of death itself. I can't be frightened to follow Alex, wherever to. I mean, first, strictly from a selfish point of view, dying is the only way I can possibly be with her again. But beyond that, Alex has, in her way, reduced all my normal maunderings about God and the hereafter to one terribly simple proposition. If there is a heaven—must be a heaven— great. If not, if this incredible little person spent eight years in pain, cursed, hopeless, only to completely disappear, poof, like that, then it is all quite pointless, all a gag, and it is of no great consequence to me whether or not I'm asked to participate in life as straight man or comic.

MARY ANN TAYLOR-HALL

In the novel Come and Go, Molly Snow, *familiar songs, even RV bumper stickers, take on new meaning for Kentucky bluegrass fiddler Carrie Marie Mullins after her five-year-old daughter Molly is killed in her own driveway.*

from Come and Go, Molly Snow

Oh, all the old songs I've sung in my day, all the times I've sent my fiddle fly-ing above the old words, *death is only a dream,* the old words, full of assur-ance. *On the opposite shore she'll be waiting for me.*

I never paid much attention. It was always more the music that got into my heart, not the words. I don't know what the ones [country music fans] at Justice's think. The ones at the festivals, sitting in plastic-webbed lawn chairs, passing beers around out of their coolers like the loaves and the fishes. Some have stickers on their RVs testifying, "No End to What Jesus Can Do." But some wear black baseball caps that say, "Shit Happens."

I don't much care anymore about this life or even about God. I just want to know what comes next. I want to know if the circle will be unbroken. I thought I knew more or less what that question was about, singing it. Now I know that love is a circle and either death breaks it or it doesn't and no one knows. It could be either way. Maybe the circle will be unbroken, but not in any way I can imagine.

What if it turns out that death is just the end of this tiny flame of con-sciousness, and then the body goes back to nature?

Then it's better to stay alive, so that I can remember her. Carry her mem-ory inside me as long as I'm alive, the way I carried *her.* Keep her safe, preserve her. I wasn't able to keep her safe in her real life. I let her out into the real world. I thought I was giving her life, but it wasn't enough to shake a stick at. I gave her death.

Not your fault, they always rush to say. *Not your fault, you must not blame yourself.* "Something terrible could happen to every one of us a hundred times a day," Ona told me. "The miracle is that mostly it don't."

"You can't watch them every second," my mother said. "You've got to trust to luck, a little." But you can't. You can't trust to luck.

Maybe the accident was—pure accident, one of the many things that just come down out of the sky and happen to people for no reason at all, except they were walking past the building when the bomb went off, sitting on the plane, looking at the clouds, when the engines failed.

That's not how it feels, though.

3

A Storm in the Heart: Pain and Despair

I used to wake up eager to start the day. Not anymore, not since Allie was killed. Now I lie in bed as long as I can, pondering the mystery and horror that happened to Allie and us. I'm like a hurt animal licking its wounds in a cave.

Sometimes Allie's death is the first thought that comes to my mind when I wake up; other times it's not. Sometimes it comes to me suddenly and sharply, my heart shrieking, "Allie is dead, Allie is dead, Allie is dead." Sometimes it floats to the surface of my consciousness slowly.

The same thoughts revolve over and over. How can it be? How can my lively sixteen-year-old son be gone forever? It makes no sense that this life which I cared for with all my heart and soul was wiped out in one cataclysmic moment. What makes life? Where did it go? What can I do to bring it back? There must be something.

I go over events of his life and decisions Peter and I made about schools, friends, neighborhoods, trying to decide what we could have done differently to avert this disaster. I review every detail of the accident—the car, the day, the scene, what I said and thought driving there and back, who Allie was with, who he was following. I may be wrong, but my impression is that there was a spectral hush at the scene as if all the police, rescue workers, and spectators were silenced by the horror of sudden death on a warm spring evening.

My thoughts travel to the future which stretches ahead, a barren vista of grief. What can I do to make my life tolerable after this? Whatever I plan, whatever I do, Allie will always be dead. I will live the rest of my life looking backwards. I cannot bear to contemplate this for long. So I come back to today. How will I navigate the grief today until I can return to the anesthesia of sleep? And tomorrow I'll start all over again.

MARY

51

TERRY ANDERSON

Anderson, chief Middle East correspondent of the Associated Press, was kidnapped off a street in Beirut in March 1985 and held hostage in Lebanon for almost seven years. Much of that time he was blindfolded and chained. After his release, former colleagues asked how he bore it. Grieving parents can well understand his answer.

from a syndicated column by Bill Hall,
originally appeared in the *Lewiston Tribune* (Idaho)

"You just do what you have to do. You wake up every day, and you summon up the energy from somewhere, even when you think you haven't got it, and you get through the day. And you do it day after day after day."

STUNNING PAIN

ANN K. FINKBEINER

A science journalist, Finkbeiner took her eighteen-year-old son, T. C. Colley, to the Baltimore train station, kissed him good-bye, and told him she was proud of him. He was eager to get back to his girlfriend and his school, the Rhode Island School of Design, after Christmas vacation. Twenty minutes later, a freight train hit T. C.'s train, killing him and fifteen other passengers, many of them also college students.

from *After the Death of a Child: Living with Loss Through the Years*

With reality comes pain, and the pain, when it comes, is stunning. The pain is actually physical, mostly in your stomach and chest. Your chest feels crushed and you can't seem to catch your breath. I remember feeling pinned like a butterfly, or somehow eviscerated. One woman drew an arc that started at her head and ended at her knees and said, "His death was cut out of *here.*" The pain comes in waves—moves in, backs off, then in again. People try describing it with superlatives or metaphors, then give up the attempt. And no one wants to try too hard anyway; they'd much rather talk about how, with time, the waves of pain gradually became less frequent. "Now when I think of him," one woman said, "I don't get that *wrenching,* I don't know the word to use, that *wrenching* feeling."

GORDON LIVINGSTON

Livingston, a psychiatrist and writer, lost two of his sons—one to suicide, the other to leukemia. The following is taken from the journal he began keeping when the family was given six-year-old Lucas's cancer diagnosis.

from *Only Spring: On Mourning the Death of My Son*

May 29, 1992 [ten days after Lucas died]

. . . The pictures in my mind of Lucas dying will give me no rest. How can I erase, or at least soften, these images and remember him as he was in health, his sweet face, happy smile? How could they have put him and us through those changes? I never felt warned about those possibilities in the dry words of the "informed consents." What is the process now other than waiting for time to pass? Should I try to get back to work next week? Would it help to travel far away or will I just miss him in a different place? I need some faith in God, but where was He when we needed him, when so many were praying on our behalf? I feel old, as if I have lived too long, seen too much, suffered beyond any hope of redemption. I am empty, barely capable of loving those who need me. My best hope for immortality lies in a church-yard. And the world goes on as if nothing has happened. I don't want to be a part of it. . . .

May 30, 1992

Lucas was brave, now I must be brave. I'm not quite sure what that means, but facing the loss and finding reasons to live seem the main tasks. The hole in my life left by his death is beyond filling. It is a void stretching into what-ever future I have left. I cannot see a child on the street or boys playing soc-cer or teenagers hanging out at the mall without thinking of what was denied my wholly innocent son. The fact that he had a wonderful life for the six years he was ours is insufficient consolation. He deserved much more. . . .

June 17, 1992

. . . The loss of my sons has brought me to the edge of an abyss. I stare into it and see only darkness. I would fill it with faith, but whatever belief I had in a just universe has been undone. I, of all people, should have been aware of what a fantasy this notion was. God knows I have seen enough injustice and random death. But I guess I harbored an unconscious belief that the really terrible, life-decimating tragedies were reserved for others. Now I wonder about curses and stigmata.

I've always felt lucky because I've always been lucky. When this happens, at some point you start to feel that you deserve it, that you've somehow earned it. I don't feel lucky anymore.

I told Clare tonight that "I think about him all the time, don't you?" The answer, of course, was yes, and we both began to cry. I said something about being sure he was all right. She said, "I hope so. . . . I just want him back." I start to tell her how sorry I am, but she knows that and I can't even think the words without remembering Emily [Lucas's sister] at his bedside when he died: "I'm so sorry, Luke. I'm so sorry." I don't see how I'm going to get past this.

June 23, 1992
. . . What I feared most has happened. Lucas is now forever a six-year-old boy who died. We miss him now as he was and still would be were he with us. In a year he would have been so much different from the child we mourn. In five years we would hardly recognize him and will have only the memories of his angelic countenance smiling forever at us from his photographs—as he was and always now will be. So it's not just the grindstone of time that will dull our pain; it's his not keeping up with us or with the world that will finally, sadly, inevitably bring us some peace. That and the hope that we will see him again on the other side.

October 7, 1992
I labor to write a paragraph or two each day about Lucas's life, trying to fix all my memories of him. Emily said to Clare on Saturday, "Sometimes I can't believe he was really here." I know what she means. I look at his picture now and it is beyond my comprehension that he no longer lives on this earth except in our hearts. Clare took some rolls of film to be developed, and, unexpectedly, one of them contained some random pictures of the inside of the car that Lucas had apparently taken. It felt to us like a message about his continuing presence in which we so much want to believe. . . .

February 10, 1993
. . . Sometimes at night I think about driving to the airport, getting into the airplane, and flying west at one thousand feet in the darkness, until I meet the mountains. It would happen near Frederick, where Clare and I were married, lending the end a certain symmetry. I could not, of course, inflict

that upon my family, but the idea that I might thereby join Lucas fills me with anticipation. I have had patients who have lost children and told me of a wish to follow them. Now I understand.

August 23, 1993
. . . Memory burdens me like an anchor I cannot raise. It was not always so. My few earthly attachments allowed me to move through the present without fear on the way to a future that held, I imagined, some perfect combination of peace and excitement. That is gone now. I am weighted by the past and advance only haltingly and with great effort toward whatever time is left—full of obligation, but without promise of the joy that I so freely savored.

JAN KOCHANOWSKI

Some critics call Kochanowski (1530–84) the greatest poet of the entire Slavic world up to the beginning of the nineteenth century. But in his middle age, when his youngest child, Ursula, died at two and a half, Kochanowski astounded his admirers: he wrote about his grief. In rural Poland at that time, "the death of a small child was a sad but fairly regular occurrence," translator Stanislaw Baranczak writes in his preface to Laments. *Elegies were reserved for important people. "Therefore, the poet's reaching for this genre . . . in order to mourn a* child's *death (and to make things worse, his own child, a very young daughter unknown to anybody beyond the immediate family) was tantamount, at best, to a serious artistic error. Indeed, the initial reaction to the publication of* Laments *in 1580 was definitely cold."*

from *Laments*, translated by Stanislaw Baranczak and Seamus Heaney

Lament 1

All Heraclitus' tears, all threnodies
And plaintive dirges of Simonides,
All keens and slow airs in the world, all griefs,
Wrung hands, wet eyes, laments and epitaphs,
All, all assemble, come from every quarter,
Help me to mourn my small girl, my dear daughter,
Whom cruel Death tore up with such wild force
Out of my life, it left me no recourse.

So the snake, when he finds a hidden nest
Of fledgling nightingales, rears and strikes fast
Repeatedly, while the poor mother bird
Tries to distract him with a fierce, absurd
Fluttering—but in vain! the venomous tongue
Darts, and she must retreat on ruffled wing.
"You weep in vain," my friends will say. But then,
What is not vain, by God, in lives of men?
All is in vain! We play at blindman's buff
Until hard edges break into our path.
Man's life is error. Where, then, is relief?
In shedding tears or wrestling down my grief?

SORROW IS NO LONGER THE ISLANDS BUT THE SEA

NICHOLAS WOLTERSTORFF

A Christian philosopher, Wolterstorff wrote several scholarly books, but this memoir charted his grief and questioning in the first year after his twenty-five-year-old son Eric died in a mountain-climbing accident.

from *Lament for a Son*

The world looks different now. The pinks have become purple, the yellows brown. Mountains now wear crosses on their slopes. Hymns and psalms have reordered themselves so that lines I scarcely noticed now leap out: "He will not suffer thy foot to stumble." Photographs that once evoked the laughter of delighted reminiscence now cause only pain. Why are the photographs of him as a little boy so incredibly hard for me to look at? This one here, holding a fish longer than he is tall, six years old? Why is it easier to look at him as a grownup? The pleasure of seeing former students is colored by the realization that they were his friends and that while they thrive he rots.

Something is *over*. In the deepest levels of my existence something is finished, done. My life is divided into before and after. A friend of ours whose husband died young said it meant for her that her youth was over. My youth was already over. But I know what she meant. Something is over.

Especially in places where he and I were together this sense of something *being over* washes over me. It happens not so much at home, but other places. A moment in our lives together of special warmth and intimacy and vividness, a moment when I specially prized him, a moment of hope and expectancy and openness to the future: I remember the moment. But instead of lines of memory leading up to his life in the present, they all enter a place of cold inky blackness and never come out. The book slams shut. The story stops, it doesn't finish. The future closes, the hopes get crushed. And now instead of those shiny moments being things we can share together in delighted memory, I, the survivor, have to bear them alone.

So it is with all memories of him. They all lead into that blackness. It's all over, over, over. All I can do is *remember* him. I can't *experience* him. The person to whom these memories are attached is no longer here with me, standing up. He's only in my memory now, not in my life. Nothing new can happen between us. Everything is sealed tight, shut in the past. I'm still here. I have to go on. I have to start over. But this new start is so different from the first. Then I wasn't carrying this load, this thing that's over.

Sometimes I think that happiness is over for me. I look at photos of the past and immediately comes the thought: that's when we were still happy. But I can still laugh, so I guess that isn't quite it. Perhaps what's over is happiness as the fundamental tone of my existence. Now sorrow is that.

Sorrow is no longer the islands but the sea.

PAULA TRACHTMAN

Paula Trachtman wrote this piece and compiled the anthology in which it appears in memory of her daughter Amy.

from "An Absence of Amy," in Out of Season: An Anthology of Work by and about Young People Who Died, edited by Paula Trachtman

I tell the psychiatrist of the things I do. Bring flowers, landscape the grave, try to get her poems published. "What," I ask, "is the point? She is dead. It's all so meaningless." Being the father of a beloved daughter, he looks away from me, pushing away my pain, which is palpable, and mutters, "Maybe it isn't."

"What," this kind man probes, "is it that you want?"

"I want Amy not to be dead."

"Of course," he says, "but what else?"

"Nothing."

He sighs. Like a sin eater, he is paid to take the burden upon himself so a lightness of being can come upon me. But we know this is impossible. I tell him of something I read in *The New York Times*. There was a support group for parents who had suffered the loss of a child. When one woman broke down after telling of the death of her daughter, an only child, in a car crash, another member of the group touched her gently and said quietly, "I know exactly how you feel."

The woman blazed with anger, threw off the comforting hand and hissed, "How could you? She was *my* daughter!" I explain that this is my exact reaction. No one can share grief. Only the bereft know the loss, each relationship is unique. Only *I* remember how my baby gurgled with joy at age three months and gave me a drooly, lop-sided grin when I entered her pretty sunshine-yellow room. Her universe existed as soon as I affirmed her reality by responding to her tentative morning sounds. A hesitation would call forth a whimper, and then heartbreaking cries. She did not exist if I didn't appear. Now I do not exist because she can never appear in answer to my cries.

JANE KENYON

Readers of Kenyon are aware that she struggled with depression. Clearly she knew her adversary well.

from *Otherwise: New and Selected Poems*

Now Where?

It wakes when I wake, walks
when I walk, turns back when I
turn back, beating me to the door.

It spoils my food and steals
my sleep, and mocks me, saying,
"Where is your God now?"

And so, like a widow, I lie down
after supper. If I lie down
or sit up it's all the same:

the days and nights bear me along.
To strangers I must seem
alive. Spring comes, summer;

cool clear weather; heat, rain. . . .

TOM CRIDER

This writer's only child, Gretchen, died in an apartment fire at age twenty-one.

from *Give Sorrow Words: A Father's Passage through Grief*

At night when he can't sleep, he reads books on death and religion. Some of them say she is not really dead. Some say God has other plans for her. He has never believed in a God who controls human lives or decrees their deaths, and he's always felt the idea of immortality was wishful thinking. Now, with his mind and emotions in turmoil, he seems to be scavenging for ways to keep her from having vanished. He finds himself ready to believe just about anything. He's like a beggar in winter, clawing through box after box of old coats, looking for one that fits. . . .

I walk through the valley of the shadow of death, but, unlike the psalmist, I fear evil everywhere.

It's deeper than fear, really, it's dread. He feels like a dog who's lived through being run over once and who jumps at the slightest sound to make sure nothing is coming at him again. When the phone rings, his heart bounds. He thinks someone else has died: Mieke, his mother, his brother, a friend. In a store or on a street, he hears a child scream, but instead of delight, he hears horror, and turns to see if the child needs help. Several times a day, spurts of fright splash up from a sea of dread.

In addition to the expected definition of *dread*—"to anticipate with anxiety, alarm, or apprehension; fear intensely," he finds this also: "fear mixed with awe or reverence."

Yes, there is awe in what I feel. It's what I imagine a mole might feel when the top of its burrow is scraped away by a grizzly. It comes from being one who is tiny in the presence of a greater, malevolent power. This power snatched my daughter Gretchen away from me. What will it do next? . . .

At the health club a guy asks him, "Do you have any children?" He hesitates before saying, "No." Would someone waiting to play racquetball want to hear what happened to Gretchen?

He feels the role of father, a silk robe he once wore, slipping from his shoulders. Everything it meant to be a father is gone, suddenly and forever.

When Gretchen was born, her infant life gave his a bright new purpose. She depended upon him for shelter, food, guidance, and love. Her development into genius or ignoramus, aggressor or peacemaker, may not have been entirely up to him, but it felt that way. And he believed he'd have some influence, through his child, her children, and her children's children, on the future of the human race.

Now, for him, in addition to his only child, his fatherhood and all that it meant has vanished. He has no daughter or son to care for and no lineage going out from himself into the future. He still has a lingering fatherly pride and love, but the object of it is gone, and he stands on a severed branch of the family tree.

ERIC CLAPTON

In this beautifully melodic song, blues/rock guitarist and singer Eric Clapton wonders if his son Conor, who died at four and a half, would still recognize him. It's a question that haunts many bereaved parents—especially those who lose young children. Where are they? And after a while, will they know us? Conor fell to his death from the fifty-third floor of his mother's New York apartment after climbing unnoticed onto a window ledge. A housekeeper, cleaning windows, had left one open to dry. Afterwards, Clapton wrote a cycle of songs for Conor, believing that somehow, in some spiritual way, his son would hear them. "I have to pay my respects to that boy, in my way," he later told an interviewer, "and let the world know what I thought about him."

from the compact disc *Eric Clapton Unplugged*

Tears in Heaven

Would you know my name
if I saw you in heaven?
Would it be the same
if I saw you in heaven?
I must be strong
and carry on
'cause I know
I don't belong
here in heaven.

Would you hold my hand
if I saw you in heaven?
Would you help me stand
if I saw you in heaven?
I'll find my way
through night and day
'cause I know
I just can't stay
here in heaven.

Time can bring you down;
time can bend your knees.
Time can break your heart;
have you begging please
. . . begging please.

Beyond the door
there's peace I'm sure
and I know
there'll be no more
tears in heaven.

C. S. LEWIS

*After his wife died, Lewis—author of the Narnia stories, as well as schol-
arly and religious books—turned understandably to what he knew best.
He tried to blunt his grief by writing about it. The result,* A Grief Observed, *has been a staple in grief literature since 1963.*

from *A Grief Observed*

No one ever told me that grief felt so like fear. I am not afraid, but the sensation is like being afraid. The same fluttering in the stomach, the same restlessness, the yawning. I keep on swallowing.

At other times it feels like being mildly drunk, or concussed. There is a sort
of invisible blanket between the world and me. I find it hard to take in what
anyone says. Or perhaps, hard to want to take it in. It is so uninteresting. Yet
I want the others to be about me. I dread the moments when the house is
empty. If only they would talk to one another and not to me. . . .

. . . Do I hope that if feeling disguises itself as thought I shall feel less? Aren't all these notes the senseless writhings of a man who won't accept the fact that there is nothing we can do with suffering except to suffer it? Who still thinks there is some device (if only he could find it) which will make pain not to be pain. It doesn't really matter whether you grip the arms of the dentist's chair or let your hands lie in your lap. The drill drills on.

J. D. McCLATCHY

This section is excerpted from a much longer piece; it is typical of McClatchy's intricate poetry, with its layers of meaning.

from "Fog Tropes," in *Poets for Life: Seventy-Six Poets Respond to AIDS*, edited by Michael Klein

When my daughter died, from the bottom
Of every pleasure something bitter
Rose up, a sour taste of nausea,
The certain sense of having failed
Not to save her but in the end to know
I could not keep her from passing
As through the last, faintest intake
Of breath to somewhere unsure of itself,
The dim landscape that grief supposes.
I remember how, in the hospital,
Without a word she put her glasses on
And stared ahead, just before she died.

I take mine off these days, to see
More of my solitude, its incidental
Humiliations. Nothing satisfies
Its demand that she appear in order
To leave my life over and over again.
If, from my car, I should glimpse her
In a doorway, bright against the dark
Inside, and stop and squint at the glare—
It's a rag on a barbed-wire fence.
Or I spot her in a sidewalk crowd

But almost at once she disappears
The way one day slips behind the next.
I've come to think of her now, in fact,
Or of her ghost I guess you'd have to say,
As the tear that rides and overrides
My eye, so that the edges of things go
Soft, a girl is there and not there.

RITA DOVE

The first African American to be named poet laureate of the United States (1993–1995), Dove explores the Greek myth of Persephone in a book of sonnets, Mother Love: Poems, *published in 1995. In this myth—the ancients' explanation for the seasons—Hades kidnaps lovely Persephone and drags her down with him into the Underworld to be his bride. Her mother, Demeter, is so distraught with grief she ignores her duties as goddess of agriculture, and the crops wither. Zeus strikes a bargain: Hades must return Persephone to her mother six months a year. Every fall and winter Demeter is allowed to grieve the loss of her only daughter, letting vegetation die. But in spring and summer, when Persephone returns, Demeter must make the earth blossom and bear fruit. Demeter thinks herself inconsolable. Only a bereaved parent realizes how blessed she is.*

from *Mother Love: Poems*

Demeter Mourning

Nothing can console me. You may bring silk
to make skin sigh, dispense yellow roses
in the manner of ripened dignitaries.
You can tell me repeatedly
I am unbearable (and I know this):
still, nothing turns the gold to corn,
nothing is sweet to the tooth crushing in.

I'll not ask for the impossible;
one learns to walk by walking.
In time I'll forget this empty brimming,

I may laugh again at
a bird, perhaps, chucking the nest—
but it will not be happiness,
for I have known that.

ANNE MORROW LINDBERGH

On a March evening in 1932, kidnappers took the eighteen-month-old son of American aviator hero Charles ("Lucky Lindy") Lindbergh and his wife, leaving behind a ransom demand on the nursery windowsill. Negotiations went on for an interminable ten weeks, but soon after the Lindberghs paid the ransom, their child's dead body was found in woods near their home. The boy's distraught mother, Anne Morrow Lindbergh, pregnant with a second child, was used to keeping a journal. In the suspenseful weeks before her baby was found, she wrote, "I found it necessary, while trying to keep a surface composure for my husband, my family, and those working for and with us, to give way somewhere to the despair banked up within me." Later it was a place to spill her grief.

from Hour of Gold, Hour of Lead:
Diaries and Letters of Anne Morrow Lindbergh 1929–1932

Saturday, July 16, 1932

. . . I feel obsessed now when I say good-by to people—that I will not see them again. Something in me that says perpetually: "Seize this while you have it, remember that gesture, it is the last time." Something in me that wants to make everything significant because, perhaps, I did not make significant enough the few hours I had with Charlie, spending them recklessly, looking ahead to endless years of him.

But you are always fooled—it is not what you expect that waits for you. . . .

Sunday, July 17, 1932

. . . I am in a kind of stupor now about the baby. I do not go up to his room or look at his things or write in his record or go over the pictures. I feel in a kind of hopeless numbness. He is gone. I can't get him back that way or any other way. He is just gone. There is nothing to do. How futile to try to hang on to him by these scraps. How futile to hope that a miniature would have some of him—and even so, what comfort would it be in the face of that complete loss. The picture gets dimmer and I, hopeless, do not fight the inevitable.

Perhaps the numbness is partly physical protection. Perhaps Emily Dickinson's . . .

> "This is the hour of lead
> Remembered if outlived
> As freezing persons recollect
> The snow—
> First chill, then stupor, then
> The letting go."

Sunday, September 18, 1932
Can hardly bear to think of the little, real body that was Charlie going to nothing. Why is it harder to think of his going to nothing than to think of his coming from nothing? One direction is just as dark as the other.

STÉPHANE MALLARMÉ

"In 1879, we had the immense sorrow of losing my little brother, an ex-quisite child of eight," Geneviève, Stéphane Mallarmé's surviving child, recalled in her memoir. "I was quite young then, but the deep and silent pain I felt in my father made an unforgettable impression on me: 'Hugo [Victor Hugo—see p. 15],' he said, 'was happy to have been able to speak (about the death of his daughter); for me, it's impossible.'" Although the French poet could not speak of Anatole, Mallarmé did plan to memorialize his son's life in *written words. He would construct a tomb of poetry for his son. But written words failed Mallarmé too. The project never came to fruition. Fragments of intended poems, like those below, were all he could manage.*

from A Tomb for Anatole, translated by Paul Auster

> father and mother
> vowing
> to have no other
> child
> —grave dug by him
> life ends here

*   *   *

family perfect
balance
   father son
   mother daughter

broken —
three, a void
among us,
     searching . . .

     *   *   *

no more life for

    —

me
    and I feel
I am lying in the grave
beside you.

   *   *   *

    child
sister remains, who
will lead to a future
brother
   — she exempt from
this grave for
father mother and son
— by her marriage.

MARGARET OLIPHANT

Margaret Oliphant wrote nearly one hundred novels in nineteenth-century England, but her most poignant writing is found in an auto-biographical sketch in which she wrote about the deaths of her six children. This passage describes her feelings after the death of her first child, Margaret, at age ten, in 1864.

from *Angels and Absences: Child Deaths in the Nineteenth Century* by Laurence Lerner

The hardest moment in my present sad life is the morning, when I must wake up and begin the dreary world again. I can sleep during the night, and

I sleep as long as I can; but when it is no longer possible, when the light can no longer be gainsaid, and life is going on everywhere, then I, too, rise up to bear my burden. How different it used to be! When I was a girl I remember the feeling I had when the fresh morning light came round. Whatever grief there had been the night before, the new day triumphed over it. Things must be better than one thought, must be well, in a world which woke up to that new light, to the sweet dews and sweet air which renewed one's soul. Now I am thankful for the night and the darkness, and shudder to see the light and the day returning.

JOHN TITTENSOR

In 1982, this Australian writer lost his only children, Jonathan and Emma, aged nine and seven, in a house fire.

from Year One: A Record

June 4 [1983]
As their first anniversary approaches, I remind myself that it's only in our own time that people have come to expect their children to live to maturity as a matter of course. My own mother was one of six children, two of whom became ill and died in the first year of their lives; in the 1920s this wasn't re-garded as exceptional. The only trouble: *this knowledge is no consolation whatsoever.*

LUCIE DUFF GORDON

Lucie Duff Gordon lived in the social and intellectual center of Victorian society until she left for Egypt in 1862 to relieve her suffering from tuber-culosis. She fell in love with Egypt and supported herself there by writing Letters from Egypt, *which captivated British readers and is still being read. In 1845, Lucie's second child, Maurice, barely six months old, died of a fever. Excerpts from letters describe her despair.*

from A Passage to Egypt: The Life of Lucie Duff Gordon by Katherine Frank

"I find it still impossible to shake off the depression caused by my boy's death. The more I think of it, the worse it seems to me and the harder to bear. People torment me with the stupid and senseless consolation of 'You can easily have another.' I have too little faith in the mercy of Providence to incur the risk of having my heart broken over again . . . The misfortune, the sorrow is *there, c'est un fait accompli,* it may be borne, like everything else, but it can't be repaired.". . .

. . . [I feel] "indifferent to everything and almost everyone, for I cannot disguise from myself that I care less even for my [remaining] child."

LOATHING LIFE

W. E. B. DU BOIS

Social critic, black advocate, and founder of the NAACP, Du Bois lost his two-year-old son Burghardt to nasopharyngeal diphtheria. The night before Burghardt died, his father frantically tried to find one of the two or three black physicians living on the other side of town—with no success. Like Samuel Clemens, another bereaved father, Du Bois took early solace in the certainty that his child would now at least be spared the cruelties of life.

from *The Souls of Black Folk*

I saw his breath beat quicker and quicker, pause, and then his little soul leapt like a star that travels in the night and left a world of darkness in its train. The day changed not; the same tall trees peeped in at the windows, the same green grass glinted in the setting sun. Only in the chamber of death writhed the world's most piteous thing—a childless mother. . . .

We could not lay him in the ground there in Georgia, for the earth there is strangely red; so we bore him away to the northward, with his flowers and his little folded hands. In vain, in vain!—for where, O God! beneath thy broad blue sky shall my dark baby rest in peace,—where Reverence dwells, and Goodness, and a Freedom that is free?

All that day and all that night there sat an awful gladness in my heart,—nay, blame me not if I see the world thus darkly through the Veil,—and my soul whispers ever to me, saying, "Not dead, not dead, but escaped; not bond, but free." No bitter meanness now shall sicken his baby heart till it die a living death, no taunt shall madden his happy boyhood. . . . Well sped, my boy, before the world had dubbed your ambition insolence, had held your ideals unattainable, and taught you to cringe and bow. Better far this nameless void that stops my life than a sea of sorrow for you.

Idle words; he might have borne his burden more bravely than we,—aye, and found it lighter too, some day; for surely, surely this is not the end. Surely there shall yet dawn some mighty morning to lift the Veil and set the prisoned free. Not for me,—I shall die in my bonds,—but for fresh young souls who have not known the night and waken to the morning; a morning when men ask of the workman, not "Is he white?" but "Can he work?" When men ask artists, not "Are they black?" but "Do they know?" Some morning this may be, long, long years to come. But now there wails, on that dark shore within the Veil, the same deep voice, *Thou shalt forego!* And all have I foregone at that command, and with small complaint,—all save that fair young form that lies so coldly wed with death in the nest I had builded.

If one must have gone, why not I? Why may I not rest me from this restlessness and sleep from this wide waking? Was not the world's alembic, Time, in his young hands, and is not my time waning? Are there so many workers in the vineyard that the fair promise of this little body could lightly be tossed away? The wretched of my race that line the alleys of the nation sit fatherless and unmothered; but Love sat beside his cradle, and in his ear Wisdom waited to speak. Perhaps now he knows the All-love, and needs not to be wise. Sleep, then, child,—sleep till I sleep and waken to a baby voice and the ceaseless patter of little feet—above the Veil.

THERE ARE NO WORDS FOR THIS

JULIAN BARNES

The man speaking here in Barnes's novel has just lost his wife, not a child. But he's not alone in being told that he'll "come out of it" someday and in finding that grief needs a language of its own.

from *Flaubert's Parrot*

There's no glory in it. Mourning is full of time; nothing but time. . . . I've tried drink, but what does that do? Drink makes you drunk, that's all it's ever been able to do. Work, they say, cures everything. It doesn't; often, it doesn't even induce tiredness: the nearest you get to it is a neurotic lethargy. And there is always time. Have some more time. Take your time. Extra time. Time on your hands.

Other people think you want to talk. "Do you want to talk about Ellen?" they ask, hinting that they won't be embarrassed if you break down.

Sometimes you talk, sometimes you don't; it makes little difference. The words aren't the right ones; or rather, the right words don't exist. "Language is like a cracked kettle on which we beat out tunes for bears to dance to, while all the time we long to move the stars to pity." You talk, and you find the language of bereavement foolishly inadequate. You seem to be talking about other people's griefs. I loved her; we were happy; I miss her. . . .

"It may seem bad, Geoffrey, but you'll come out of it. I'm not taking your grief lightly; it's just that I've seen enough of life to know that you'll come out of it." The words you've said yourself. . . . And you do come out of it, that's true. After a year, after five. But you don't come out of it like a train coming out of a tunnel, bursting through the Downs into sunshine and that swift, rattling descent to the Channel; you come out of it as a gull comes out of an oil-slick. You are tarred and feathered for life.

JIM SIMMERMAN

Simmerman brings a dark beauty here to the familiar expression "Action speaks louder than words."

from The Bread Loaf Anthology of Contemporary American Poetry,
edited by Robert Pack, Sydney Lea, and Jay Parini

Child's Grave, Hale County, Alabama

Someone drove a two-by-four
through the heart of this hard land
that even in a good year
will notch a plow blade worthless,
snap the head off a shovel,
or bow a stubborn back.
He'd have had to steal
the wood from a local mill
or steal, by starlight, across
his landlord's farm, to worry
a fencepost out of its well
and lug it the three miles home.
He'd have had to leave his wife
asleep on a corn shuck mat,
leave his broken brogans

by the stove, to slip outside,
quiet as sin, with the child
bundled in a burlap sack.
What a thing to have to do
on a cold night in December,
1936, alone
but for a raspy wind
and the red, rock-ridden dirt
things come down to in the end.
Whoever it was pounded
this shabby half-cross
into the ground must have toiled
all night to root it so:
five feet buried with the child
for the foot of it that shows.
And as there are no words
carved here, it's likely that
the man was illiterate,
or addled with fatigue,
or wrenched simple-minded
by the one simple fact.
Or else the unscored lumber
driven deep into the land
and the hump of busted rock
spoke too plainly of his grief:
forty years layed by and still
there are no words for this.

MOISHE LANG

Lang, a therapist, points out to other therapists that silence is not always what it seems.

from "The Shadow of Evil," in *The Family Therapy Networker*,
September/October 1995

In the "talking cure" of therapy, silence is usually associated with defensiveness, resistance, negativism, denial and shame. But silence may also be a mark of profound respect, a recognition that ordinary language is inadequate before certain vast and terrible realities. This taboo applies not only to what is forbidden, but to what is sacred, as well.

HANGING ON TO GRIEF

RUSSELL BANKS

In The Sweet Hereafter, *later made into a movie of the same name, a town loses its children when a veteran school-bus driver brakes—for a dog?—and the bus plunges over an embankment into a frozen water-filled sandpit below. Garage-owner Billy Ansel, the narrator here, is in his pickup directly behind the bus, waving to his twins, when the bus skids off the road. Already widowed, he goes home to an empty house.*

from *The Sweet Hereafter*

Mourning can be very selfish. When someone you love has died, you tend to recall best those few moments and incidents that helped to clarify your sense, not of the person who has died, but of your own self. And if you loved the person a great deal, as I loved Lydia and my children, your sense of who you are will have been clarified many times, and so you will have many such moments to remember. I have learned that.

Nights now I can sit in my living room alone, looking at the glass of the picture window, with the reflection of my body and the drink in my hand and the chair and lamp beside me glaring flat and white back at me, and I am in no way as real in that room as I am in my memories of my wife and children. Sometimes it's not as if they have died so much as that I myself have died and have become a ghost. You might think that remembering those moments is a way of keeping my family alive, but it's not; it's a way of keeping myself alive. Just as you might think my drinking is a way to numb the pain; it's not; it's a way to feel the pain.

One night early after the accident, Ansel drives to the garage lot where the school bus now sits.

I don't know why I was there, staring with strange loathing and awe at this wrecked yellow vehicle, as if it were a beast that had killed our children and then in turn been slain by the villagers and dragged here to a place where we

could all come, one by one, and verify that it was safely dead. But I did want
to see it, to touch it with my hands, maybe, in a primitive way to be sure finally that we had indeed killed it.

I got out of my truck, leaving the motor running and the headlights on,
and walked slowly toward the bus. It was very cold; my shoes squeaked
against the hard-packed snow on the ground, and my breath glided out in
front of me in pale thin strips. There were several other vehicles parked in
the darkness in the back lot—customers' cars scheduled to be repaired but
crowded out of the garage and a couple of wrecks stashed there for parts or
being rebuilt for the demolition derby. The orange plastic tape that the state
police had wrapped around the bus to warn people away from it looked like
tangled lines from the harpoons we had stuck it with.

For a moment I stood at the side of the bus, looking up at the windows;
and then I heard the children inside. Their voices were faint, but I could
hear them clearly. They were alive and happy, going to school, and Dolores
was moving through the gears, driving the bus up hill and down, cheerfully
doing her duty; and I longed to join them, felt a deep aching desire to be
with them, the first clear emotion I had felt since the accident; I wanted simply to pull the door open and walk inside and smell the wet wool and rubber boots and the lunches carried in paper sacks and tin boxes, hear their
songs and gossip and teasing; I wanted to be with them in death, with my
own children, yes, but with all of them, for they seemed at that moment so
much more believable than I myself was, so much more alive.

PHILLIPS BROOKS

*Writing to a friend on the death of his mother in 1891, Brooks gives
advice that applies equally well to bereaved parents.*

from In the Midst of Winter: Selections from the Literature of Mourning,
edited by Mary Jane Moffat

May I try to tell you again where your only comfort lies? It is not in forgetting the happy past. People bring us well-meant but miserable consolations
when they tell us what time will do to help our grief. We do not want to lose
our grief, because our grief is bound up with our love and we could not cease
to mourn without being robbed of our affections.

FYODOR DOSTOEVSKY

Alexey, Dostoevsky's fourth child, died May 16, 1878, shortly before his fourth birthday. An epileptic himself, Dostoevsky felt responsible because Alexey died of a prolonged epileptic seizure. In January 1879, The Brothers Karamazov *began to be published in serial form. Dostoevsky had to be thinking of his own Alexey when he wrote the following scene at the beginning of the book. In it a grieving mother has made a pilgrimage to Father Zossima, a revered elder of the church. Like Melville (see p. 18), Dostoevsky refers here to the biblical verse about Rachel weeping for her children who are no more.*

from The Brothers Karamazov, translated by Constance Garnett,
edited by Ralph E. Matlaw

"But here is one from afar." He pointed to a woman by no means old but very thin and wasted, with a face not merely sunburned but almost blackened by exposure. She was kneeling and gazing with a fixed stare at the elder; there was something almost frenzied in her eyes.

"From afar off, Father, from afar off! From two hundred miles from here. From afar off, Father, from afar off!" the woman began in a singsong voice as though she were chanting a dirge, swaying her head from side to side with her cheek resting in her hand.

There is silent and long-suffering sorrow to be met with among the peasantry. It withdraws into itself and is still. But there is also a grief that breaks out, and from that minute it bursts into tears and finds vent in wailing. This is particularly common with women. But it is no lighter a grief than the silent. Lamentations comfort only by lacerating the heart still more. Such grief does not desire consolation. It feeds on the sense of its own hopelessness. Lamentations spring only from the constant craving to reopen the wound. . . .

. . . "I have come to see you, oh Father! We heard of you, Father, we heard of you. I have buried my little son, and I have come on a pilgrimage. I have been in three monasteries, but they told me, 'Go, Nastasya, go to them' — that is to you, my dear. I have come; I was yesterday at the service, and today I have come to you."

"What are you weeping for?"

"It's my little son I'm grieving for, Father. He was three years old—three years all but three months. I grieve for my little boy, Father, for my little boy. I'm in anguish for my little boy. . . . He seems always standing before me. He never leaves me. He has withered my heart. I look at his little clothes, his little shirt, his little boots, and I wail. I lay out all that is left of him, all his little things. I look at them and wail. I say to Nikita, my husband, let me go on a pilgrimage, master. He is a driver. We're not poor people, Father, not poor; he drives our own horse. It's all our own, the horse and the carriage. And what good is it all to us now? My Nikita has begun drinking while I am away. He's sure to. It used to be so before. As soon as I turn my back he gives way to it. But now I don't think about him. It's three months since I left home. I've forgotten him. I've forgotten everything. I don't want to remember. And what would our life be now together? I've done with him, I've done. I've done with them all. I don't care to look upon my house and my goods. I don't care to see anything at all!". . .

. . . [Zossima counsels] "Mother, know that your little one is surely before the throne of God, is rejoicing and happy, and praying to God for you, and therefore weep, but rejoice."

The woman listened to him, looking down with her cheek in her hand. She sighed deeply.

"My Nikita tried to comfort me with the same words as you. 'Foolish one,' he said, 'why weep? Our son is no doubt singing with the angels before God.' He says that to me, but he weeps himself. I see that he cries like me. 'I know, Nikita,' said I. 'Where could he be if not with the Lord God? Only, here with us now he is not as he used to sit beside us before.' And if only I could look upon him one little time, if only I could peep at him one little time, without going up to him, without speaking, if I could be hidden in a corner and only see him for one little minute, hear him playing in the yard, calling in his little voice, 'Mummy, where are you?' If only I could hear him pattering with his little feet about the room just once, only once; for so often, so often I remember how he used to run to me and shout and laugh, if only I could hear his little feet I should know him! But he's gone, Father, he's gone, and I shall never hear him again. Here's his little sash, but him I shall never see or hear now."

She drew out of her bosom her boy's little embroidered sash, and as soon as she looked at it she began shaking with sobs, hiding her eyes with her fingers through which the tears flowed in a sudden stream.

"It is 'Rachel of old,'" said the elder, "'weeping for her children, and will not be comforted because they are not.' Such is the lot set on earth for you mothers. Be not comforted. Consolation is not what you need. Weep and be not consoled, but weep. Only every time that you weep be sure to remember that your little son is one of the angels of God, that he looks down from there at you and sees you, and rejoices at your tears, and points at them to the Lord God; and a long while yet will you keep that great mother's grief. But it will turn in the end into quiet joy, and your bitter tears will be only tears of tender sorrow that purifies the heart and delivers it from sin. And I shall pray for the peace of your child's soul. What was his name?"

"Alexey, Father."

SOME THINGS BRING RELIEF

RUMER GODDEN

Aging and alone in China Court, the English country estate of five generations of Quins, Deborah Quin—the main character in Godden's novel—reflects on how she has coped with the three great losses of her life: Borowis, her first love killed in World War I; Stace, her son killed in World War II; and Tracy, Stace's daughter who was taken to live in America.

from *China Court: The Hours of a Country House*

"Memory is the only friend of grief," Alice, the village girl who comes as maid-companion to Tracy, writes that on one of the tombstones she designs. Alice likes to draw tombstones for all the people she knows and Tracy colours them from her paintbox. "Memory is the only friend of grief," writes Alice. Tracy shows it to Mrs. Quin who says it is not true.

Even when one is stricken, much remains; often creature things: drinking good tea from a thin porcelain cup; hot baths; the smell of a wood fire, the warmth of firelight and candlelight. The sound of a stream can be consolation, thinks Mrs. Quin, or the shape of a tree; even stricken, she can enjoy those. To hold a skeleton leaf, see its structure, can safely lift one away from grief for a moment, marvelling; and sunrises help, she thinks, though sunsets are dangerous, and moon and stars; they stir too much. Shells are safe, and birds and most little animals, kittens or foals especially, for they are not sentimental. Dogs sometimes know too much, though it is then, after Tracy, that she gets a new puppy, Bumble. "I have been happy in food," Mrs. Quin is able to say. How ridiculous to find consolation in food, but it is true and when one is taking those first steps back, bruised and wounded, one can read certain books: Hans Andersen, and the Psalms, Jane Austen, a few other novels. Helped by those things, life reasserts itself, as it must, even when one knows one will be stricken again: Tracy, Stace, Borowis, those are her private deepest names.

AND THE REST OF THE WORLD GOES ON

W. H. AUDEN

The source of the painting Auden refers to here, The Fall of Icarus *by sixteenth-century artist Pieter Brueghel, is a Greek myth. In it, Crete's King Minos has Daedalus, an Athenian architect and skilled inventor, design a palace for him at Knossos. Angry with him later, Minos imprisons Daedalus and his son Icarus in the same palace. The two escape, using wings made of feathers and beeswax. But young Icarus disregards his father's warning and flies too close to the sun. The wax melts and Icarus falls into the sea and drowns.*

from *The Norton Anthology of Poetry*, 4th ed.,
edited by Margaret Ferguson, Mary Jo Salter, and Jon Stallworthy

Musée des Beaux Arts

About suffering they were never wrong,
The Old Masters: how well they understood
Its human position; how it takes place
While someone else is eating or opening a window or just
　　walking dully along;
How, when the aged are reverently, passionately waiting
For the miraculous birth, there always must be
Children who did not specially want it to happen, skating
On a pond at the edge of the wood:
They never forgot
That even the dreadful martyrdom must run its course
Anyhow in a corner, some untidy spot
Where the dogs go on with their doggy life and the torturer's horse
Scratches its innocent behind on a tree.

In Brueghel's *Icarus*, for instance: how everything turns away
Quite leisurely from the disaster; the ploughman may

Have heard the splash, the forsaken cry,
But for him it was not an important failure; the sun shone
As it had to on the white legs disappearing into the green
Water; and the expensive delicate ship that must have seen
Something amazing, a boy falling out of the sky,
Had somewhere to get to and sailed calmly on.

4

A Storm in the Heart: Anger and Guilt

A nobleman once asked a Chinese philosopher to grant his family a blessing. The famous scholar thought for a moment, then said, "Grandfather dies, father dies, son dies." The nobleman was horrified, but the philosopher shrugged his shoulders. "What other way would you have it?" he said.

None.

And the sense of wrongness when it's otherwise, when a child dies before its parents and grandparents, seems to be at the core of our early guilt. Children shouldn't die, and when they do, it must be someone's fault. Who better to blame than we who brought them here?

I should know. I spent a year working hard to hang Jake's death on my door.

This is the heart talking, not reason. Yes, I do hear how childish, how crazy even, my "if onlys" sound: *If only* I had pulled out of my mother's driveway five minutes earlier, *if only* I'd gone home the day before, *if only* I'd not made the trip at all. Well, of course.

Still, the wrong person died. It should have been me. That's how it feels. No matter that a stranger crossed the median strip and drove straight into me. No matter that police said my skid marks told the tale: I did everything I could. I had nowhere else to go. No matter. I was Jake's mother. My job was to protect him. I failed him. In my car, the wrong person died.

I *wanted*, I *needed* to blame myself. I needed to make sure that there wasn't something I could have done to avoid the accident. And I needed to learn, really learn, how small I was.

Adults forget how awful it feels to be small and helpless. Certainly life reminds us periodically, delivering those inevitable encounters that temporarily diminish us. We do know that horrible things happen to other people—and that they could happen to us. But young children see their parents as big, and we feel big around them. It is, in fact, our responsibility to them to be capable and strong. It is also, of course, part illusion: we

79

---

can be every bit as powerless as they. *That* is the frightening truth no one wants to face.

For me, though, it was only when I did face it—when I began to question the exaggerated sense of power I'd always thought I'd held—that I could start loosening the grip on my guilt. How had I ever convinced myself that I was big enough to protect my children from death?

At this point, and not a moment before, I was open to hearing a friend's wise summation: "If you'd known you were heading into an accident, you would have done anything to avoid it. You didn't know. If you'd been given the chance, you would have traded your life in a second for Jake's. You would have. But you weren't given that chance."

My father died some twenty years ago and my mother continues to see it as wrong—almost sinful—that she's traveled to Greece twice in the years since, seeing antiquities and architecture that my father, the art historian, knew only from books. I am always impatient when she brings this up. It seems so irrational to taint her own pleasure with such futile regret. Is she not worthy of enjoying the Parthenon? And how would her self-denial help my long-dead father?

But there it is. Some things just feel unjust. They defy reason. I no longer feel that by taking Jake to visit his grandmother, I killed him. I no longer castigate myself for surviving the accident that he didn't. I now know the humbling truth: I had a minor role in this script—a bit part, with pitifully few lines.

I am still left with guilt, but it's something else now, more akin to the way my mother feels. Like her, I don't reject life's pleasures just because Jake can't enjoy them. I walk the beach, sail the boat, pet the dog, ride the bike he would have loved. But Jake got a dirty deal. Some things just feel forever wrong. And none more than the ruthless scrambling of the *correct* sequence: "Grandfather dies, father dies, son dies."

ANNE

ANGER

ANNE TYLER

In this excerpt from Tyler's novel The Accidental Tourist, *Sarah and Macon, separated a month, talk about how they're faring soon after their twelve-year-old son Ethan was murdered in a fast-food restaurant during a holdup. It was his second night away at camp.*

from *The Accidental Tourist*

"I should have agreed to teach summer school," Sarah said. "Something to give some shape to things. I open my eyes in the morning and think, 'Why bother getting up?' "

"Me too," Macon said.

"Why bother eating? Why bother breathing?"

"Me too, sweetheart."

"Macon, do you suppose that person has any idea? I want to go see him in prison, Macon. I want to sit on the other side of the grid or the screen or whatever they have and I'll say, 'Look at me. Look. Look at what you did. You didn't just kill the people you shot; you killed other people besides. What you did goes on and on forever. You didn't just kill my son; you killed me; you killed my husband. I mean I can't even manage to put up my curtains; do you understand what you did?' Then when I'm sure that he does understand, that he really does realize, that he feels just terrible, I'm going to open my purse and pull out a gun and shoot him between the eyes."

"Oh, well, sweetheart—"

"You think I'm just raving, don't you. But Macon, I swear, I can feel that little kick against my palm when I fire the gun. I've never fired a gun in my life—Lord, I don't think I've ever *seen* a gun. Isn't it odd? Ethan's seen one; Ethan's had an experience you and I have no notion of. But sometimes I hold my hand out with the thumb cocked like when kids play cowboy, and I fold my trigger finger and feel what a satisfaction it would be."

"Sarah, it's bad for you to talk like this."

"Oh? How am I supposed to talk?"

"I mean if you let yourself get angry you'll be . . . consumed. You'll burn up. It's not productive."

"Oh, productive! Well, goodness, no, let's not waste our time on anything unproductive."

Macon massaged his forehead. He said, "Sarah, I just feel we can't afford to have these thoughts."

"Easy for you to say."

"No, it is not easy for me to say, dammit—"

"Just shut the door, Macon. Just walk away. Just pretend it never happened. Go rearrange your tools, why don't you; line up your wrenches from biggest to smallest instead of from smallest to biggest; that's always fun."

"Goddammit, Sarah—"

DOMINICK DUNNE

Dunne, known to many for his best-selling novels, gained notoriety in the past decade for his crime reporting for Vanity Fair *magazine. He's covered the big names: Claus von Bulow, Eric Menendez, O. J. Simpson. But few readers realize just how personal his interest in our justice system is. Dunne's first piece for* Vanity Fair *was his account of the trial of his own daughter's killer. In 1982, Dominique, who had played the teenage daughter in the movie* Poltergeist, *was strangled by a former boyfriend, John Sweeney. He was convicted of voluntary manslaughter only and served three and a half years in prison.*

from "Justice," in *Fatal Charms and Other Tales of Today*

On my first day back in New York after the funeral, I was mugged leaving the subway at twelve noon in Times Square. I thought I was the only person on the stairway I was ascending to the street, but suddenly I was grabbed from behind and pulled off balance. I heard the sound of a switchblade opening, and a hand—which was all I ever saw of my assailant—reached around and held the knife in front of my face. From out of my mouth came a sound of rage that I did not know I was capable of making. It was more animal than human, and I was later told it had been heard a block away. Within seconds people came running from every direction. In his panic my assailant superficially slashed my chin with the blade of his knife, but I had beaten him. I had both my wallet and my life, and I realized that, uncourageous as I am about physical combat, I would have fought before giving in. Whoever that nameless, faceless man was, to me he was John Sweeney.

C. J. HRIBAL

In this short story, a drunken boy in a Plymouth convertible hits and kills Janie's son. Docilely, she goes every day to the trial. But what she wants is to scream at the jury, "That boy killed my son! What else is there to know?"

from "The Clouds in Memphis," in *TriQuarterly,* spring/summer 1995

The boy who killed Peter was a quarterback for Presbyterian Country Day. That's how she thinks of the blond boy in the blue suit and the blue-and-maroon foulard. When they pulled him from the car he had long strings of blond hair hanging in his eyes and a chin beard of black and blond and rust-colored wires. He reeked of alcohol. She knows this because Peter was struck by a car going sixty-three in a thirty-five zone. And he was not alone. William, a friend, was with Peter when it happened. They were trying to cross Poplar Pike. They were on the curb chatting and there seemed to be a gap in traffic and Peter stepped off the curb. William started, then stopped, then made a grab for Peter's shoulder. The car—a '59 candy-apple-red Plymouth convertible, boat-sized, with a white interior and fins—spun Peter over the front grillwork and up the windshield and spat him off to one side the way you might send a penny spinning off a table. Only this penny— these were the words her attorney used in court—only this penny ended up dead.

William said he couldn't remember anything. Pieces only. He remembered the car, its looming grillwork, its shriek of brakes, the thud, like the sound of cars colliding, you know? Only it wasn't cars colliding. It was Peter. Peter and the boat. Peter with his cheek bruised and scratched, his legs bent up under him in a way that didn't seem natural unless you were a little kid playing Army and pretending you were dead. . . .

Janie doesn't want to talk about it but she can't not. Every day she goes to the trial and watches a parade of human beings she doesn't know or only vaguely recognizes all claiming to know her son or the boy who killed him. There are photographs, diagrams, calculations that remind her of high-school trigonometry problems. If Fig. A is traveling from East Memphis at fifty-nine miles per hour, and Fig. B is a stationary object on a curb near Sound Warehouse, what will the velocity of impact be at 3:38 P.M., Central Standard Time, given dry road conditions, a clear day, and six empties clinking about the floorboards behind the front seat? . . .

. . . In his offices he [her attorney] tries explaining reasonable doubt and jury of your peers and she's screaming, Jury of your peers? Jury of your peers? How about Peter's peers? How about a jury of people hit by automobiles? How about a row of bloody corpses, huh? Huh? Huh? And her attorney, the mild young man with the round face and the tortoise-shell spectacles calmly lets his blue-suited chest and shoulders absorb her beating.

There is a problem with the boy who struck and killed her son. (She can't think of him any other way.) He's the son of an appellate-court judge and is a star quarterback. The policeman at the scene recognized this. Eight hours elapsed before they gave him a Breathalyzer test. There seems to be an un-spoken agreement among all present—judge, jury, spectators, courtroom personnel—that this was a terrible accident but not, repeat not, a criminal offense. The defense attorney, a florid man with iron-gray wavy hair and a propensity for double-breasted suits, fosters this view, repeating over and over that the freshly barbered boy in front of them should not pay a life-time's worth of guilt and sorrow—he is already sorry—and certainly should not be criminally liable for a single moment's lapse of concentration, espe-cially since that stretch of Poplar Pike—a commercial street of strip malls and dry cleaners and florists and restaurants with funny names like the Halfway House and Ben's Lobster Supreme and the Normal Barbecue—has neither a consistent sidewalk nor a crosswalk.

It could, the defense attorney concludes, have happened to anybody.

Janie cannot believe what she's hearing. Why hasn't her attorney leapt to his feet? Why isn't he riddling that flimsy argument full of the holes it's so easy to poke? Why does he seem to be cooperating, even acquiescing in this clean, clinical discussion of what this one boy has so carelessly, remorselessly done to her son? And to talk of that barbered boy's suffering! Twisted, griev-ous mess—that's what her attorney said in his opening arguments, and after that Janie could barely bear listening, but she did, she did, and now it's come down to this calm reasoning, this weighing and sorting of testimonials and pitches for leniency. It could *not* have happened to anybody. Even the way he says the word is a lie. He says *any*body, not any*body*. Body body body body! Don't they see? Don't they feel it? The cold rush of metal into one's ab-domen, the whoof! of air dispersing, disappearing? The internal blossoming of organs loosed in blood?

It's a conspiracy of concern for the living body over the lifeless one. The boy in question is a prettified drunken quarterback who had the good for-tune of being born into an appellate-court judge's household. What matters most, it seems, is how to dispose of the evidence and not muck up the fu-ture for the guilty when what's done is done for the innocent.

SUSAN COHEN

Susan Cohen's daughter Theo, at age twenty, was murdered by the terrorists who blew up Pan Am Flight 103 in 1988.

from "Rage Makes Me Strong," in *Time*, July 29, 1996

The very phrase "grief process" tells it all. Bland, neutral words that have nothing to do with my personal hell. The grief therapists I encountered at first were no better than the books. There was the rabbit-eyed, frightened individual who would cower behind his desk when I was in his office and who told me to adopt a child. I couldn't even look at children then. There was the tough therapist who told me to get back into the flow of life quickly and encouraged me to get on a plane well before I was ready. My trip to the airport left me a crumpled wreck in the parking lot. There was the grief-group therapist who told me she was worried about my anger, that I should open my heart. Well, my heart was open, all right. It was an open, bleeding wound. I didn't need clichés. Most of all, I didn't need anyone telling me there was something wrong with the enormous rage I was feeling. My daughter dies in a mass murder, and I'm not supposed to feel anger? I am a skeptic by inclination, a fighter by nature, and it was beginning to dawn on me that there were a lot people making a lot of money promoting denial and passivity. Of all the emotions I have felt since Theo's murder, anger is the best. Rage gives me energy. Rage makes me strong.

JOHN WALSH

In 1981, six-year-old Adam Walsh became separated from his mother and disappeared in a mall in Hollywood, Florida. For two weeks his tortured parents waited, as the Lindberghs had waited almost fifty years before. Then came the news: Adam's headless remains had been found in a drainage canal more than one hundred miles from home. In this excerpt, John Walsh, television host of America's Most Wanted, *and his wife, Revé, get off an airplane to find reporters ready to record their grief. Sometimes anger finds several deserving targets.*

from *Tears of Rage: From Grieving Father to Crusader for Justice, the Untold Story of the Adam Walsh Case,* by John Walsh with Susan Schindehette

I couldn't understand. What did these people want to see, exactly? Two destroyed human beings on the six-o'clock news?

It was chaos. . . . Someone ushered us into a VIP lounge to give us some breathing room. Revé went into the bathroom and, in the middle of everything, suddenly found herself alone. Later, she told me that she had stood there for a long time, looking at herself in the mirror and trying to make herself believe it.

"Your little boy is dead. They cut his head off," she said, looking right into her own eyes.

When we got home, we could barely get up the driveway to our front door. Reporters were all over the lawn, camped out on our street. Cops were there to try to protect us, and they had to push people back just so we could get into the house. Like we were going to the Oscars.

Then, without our little boy, we walked across the threshold. It wasn't a home anymore. It was a building. It meant nothing now. Without Adam in it, it was nothing. A place to keep your clothes. It was now the area that we were forced to return to at night to be reminded that we were never going to take him on another trip. That he was never going to play with his toys again. That we would never again put him to bed in his room.

And then, gradually, after a few hours, the press finally went away. Some out of common decency. Others because they gave up. Then, it was only Revé and me. We didn't sleep. We were lying on the floor, crying. Hanging on to each other. Weeping.

And then, at four o'clock in the morning, there was a knock on the door. I thought it was the Hollywood police telling us that a suspect had been picked up.

But when I answered the door, it was a woman staring at me. "Mr. Walsh, I'm a reporter, and I need to get a comment about Adam's murder tonight because my editor said that if I don't get a quote from you tonight for tomorrow's editions, I'm going to be fired."

At first I just stood there. I wasn't sure of what I had heard. I was trying to catch it again.

"What? What did you just say to me? Who are you?"

And then, it sank in, and I finally lost it completely.

"You tell that fucking coward son-of-a-*bitch* to come over here right now! Because I am going to pound his ass to a bleeding *pulp!* You take your notebook and you get the hell off my lawn, do you hear me? You get out of here and leave us the hell alone!"

And that was just the beginning. That was just my baptism.

ROBERT HARLING

Written in memory of Harling's sister Susan Harling Robinson, Steel
Magnolias *is a play which was adapted for film. In it, Shelby, a young
diabetic woman, sacrifices her health and ultimately her life to bear a
child. Her mother, M'Lynn, is forced to cope with her death, sustained by
her stalwart women friends. After the funeral, M'Lynn talks to her friends
in the beauty parlor. Initially in control, her anger quickly takes over.*

from Steel Magnolias

M'LYNN: . . . Shelby, as you know, would not want us to get all mired down
and wallow in this. She would look on it as one of life's occur-
rences. We should deal with it in the best way we know how . . .
and get on with it. That's what my mind says. I wish somebody
would explain that to my heart.

TRUVY: Tommy [Shelby's brother] said you didn't leave her side.

M'LYNN: Well. I wasn't in the mood to play bridge. (*Beat.*) No, I couldn't
leave my Shelby. It's interesting. Both the boys were very difficult
births. I almost died when Jonathan was born. Very difficult
births. Shelby was a breeze. I could've gone home that afternoon
I had her. I was thinking about that as I sat next to Shelby while
she was in the coma. I would work her legs and arms to keep the
circulation going. I told the ICU nurse we were doing our Jane
Fonda. I stayed there. I kept on pushing . . . just like I always have
where Shelby was concerned . . . hoping she'd sit up and argue
with me. But finally we all realized there was no hope. At that
point I panicked. I was very afraid that I would not survive the
next few minutes while they turned off the machines. Drum
[Shelby's father] couldn't take it. He left. Jackson [Shelby's hus-
band] couldn't take it. He left. It struck me as amusing. Men are
supposed to be made of steel or something. But I could not leave.
I just sat there . . . holding Shelby's hand while the sounds got
softer and the beeps got farther apart until all was quiet. There
was no noise, no tremble . . . just peace. I realized as a woman
how lucky I was. I was there when this wonderful person drifted
into my world and I was there when she drifted out. It was the
most precious moment of my life thus far.

TRUVY: (*Putting the finishing flourishes on M'Lynn's hair.*) Well I don't know how your insides are doing. But your hair is holding up beautifully. All it needs is a lick and a promise. Did you have it done in Shreveport?

M'LYNN: No. I did it myself . . .

TRUVY: Hold it, Missy. I don't want to hear that kind of talk.

M'LYNN: Doing my own hair was so odd. I had no idea about the back . . .

TRUVY: You did a lovely job. I just smoothed out the rough spots. In fact, I'm going to be looking for temporary help when Annelle goes on maternity leave . . . interested?

M'LYNN: (*Struggling for control.*) It was just with so much going on, I didn't know if I would have time . . . would feel like coming here. But this morning I wanted to come here more than anything. Isn't that silly?

TRUVY: No.

M'LYNN: Last night I went into Shelby's closet for something . . . and guess what I found. All our Christmas presents stacked up, wrapped. With her own two hands . . . I better go.

TRUVY: (*Handing M'Lynn a mirror.*) Check the back.

M'LYNN: Perfect . . . as always. (*M'Lynn continues to gaze into the mirror.*) You know . . . Shelby. . . Shelby was right. It . . . it does kind of look like a blond football helmet. (*M'Lynn disintegrates.*)

TRUVY: Honey. Sit right back down. Do you feel alright?

M'LYNN: Yes. Yes. I feel fine. I feel great. I could jog to Texas and back, but my daughter can't. She never could. I am so mad I don't know what to do. I want to know why. I want to know why Shelby's life is over. How is that baby ever going to understand how wonderful his mother was? Will he ever understand what she went through for him? I don't understand. Lord I wish I could. It is not supposed to happen this way. I'm supposed to go first. I've always been ready to go first. I can't stand this. I just want to hit somebody until they feel as bad as I do. I . . . just want to hit something . . . and hit it hard.

ANGER *AND* GUILT

WILLIAM FAULKNER

Faulkner's firstborn child, christened Alabama after his favorite aunt, was born two months early. Anxious about both his wife, Estelle, and his baby, Faulkner asked the brusque, opinionated doctor what he should do. The small Oxford, Mississippi, hospital had no incubator and bills were adding up. Confident that he could care for them, Faulkner ultimately decided to take Alabama and his wife home to Rowan Oak—where the baby died. For that, he blamed the doctor, and his anger became legendary.

from William Faulkner: The Man and the Artist by Stephen B. Oates

The tiny child lay in a bassinet in the middle upstairs bedroom, where Malcolm and Cho-Cho [Estelle's children by a previous marriage], standing on tiptoes, looked down at her in wonder. Although Dr. Culley came every day and Faulkner and Mammy Callie tended to their every need, mother and child both took a turn for the worse. At dawn on January 20, an alarmed Mammy Callie shook Faulkner, asleep in an adjacent bedroom, and said it was the baby. They hurried to the bassinet, where Alabama was struggling to breathe. Frantically, he phoned Dr. Culley, but the doctor, curt as ever, said there was nothing he or anybody else could do for the child. Back at the bassinet, Faulkner and Mammy Callie looked on helplessly as Alabama, only ten days old, passed from this world. . . .

. . . Quietly, the family gathered for the funeral, with the dead child lying in a tiny casket before them. Then came the procession of automobiles out to the cemetery. On the way, Faulkner held the little casket in his lap, so numb from grief that he scarcely knew where they were. . . .

Back at Rowan Oak, Estelle lay in her bedroom, unaware of what had happened. Faulkner waited until she took a sedative, then entered and sat down beside her bed. Overwhelmed with grief and bitterness, he could not at first find the words to tell her. But finally it came out—"Alabama's dead, Estelle"—and then he cried. She had never seen him cry before.

"Bill," she said, "get you a drink."

"No," he said in his misery, "this is one time I'm not going to do it."

The rage came afterward, an almost paralyzing fury that fixed on Dr. Culley as the author of their misfortune. Faulkner fantasized about seeking violent retribution, as the Old Colonel [his legendary great-grandfather, a Civil War commander who was later acquitted of killing a rival in a street altercation] would likely have done. Soon fantasy became reality in his mind, and he spread an apocryphal story that he had punished the doctor for refusing to come to Rowan Oak when Faulkner had called. He claimed that right after Alabama died, he had grabbed a gun, plunged into the dawn, summoned Dr. Culley from his home, and shot him with full intention to kill. But the bullet only wounded him, Faulkner said, and he recovered and didn't press charges. Faulkner added, "The bastard deserved to die."

He told the story many times, with various embellishments, until it passed into local lore. While it wasn't true, it revealed the depth of his grief and anger—and his guilt. Deep down, he feared that he was really to blame. If only he hadn't brought Alabama home from the hospital, if only he hadn't been asleep. . . . To assuage his guilt, he later contributed an incubator to the hospital. But nothing seemed to ease the hurt inside—not his work, not even furious hacking at the bitterweeds out in the pasture.

WILLIAM SHAKESPEARE

Noble and powerful Macduff has scarcely had time to take in that his entire family has been murdered by his political enemies before Malcolm, an ally, urges retribution. "Dispute it like a man," he counsels, and "let grief convert to anger." Shakespeare, who nine years prior had lost his only son, Hamnet, well knew Macduff's rejoinder: "But I must also feel it as a man." Perhaps too, only a playwright who had lost a child would have had Macduff ask first about his children, then his wife—and know that he would feel guilty about surviving them all.

from *Macbeth*, in *The Complete Works of Shakespeare*, edited by Hardin Craig

Ross [a Scottish nobleman who here plays the messenger]:
>   I have words
> That would be howl'd out in the desert air,
> Where hearing should not latch them.

MACDUFF: What concern they?
>   The general cause? or is it a fee-grief
>   Due to some single breast?

Ross: No mind that's honest
>   But in it shares some woe; though the main part
>   Pertains to you alone.

MACDUFF: If it be mine,
 Keep it not from me, quickly let me have it.

ROSS: Let not your ears despise my tongue for ever,
 Which shall possess them with the heaviest sound
 That ever yet they heard.

MACDUFF: Hum! I guess at it.

ROSS: Your castle is surprised; your wife and babes
 Savagely slaughter'd: to relate the manner,
 Were, on the quarry of these murder'd deer,
 To add the death of you.

MALCOLM: Merciful heaven!
 [to Macduff] What, man! ne'er pull your hat upon your brows;
 Give sorrow words: the grief that does not speak
 Whispers the o'er-fraught heart and bids it break.

MACDUFF: My children too?

ROSS: Wife, children, servants, all
 That could be found.

MACDUFF: And I must be from thence!
 My wife kill'd too?

ROSS: I have said.

MALCOLM: Be comforted:
 Let's make us medicines of our great revenge,
 To cure this deadly grief.

MACDUFF: He has no children. All my pretty ones?
 Did you say all? O hell-kite! All?
 What, all my pretty chickens and their dam
 At one fell swoop?

MALCOLM: Dispute it like a man.

MACDUFF: I shall do so;
 But I must also feel it as a man:
 I cannot but remember such things were,
 That were most precious to me. Did heaven look on,

And would not take their part? Sinful Macduff,
They were all struck for thee! naught that I am,
Not for their own demerits, but for mine,
Fell slaughter on their souls. Heaven rest them now!

MALCOLM: Be this the whetstone of your sword: let grief
Convert to anger; blunt not the heart, enrage it.

SURVIVOR'S GUILT

RUDYARD KIPLING

In 1992, almost eighty years after Kipling's son, John, died on a World War I battlefield in France, his remains were discovered in an unmarked grave. Kipling Sr. and his wife had fruitlessly toured battlefield after battlefield trying to find that body. In likely atonement for having pushed young Jack to go to war, Kipling later became a founding member of the Imperial War Graves Commission, set up to carry out the enormous task of exhuming, identifying, and reburying a million British dead. He was responsible for choosing the inscription that adorned every war cemetery: "Their name liveth for evermore." But in his lifetime, there was no head-stone for his own son.

from "Young Men and War" by Christopher Hitchens, in *Vanity Fair*, February 1997

On September 27, 1915, during the Battle of Loos, a young lieutenant of the Irish Guards posted "wounded and missing." His name was John Kipling, and he was the only son of the great Bard of Empire, Rudyard Kipling. Kipling never goes out of print, because he not only captured the spirit of imperialism and the white man's burden but also wrote imperishable stories and poems—many of them to the boy John—about the magic and lore of childhood. And on that shell-shocked September day, the creator of Mowgli and Kim had to face the fact that he had sacrificed one of his great loves—his son, whom he called his "man-child"—to another of his great loves: the British Empire. You can trace the influence of this tragedy through almost every line that he subsequently wrote. . . .

John Kipling was only 16 when the war broke out. Pressed by his father to volunteer, he was rejected on the grounds of poor eyesight. . . . The proud and jingoistic father used his influence with the high command to get young

John commissioned anyway. His mother's diary recorded that "John leaves at noon. . . . He looks very straight and smart and young, as he turned [*sic*] at the top of the stairs to say: 'Send my love to Dad-o.'"

He didn't last more than a few weeks. The village of Loos, where he disappeared, was also where the British found out about modern warfare; it was at Loos that they first tried to use poison gas as a weapon of combat. . . .

Accounts of the boy's last moments differ, but Kipling's friend H. Rider Haggard (creator of *King Solomon's Mines* and *She*) took a lot of trouble interviewing witnesses. He recorded in his diary that one of them, a man named Bowe, "saw an officer who *he could swear* was Mr. Kipling leaving the wood on his way to the rear and trying to fasten a field dressing round his mouth which was badly shattered by a piece of shell. Bowe would have helped him but for the fact that the officer was crying with the pain of the wound and he did not want to humiliate him by offering assistance. I shall not send this on to Rudyard Kipling—it is too painful.". . .

Haggard may have wished to spare Kipling pain, but one has to say that Kipling did not try to spare himself. His whole personality as an author underwent a deep change. At different stages, one can see the influence of parental anguish, of patriotic rage, of chauvinistic hatred, and of personal guilt. A single couplet almost contrives to compress all four emotions into one: "If any question why we died, / Tell them, because our fathers lied."

GEORGE McGOVERN

In mid-December of 1994, Eleanor and George McGovern's forty-five-year-old daughter Terry was found frozen to death in a parking lot in Madison, Wisconsin. She had fallen asleep in a snowbank while in an alcoholic stupor. After years of unsuccessful attempts to help Terry treat her alcoholism and depression, the McGoverns "had decided—with the encouragement of a counselor—that it might be best for both Terry and us not to be deeply involved for a time."

from Terry: My Daughter's Life-and-Death Struggle with Alcoholism

Why did it take her death to trigger this search for understanding of the affliction that scarred her troubled life and in the end brought her to an untimely grave? Why couldn't I have gained my present knowledge and understanding of my daughter and her disease in time to have helped her more effectively than I did?

I can't give satisfying answers to these questions. What I can tell you is that the sorrow of losing one of your children is almost unbearable. It is sad beyond any measure that I had imagined.

If you have a troubled or addicted daughter or son, do not ever imagine that you or your child might be better off if death were to steal her or him away. Death is devastating and final and agonizing for a parent. There is no way you can avoid a full measure of painful regrets and might-have-beens.

Your friends and counselors will tell you: "Don't blame yourself. It's not your fault—you did the best you could." This advice is well meant and may even be true. It doesn't help much. You'll be sad, and you will hurt when you lie down to sleep, when you awake in the night, when you rise in the morning, when you go to a beach where she swam, when you drive past her school, when you hear her children laughing, when you see a Christmas tree, or whenever you recall her dancing eyes, her lingering embrace, her glorious smile when she saw you at the airport—or her anguish when she fell from intoxication. I'm especially sad on June 10—her birthday—and on December 13, when she died in the snow.

JOHN EDGAR WIDEMAN

In Wideman's closely autobiographical short story, his narrator, a bereaved mother, worries about her brother Tom. He's lost a child too—not to death, but to a life sentence in prison. Somehow the feeling of guilt reads the same.

from "Welcome," in *The Stories of John Edgar Wideman*

Her brother had said: No matter how much you love them you only get one chance, so if something happens and you lose one, no matter how, no matter who's to blame, you're guilty forever because you had that one chance, that precious life given to you to protect, and you blew it. I know you must understand, Sis. And she did and didn't and reached out to touch him, but he wasn't asking for that. His eyes in another country that quick.

BARBARA LAZEAR ASCHER

After her thirty-one-year-old brother Bobby died of AIDS, Ascher began attending a grief-healing group. She later wrote: "When I tell the other members that just the other day someone close to me grew impatient and said,

'You can't possibly still be grieving. You and your brother weren't even that close,' there is a unanimous nodding of heads. 'Nobody wants to be with a sad person,' says the attorney. 'They grow impatient after two weeks.'"

from Landscape Without Gravity: A Memoir of Grief

My friend was not wrong, my brother and I were not close. The passion of our attachment when he was a young boy turned to later disenchantment. Now that old passion returns and fuels my remorse. I turn the anger, that integral aspect of grief, against myself. Whereas many mourners shake their fists in fury at the space their beloveds have left behind—"How could you go and leave me?"—I am my own accuser. Why had I not been larger-hearted? Why hadn't I included Bobby in my life? Why had there been limits and conditions on my love? I become aware of my most grievous crime: I had been ashamed of him.

Now I am ashamed of myself. Such guilt and ambivalence complicate and extend grief. But how could an outsider understand that no, my brother and I were not close and that is precisely why I grieve. . . .

Each of us in the grief-healing group has experienced the if-only stage of grief. Over and over I think, if only I had not been so distant. If only I had insisted on intimacy and involvement. If only I had not run from the pain in his eyes during that last visit. If only I had moved toward rather than away from it by putting my arms around him, by telling him that I loved him and had always loved him. If only I had accepted him with all his eccentricities and excesses. If only I had been an extraordinary rather than ordinary sister. . . .

I try to remind myself that relationships among the living are two-sided. There were others who knew and, yes, loved Bobby better. I was important in his life, but not central. In forgiving myself, I have to accept that. There is a form of aggrandizement in remorse as though things would have been completely different if the mourner had done what had been left undone. The fact is that I might be suffering fewer regrets now if I had performed the "if onlys" then but they might have made no difference in our relationship. . . .

The minister introduces us to an exercise "that has helped ease mourners' guilt." He instructs us, "Close your eyes and talk to the dead person. Express your regrets and then respond as you think the deceased might respond." Since the deceased is not in a position to forgive us, we are going to have to forgive ourselves. I try and a flood of remorse washes over me. As I want to stop it I know that I mustn't, that it has to wash over and away, like a river.

PAUL NEWMAN

Soon after his son's death in 1978, Newman donated or raised $500,000 to set up the Scott Newman Foundation at the University of Southern California, which finances the production of antidrug movies for children. He continues to support it with some of the profits from the Newman's Own food line.

from *Paul Newman: A Biography* by Eric Lax

Newman has always been guarded in discussing the details of his and [his late son] Scott's estrangement. How does a young man find himself under a shadow so large? A father trying to help is often viewed by the son as a father trying to hinder. Scott was nineteen when Butch Cassidy, one of a generation of moviegoers' great romantic characters, held the land in thrall. By all accounts the two by that time had pretty much broken with each other. Scott was as handsome as Paul. He tried his hand at acting, worked as a stuntman, and under the name William Scott was a part-time nightclub singer.

Newman was at Kenyon College, directing a student play, when the call came telling him that Scott had died of an accidental overdose of drugs and alcohol.

When asked a few years after the event how he reacted to the moment, Newman replied tensely, "In a way, I had been waiting for the call for ten years. Somehow, my body mechanism built me an anesthetic for when it really happened. I was . . . a lot of things when I got that call. I was probably more pissed off than anything. . . . Scott and I had simply lost the ability to help each other. I had lost the ability to help him, and he had lost the ability to help himself. I had simply lost my ability to make a difference. Any kind of difference. . . . I just realized that whatever I was doing in trying to be helpful was not being helpful at all. In fact, it could have been harmful."

"We were like rubber bands," he said on another occasion, "one minute close, the next separated by an enormous and unaccountable distance. I don't think I'll ever escape the guilt."

ANN K. FINKBEINER

A bereaved parent and science writer, Finkbeiner drew her book from grief research and from interviews with other parents. "The guilt is because of the natural order of things," Emily, whose daughter committed suicide, told Finkbeiner. "The child should still be here and if anybody should go, it should be the parent. You feel guilt about anything."

from *After the Death of a Child: Living with Loss Through the Years*

Parents whose children commit suicide do feel more guilt than parents whose children die in other ways. But regardless of how their children died, bereaved parents feel guilty. If researchers agree on nothing else, they agree on this. One of the earliest studies, done in 1944, found that all bereaved people, not just parents, feel guilty. Several studies since then have compared people whose spouses or parents have died with people whose children have died, and found parents with more feelings of guilt.

Parents of babies who died of sudden infant death syndrome still have, years later, what one researcher called a "gnawing sense of responsibility for the child's death." Parents of children who died suddenly feel more guilt than parents of children whose deaths were anticipated, and parents of children who committed suicide feel most guilty of all. Parents of older children feel more guilt than parents of younger children. Fathers and mothers feel equally guilty. Less religious parents feel more guilt than more religious parents. Even grandparents feel guilty.

In general, the researchers say what Emily said: parents can feel guilty about *anything*. Sally and Chris [other bereaved parents] felt guilty for the usually harmless, completely human reactions of anger and inattentiveness. Emily felt guilty for not having said, "I love you," even though her daughter had already died. Perhaps their guilt over these specific instances stands in for guilt over general argumentiveness, inattention, and insufficient affection. But what parent is innocent of any of this?

FRANCES GUNTHER

Gunther's ex-husband, John Gunther, wrote a classic memoir, Death Be Not Proud, *after their son Johnny died in 1947, at seventeen, from a brain tumor. The book ends with "A Word From Frances."*

from "A Word From Frances," in *Death Be Not Proud: A Memoir* by John Gunther

My grief, I find, is not desolation or rebellion at universal law or deity. I find grief to be much simpler and sadder. Contemplating the Eternal Deity and His Universal Laws leaves me grave but dry-eyed. But a sunny fast wind along the Sound, good sailing weather, a new light boat, will shake me to tears: how Johnny would have loved this boat, this wind, this sunny day! . . .

. . . Missing him now, I am haunted by my own shortcomings, how often I failed him. I think every parent must have a sense of failure, even of sin, merely in remaining alive after the death of a child. One feels that it is not right to live when one's child has died, that one should somehow have found the way to give one's life to save his life. Failing there, one's failures during his too brief life seem all the harder to bear and forgive. How often I wish I had not sent him away to school when he was still so young that he wanted to remain at home in his own room, with his own things and his own parents. How I wish we had maintained the marriage that created the home he loved so much. How I wish we had been able before he died to fulfill his last heart's desires: the talk with Professor Einstein, the visit to Harvard Yard, the dance with his friend Mary.

These desires seem so simple. How wonderful they would have been to him. All the wonderful things in life are so simple that one is not aware of their wonder until they are beyond touch. Never have I felt the wonder and beauty and joy of life so keenly as now in my grief that Johnny is not here to enjoy them.

WILLIAM WORDSWORTH

Eventually the pain does abate. Almost against our will, we begin to enjoy bits and pieces of life again. And like Wordsworth, whose four-year-old daughter Catharine died in 1812, we feel guilty.

from *The Norton Anthology of Poetry*, 4th ed.,
edited by Margaret Ferguson, Mary Jo Salter, and Jon Stallworthy

Surprised by Joy

Surprised by joy—impatient as the Wind
I turned to share the transport—Oh! with whom
But thee, deep buried in the silent tomb,
That spot which no vicissitude can find?
Love, faithful love, recalled thee to my mind—
But how could I forget thee? Through what power,
Even for the least division of an hour,
Have I been so beguiled as to be blind
To my most grievous loss!—That thought's return

Was the worst pang that sorrow ever bore,
Save one, one only, when I stood forlorn,
Knowing my heart's best treasure was no more;
That neither present time, nor years unborn
Could to my sight that heavenly face restore.

JUDITH GUEST

*In Guest's novel, seventeen-year-old Conrad Jarrett can't forgive himself
for surviving the sailboat accident that killed his older brother, Buck. Already he's tried suicide. When he reads in the paper that a depressed friend
has killed herself, Con "loses it." He calls Berger, his therapist, and begs to
see him quickly. Here Berger tries to get him talking.*

from Ordinary People

"I can't!" he cries. "I can't!" He drops his head on his arms. "You keep at me,
make me talk about things I can't talk about, I can't!"

"Is that what you came here to tell me?"

He lifts his head, holding himself tight. Control. Control is all. He tries
to clamp his throat shut over it, to stifle the sound, but he cannot and he begins to sob, a high, helpless coughing sound. There is no control any more,
everything is lost, and his body heaves, drowning. His head is on his arms
again. . . .

"Ah, God, I don't know. I don't know, it just keeps coming, I can't make
it stop!"

"Don't, then."

"I can't! I can't get through this! It's all hanging over my head!"

"What's hanging over your head?"

"I don't know!" He looks up, dazed, drawing a deep breath. "I need
something, I want something—I want to get off the hook!"

"For what?"

He begins to cry again. "For killing him, don't you know that? For letting him drown!"

"And how did you do that?" Berger asks. . . .

. . . "I don't know, I just know that I did!" Head cradled on his arms
again, he sobs. Cannot think, cannot think, no way out of this endless turning and twisting. Hopeless.

"You were on opposite sides of the boat," Berger says, "so you couldn't even see each other. Right?"

He nods his head as he sits up. He scratches his cheek, staring at Berger through the slits of his eyes. The itching creeps downward, under his pajama top.

"And he was a better swimmer than you. He was stronger, he had more endurance."

"Yes."

"So, what is it you think you could have done to keep him from drowning?"

Tears flood his eyes again. He wipes them roughly away with his hand.

"I don't know. Something."

It is always this way. His mind shuts down. He cannot get by this burden, so overpowering that it is useless to look for a source, a beginning point. There is none.

"You don't understand," he says. "It has to be somebody's fault. Or what was the whole goddamn point of it?"

"The point of it," Berger says, "is that it happened."

"No! That's not it! That is too simple—"

"Kiddo, let me tell you a story," Berger says. "A very simple story. About this perfect kid who had a younger brother. A not-so-perfect kid. And all the time they were growing up, this not-so-perfect kid tried to model himself after his brother, the perfect kid. It worked, too. After all, they were a lot alike, and the not-so-perfect kid was a very good actor. Then, along came this sailing accident, and the impossible happened. The not-so-perfect kid makes it. The other kid, the one he has patterned his whole life after, isn't so lucky. So, where is the sense in that, huh? Where is the justice?"

"There isn't any," he says dully.

Berger holds up his hand. "Wait a second, let me finish. The justice, obviously, is for the not-so-perfect kid to become that other, perfect kid. For everybody. For his parents and his grandparents, his friends, and, most of all, himself. Only, that is one hell of a burden, see? So, finally, he decides he can't carry it. But how to set it down? No way. A problem without a solution. And so, because he can't figure out how to solve the problem, he decides to destroy it." Berger leans forward. "Does any of this make sense to you?"

"I don't know," he says. "I don't know."

"It is a very far-out act of self-preservation, do you get that, Con? And you were right. Nobody needs you to be Buck. It's okay to just be you."

"I don't know who that is any more!" he cries.

"Yeah, you do," Berger says. "You do. Con, that guy is trying so hard to get out, and he's never gonna be the one to hurt you, believe me. Let him talk. Let him tell you what you did that was so bad. Listen, you know what you did? You hung on, kiddo. That's it. That's your guilt. You can live with that, can't you?"

ANNE RIVERS SIDDONS

In Siddons's novel, five-year-old Stephen drowns in a friend's swimming pool, in full view of three children and a baby-sitter, who all thought he was "playing at snorkeling." Here his mother, Kate, recalls an early conversation with her husband about blame.

from *Outer Banks*

I know that many marriages do not survive the anguish and guilt and outrage of a child's death, but it never occurred to Alan or me that ours might not. We clung together like survivors in a life raft. I remember something he said to me late in that first night, after they had taken Stephen's little blue body away to the funeral home and I had fought my way up out of the sedative our GP friend had given me.

When I got to the surface, Alan's was the face that I saw, and as memory swept over me like a cold, black salt sea, he held me fast and said, "One thing we will not do is blame ourselves. Of course it wouldn't have happened if we hadn't gone to that terrible fucking party, but I want you to remember this, Kate: neither of us wanted Stephen to die. Either one of us would have died to prevent it. So we can cry, and we can mourn, and we can stand it or not, but we are not going to blame ourselves or each other. And we are going to get through this one minute at a time, and one hour, and one day. Just like that. Together."

5

Parents, Lost in the Storm Together

That first year after Jake died, I cried so much I thought I'd damage my eyes. But *my* crying felt therapeutic. Tom's wailing, coming from another floor, was something else, something so disturbing, so dreadfully sad, that I'd feel nauseous hearing him. And powerless. I was like a bystander who watches a parent bully a child: I could intervene, but I couldn't really help. Like me, Tom wanted to be alone when he cried. Neither of us wanted the other to soulfully empathize, to rub the shoulder, to kiss the top of the head, to murmur, "I know, I know." That could come afterwards. When we cried, we wanted to have an all-out good cry, and sympathy was like a pesky fly, diverting us from the business at hand, which was to spew out all those saved-up tears, as if the tears themselves were the cause of our pain. Any sympathizer—even sweet little Hollis, who rushed to comfort either parent she heard sobbing—just interrupted the flow, made us stop before we wanted to, before we felt any better. Who would have dreamed that sympathy could be so unhelpful?

That first year especially, I indulged my grief. I was shocked when another bereaved mother asked, "When is it going to get better? I can't stand this pain." What made her think it would get better, and if so, anytime soon? I *expected* pain. I just avoided what I could and tried to steel myself for the rest. But grief always seemed to surprise Tom, to hit him like "a two-by-four to the back of the head," he'd say. Unprepared, he would buckle from its blow. Still, from the start, I envied him his ability to push his grief aside. It seemed both healthier and easier than what I did. He could enjoy playing with a neighbor's three-year-old boy and not see Jake in him. At least not right away. He could lose himself in a movie about adolescent boys, be short-tempered the rest of the evening, and see no cause and effect. He could go to work on the third anniversary of the accident and be surprised at the ferocity of his "Jake attack" on the beltway coming home. I tried to accustom myself to a lifetime of pain; Tom seemed ever amazed at its continuing strength.

These days, nine years after Jake's death, we hardly ever cry, either of us. It's not, as I once feared, that we've finally damaged our eyes. We've just learned to live with the pain. That is, like a shadow, it goes where we go. Friends say they don't know how we do it, live this way. *Is there a choice?* we ask.

ANNE

Peter and I had our share of friction in our twenty-four years of marriage before Allie died. I thought he should communicate more; he thought I was too critical. I thought he was too laid back about money; he thought I was neurotic. I wanted to talk before making love; he could skip the talking. We disagreed about the children too. He thought I was too soft; I was sure he was too tough. But by May 1991, with Hilary set to enter her senior year of college and Allie his senior year of high school, we had smoothed the rough edges of our marriage and the future looked bright.

Then tragedy struck. Although oblivion seemed infinitely preferable to suffering Allie's loss, I knew I had to hold on to life and sanity for Hilary's sake, and I wanted Peter to hang on with me. I was terrified that he would succumb to despair. We knew immediately that it was impossible to console each other. Allie is an inconsolable loss. The best we could do was stick together and try not to cause each other any more pain.

Seven years later we feel grounded again, but life is very different. The future is a thing of the past, as writer Peter De Vries puts it. We live from day to day, bearing our burden of grief, finding solace when and where we can. We talk about Allie a lot—sharing memories, fantasies of how things might have been, and the terrible longing. There are other parents who understand what it is to lose a child. Only Peter knows what it is to lose Allie. Peter understands that I have lost my zest for life and feel like I'm going through empty motions. It's impossible to live wholeheartedly with a heart that is broken.

We are kinder and gentler to each other and argue less. My expectations are lower. I used to think that Peter could make me happy if he would just adjust a little here and there. Now I know that unless he can figure out a way to get Allie back, happiness is out of the question, so why should I bug him? I look back on what I now know as the best time in my life and regret that I wasted any of it being angry. I can hardly recall what seemed so important. When you have lost what you value most, very little seems worth fighting about.

MARY

MARRIAGE: FOR BETTER AND WORSE

LYNN DARLING

*We solemnly pledge our vows. And as Darling points out in a long
personal essay, marriage eventually tests every one of them.*

from "For Better and Worse," in *Esquire*, May 1996

Every marriage has a story, says a friend of mine, a plot twist, "a critical moment that changes things, like a tree after a bad storm, the event that colored
their whole lives—Bill had to go to war; we lost the money when the mar-
ket crashed. So that where you end up is not where you began, which is both
the heaven and the hell of marriage. You are not who you were and she is not
who she was, and the balance on any given day, of whether that is a good or
a bad thing, shifts precariously."

My marriage assumed its final form on a day in April laced in green when
my husband walked to a lectern in a Washington church and delivered the
eulogy for his twelve-year-old and only son.

He talked about his son's short life, and at the end he asked the congregation to say the boy's name out loud together one last time. And all that I
know about love and courage and timeless sorrow I learned from looking at
his face as he listened while we did as he asked.

I sat in a pew with the boy's mother, whose strength and generosity still
astound me, and his two sisters, my stepdaughters, just entering their own
spring. Around us was a force of people who had buoyed this family and
kept them afloat for a terrible week and would continue to do so in the years
ahead. This was the community in which my husband and I had taken our
place together. . . .

My husband and I would never be the same after what happened to his
son. The moment when I understood the horror and the beauty of that fact,
the way in which we had been changed, the way in which our knowledge of
each other was unfathomably deepened, the way in which we were inextri-
cably a part of each other, was the moment when I felt I finally knew what
it meant to be married.

ANNE RIVERS SIDDONS

Kate, in another excerpt from Siddons's novel Outer Banks, *recalls a day soon after her five-year-old son drowned (see p. 101).*

from *Outer Banks*

When Stephen died, someone gave me a copy of Juliana of Norwich's *Book of Hours,* intending, no doubt, that I should find comfort in the words of that terrible old abbess. It was a long time before I could read that or anything, but when I did, I opened it to the passage that goes, "All shall be well, and all shall be well, and all shall be exceedingly well." I threw the book into the fireplace in a cold, trembling rage, and was about to set fire to it when Alan rescued it and read the passage. He cried then, terrible, tearing sobs that went on and on and on, rising sometimes into a kind of wail I had never heard before. It frightened me badly; I had cried, torrents, rivers, seas of hopeless, anguished tears. But he had not, until then.

We talked about it later, after the awful crying had stopped, and he was calm again, limp and somehow clean and light.

"I hated her for saying that," I said, by way of explaining why I had attempted to burn the book. "'All shall be exceedingly well.' It's horrible. Nothing shall be well. It's the worst thing that ever happened. How can anything be well again?"

"It's not the worst thing that ever happened, Katie," he said. "It's just the worst thing that ever happened to you. To us. And now, nothing this bad can ever happen to us again. I think that's what she meant. She wasn't stupid; she lived a godawful life. And my dear love, for a very long time all was most exceedingly well with us. And may be again, who knows?"

I was angry with him for days. I did not want optimism. It was a long time before I saw that it was not that; it was the only way Alan could stay alive in those unspeakable days. But from the moment he spoke the words, I knew in my savage heart that he had been right when he said that indeed, for us, all had been, until then, exceedingly well.

GRIEVING SEPARATELY

NICHOLAS WOLTERSTORFF

In his memoir of his son Eric (see p. 56), Wolterstorff is unsparingly honest about the loneliness of grief.

from *Lament for a Son*

I have been daily grateful for the friend who remarked that grief isolates. He did not mean only that I, grieving, am isolated from you, happy. He meant also that *shared* grief isolates the sharers from each other. Though united in that we are grieving, we grieve differently. . . . I may find it strange that you should be tearful today but dry-eyed yesterday when my tears were yesterday. But my sorrow is not your sorrow.

There's something more: I must struggle so hard to regain life that I cannot reach out to you. Nor you to me. The one not grieving must touch us both. It's when people are happy that they say, "Let's get together."

GRIEVING DIFFERENTLY

GWENDOLYN PARKER

In this novel, Sirus and Aileen's only child, Mattie, has only recently died in a freak fall from her backyard slide.

from *These Same Long Bones*

"Have you seen Sirus and Aileen recently?" Emma asked when time had had enough of a visit. "How are they doing?"

Jason thought about them. As between the two of them, he thought, Aileen looked better. She had an almost haunted look in her eyes, particularly when she saw other children, but at least it was a look that seemed alive. It was different with Sirus. "He looks like he's the one who died," some people said about him. "He ain't dead, just grieving," Jason would say to defend him, but as all these months had gone by, Jason himself felt less and less sure. He didn't want to admit that Sirus was failing, but he had seen it enough times in his work. You could tell it sometimes right out at the interment, right while somebody stood over the grave. The preacher would throw a piece of earth on the coffin, talking about dust to dust, and for some, it was as if they'd been slapped, and they'd let out a yell. They'd fall to the ground, screaming, and their kinfolks would have to drag them up to their feet. Sometimes they'd be like that all the way to the car, moaning, clutching at other people's hands. Later, they were the ones who did just fine.

With others, it was as if the sound of that clod of earth was a voice calling to them, and they'd hear it and turn and then something inside them would climb down and lie beside their loved one inside the grave. And after that, all of the light in their eyes would be gone. Other children, parents, even husbands or wives couldn't reach those people who'd climbed down into a grave after their heart. He worried that this was what was happening to Sirus.

ANNE MORROW LINDBERGH

The following excerpt is from the journal Lindbergh kept after her young son was kidnapped and killed (see p. 64).

from Hour of Gold, Hour of Lead:
Diaries and Letters of Anne Morrow Lindbergh 1929–1932

Hopewell, Tuesday, May 17, 1932
. . . C.'s [Charles's] grief is different from mine and, perhaps, more fundamental, as it is not based on the small physical remembrances. There is something very deep in a man's feeling for his son, it reaches further into the future. My grief is for the small intimate everyday person. How much of it is physical and can be allayed by another child? . . .

Englewood, Thursday, June 9, 1932
. . . I think, analyzing it, that women take and conquer sorrow differently from men. They take it willingly, with open arms they blend and merge it into every part of their lives; it is diffused and spread into every fiber, and they build from that and with that. While men take the concentrated bitter dose at one draught and then try to forget—start to work at something objective and entirely separate. So C. says, "Write about Baker Lake—that has no connection."

But that is just it—it has no connection; my heart is not in it. I can only work from the one strong emotion in me: my love for that boy, and the things that grow from it—wanting a home, wanting children, things to give and do for them, for Charles and my home. . . .

IAN McEWAN

In this novel by McEwan, a father loses his three-year-old daughter Kate in
a busy grocery store one Saturday morning. She does not reappear ever, alive
or dead, and her father is able to prolong hope and defer grieving longer
than most bereaved parents. Still, this passage illustrates how differently par-
ents can grieve the same loss and why sorrow is such lonely business.

from The Child in Time

He anesthetized himself with activity.

He went everywhere alone, setting out each day shortly after the late winter dawn. The police had lost interest in the case after a week. Riots in a northern suburb, they said, were stretching their resources. And Julie stayed at home. She had special leave from the college. When he left in the morning she was sitting in the armchair in the bedroom, facing the cold fireplace. That was where he found her when he came back at night and turned on the lights.

Initially there had been bustle of the bleakest kind: interviews with senior policemen, teams of constables, tracker dogs, some newspaper interest, more explanations, panicky grief. During that time Stephen and Julie had clung to one another, sharing dazed rhetorical questions, awake in bed all night, theorizing hopefully one moment, despairing the next. But that was before time, the heartless accumulation of days, had clarified the absolute, bitter truth. Silence drifted in and thickened. Kate's clothes and toys still lay about the flat, her bed was still unmade. Then one afternoon the clutter was gone. Stephen found the bed stripped and three bulging plastic sacks by the door in her bedroom. He was angry with Julie, disgusted by what he took to be a feminine self-destructiveness, a willful defeatism. But he could not speak to her about it. There was no room for anger, no openings. They moved like figures in a quagmire, with no strength for confrontation. Suddenly their sorrows were separate, insular, incommunicable. They went their different ways, he with his lists and daily trudging, she in her armchair, lost to deep, private grief. Now there was no mutual consolation, no touching, no love. Their old intimacy, their habitual assumption that they were on the same side, was dead. They remained huddled over their separate losses, and unspoken resentments began to grow.

At the end of a day on the streets, when he turned for home, nothing pained Stephen more than the knowledge of his wife sitting in the dark, of how she would barely stir to acknowledge his return, and how he would have neither the good will nor the ingenuity to break through the silence. He suspected—and it turned out later he was correct—that she took his efforts to be a typically masculine evasion, an attempt to mask feelings behind displays of competence and organization and physical effort. The loss had driven them to the extremes of their personalities. They had discovered a degree of mutual intolerance which sadness and shock made insurmountable. They could no longer bear to eat together. He ate standing up in sandwich bars, anxious not to lose time, reluctant to sit down and listen to his thoughts. As far as he knew she ate nothing at all. Early on he brought home bread and cheese, which over the days quietly grew their separate molds in the unvisited kitchen. A meal together would have implied a recognition and acceptance of their diminished family.

It came to the point where Stephen could not bring himself to look at Julie. It was not only that he saw haggard traces of Kate or himself mirrored in her face. It was the inertia, the collapse of will, the near ecstatic suffering which disgusted him and threatened to undermine his efforts. He was going to find his daughter and murder her abductor. He had only to keep walking, remain attentive, and he would surely enter the force field that would warn him that she was nearby. He had only to act on the correct impulse and show the photograph to the right person and he would be led to her. If there were more daylight hours, if he could resist the temptation which was growing each morning to keep his head under the blankets, if he could walk faster, maintain his concentration, remember to glance behind now and then, waste less time eating sandwiches, trust his intuition, go up side streets, and move faster, cover more ground, run even, run . . .

WALL OF SILENCE

WINSTON CHURCHILL

The Churchills' fourth child, Marigold, died at two years and nine months of septicemia. A young French governess was slow to call the doctor and slower yet to telegraph Clementine, "Duckadilly's" mother, away in Scotland with her husband. Seven months later Winston wrote home to his wife.

from *The Last Lion: Winston Spencer Churchill: Visions of Glory 1874–1932*
by William Manchester

"I pass through again those sad scenes of last year when we lost our dear Duckadilly. Poor lamb—it is a gaping wound, whenever one touches it & removes the bandages & plasters of daily life." To the end of her life Clementine could never speak of her lost child. Mary, the last of the Churchills' children, was born that autumn. She grew up puzzled by the identity of the little girl whose framed picture stood on her mother's dressing table, wondering who she could be.

ROBERT FROST

Frost was twenty-six when Elliott, his firstborn, died of cholera at almost four years old. He was sixty-six when son Carol, plagued by depression, killed himself at age thirty-eight. In between, Frost and his wife, Elinor, also lost a two-day-old infant, as well as daughter Marjorie, twenty-nine, who died from septicemia. Of their two surviving children, one was later committed to a mental hospital. No wonder then, in his last interview, Frost stoically said: "I don't take life very seriously. It's hard to get into this world and hard to get out of it. And what's in between doesn't make much sense. If that sounds pessimistic, let it stand."

from *The Poetry of Robert Frost: The Collected Poems, Complete and Unabridged*, edited by Edward Connery Lathem

Home Burial

He saw her from the bottom of the stairs
Before she saw him. She was starting down,
Looking back over her shoulder at some fear.
She took a doubtful step and then undid it
To raise herself and look again. He spoke
Advancing toward her: "What is it you see
From up there always?—for I want to know."
She turned and sank upon her skirts at that,
And her face changed from terrified to dull.
He said to gain time: "What is it you see?"
Mounting until she cowered under him.
"I will find out now—you must tell me, dear."
She, in her place, refused him any help,
With the least stiffening of her neck and silence.
She let him look, sure that he wouldn't see,
Blind creature; and a while he didn't see.

But at last he murmured, "Oh," and again, "Oh."

"What is it—what?" she said.

                        "Just that I see."

"You don't," she challenged. "Tell me what it is."

"The wonder is I didn't see at once.
I never noticed it from here before.
I must be wonted to it—that's the reason.
The little graveyard where my people are!
So small the window frames the whole of it.
Not so much larger than a bedroom, is it?
There are three stones of slate and one of marble,
Broad-shouldered little slabs there in the sunlight
On the sidehill. We haven't to mind *those.*
But I understand: it is not the stones,
But the child's mound—"

                        "Don't, don't, don't, don't," she cried.

She withdrew, shrinking from beneath his arm
That rested on the banister, and slid downstairs;
And turned on him with such a daunting look,
He said twice over before he knew himself:
"Can't a man speak of his own child he's lost?"

"Not you!—Oh, where's my hat? Oh, I don't need it!
I must get out of here. I must get air.—
I don't know rightly whether any man can."

"Amy! Don't go to someone else this time.
Listen to me. I won't come down the stairs."
He sat and fixed his chin between his fists.
"There's something I should like to ask you, dear."

"You don't know how to ask it."

                        "Help me, then."

Her fingers moved the latch for all reply.

"My words are nearly always an offense.
I don't know how to speak of anything

So as to please you. But I might be taught,
I should suppose. I can't say I see how.
A man must partly give up being a man
With womenfolk. We could have some arrangement
By which I'd bind myself to keep hands off
Anything special you're a-mind to name.
Though I don't like such things 'twixt those that love.
Two that don't love can't live together without them.
But two that do can't live together with them."
She moved the latch a little. "Don't—don't go.
Don't carry it to someone else this time.
Tell me about it if it's something human.
Let me into your grief. I'm not so much
Unlike other folks as your standing there
Apart would make me out. Give me my chance.
I do think, though, you overdo it a little.
What was it brought you up to think it the thing
To take your mother-loss of a first child
So inconsolably—in the face of love.
You'd think his memory might be satisfied—"

"There you go sneering now!"

      "I'm not, I'm not!
You make me angry. I'll come down to you.
God, what a woman! And it's come to this,
A man can't speak of his own child that's dead."

"You can't because you don't know how to speak.
If you had any feelings, you that dug
With your own hand—how could you?—his little grave;
I saw you from that very window there,
Making the gravel leap and leap in air,
Leap up, like that, like that, and land so lightly
And roll back down the mound beside the hole.
I thought, Who is that man? I didn't know you.
And I crept down the stairs and up the stairs
To look again, and still your spade kept lifting.
Then you came in. I heard your rumbling voice
Out in the kitchen, and I don't know why,

But I went near to see with my own eyes.
You could sit there with the stains on your shoes
Of the fresh earth from your own baby's grave
And talk about your everyday concerns.
You had stood the spade up against the wall
Outside there in the entry, for I saw it."

"I shall laugh the worst laugh I ever laughed.
I'm cursed. God, if I don't believe I'm cursed."

"I can repeat the very words you were saying:
'Three foggy mornings and one rainy day
Will rot the best birch fence a man can build.'
Think of it, talk like that at such a time!
What had how long it takes a birch to rot
To do with what was in the darkened parlor?
You *couldn't* care! The nearest friends can go
With anyone to death, comes so far short
They might as well not try to go at all.
No, from the time when one is sick to death,
One is alone, and he dies more alone.
Friends make pretense of following to the grave,
But before one is in it, their minds are turned
And making the best of their way back to life
And living people, and things they understand.
But the world's evil. I won't have grief so
If I can change it. Oh, I won't, I won't!"

"There, you have said it all and you feel better.
You won't go now. You're crying. Close the door.
The heart's gone out of it: why keep it up?
Amy! There's someone coming down the road!"

"*You*—oh, you think the talk is all. I must go—
Somewhere out of this house. How can I make you—"

"If—you—do!" She was opening the door wider.
"Where do you mean to go? First tell me that.
I'll follow and bring you back by force. I *will*!—"

TAKING SOLACE WHERE WE CAN

MICHAEL DORRIS

In 1990 Dorris's adopted son Abel, the son born with fetal alcohol syndrome whom he wrote about in The Broken Cord, *was hit by a car while coming home from work. Two weeks later, twenty-three-year-old Abel died, never having regained consciousness. In this short story, a young boy and his friend drown in a pond created by the boy's father, who did landscaping for a living. "Where on the property do you want it situated?" the father had asked his wife, Martha, when they'd saved enough to buy twelve acres. Behind the house, he persisted, or beyond the hill for privacy? She'd opted for privacy.*

from "The Benchmark," in *Working Men: Stories*

Later, men came, dragged the pond, and found the neighbor boy. The two were buried side by side. No word of blame was hurled. None was needed. Everyone knew which man had dug the hole. Martha and I did the bare minimum for Sam and Gloria [their remaining children], and had nothing left. For weeks after the service, we hardly saw each other. I for one was fearful of what might erupt if we spoke.

You had to have the pond so far away, I might easily have unleashed, and then that accusation could never again be caged. . . .

We lived an ordinary life thereafter. Martha joined clubs of women and I worked steady. . . .

I took for granted the patterns, the pathways worn by repetition. Divert a stream and eventually the shape of rocks will alter. Veins appear, then channels carved so deep they seem the natural order. I trusted in the warm wall of my wife beside me in sleep, in the last cup of evening coffee saved for breakfast and in the appearance of supper at five-thirty each night. My half of labor met and fit with Martha's. I depended on her sensible gifts—long johns and caps and heavy gloves—and gave her the same. We maintained our truce without ever declaring the war. And if something was missing, it was replaced by this reliability. We spared each other surprise, and each was grateful.

RICHARD FORD

Frank Bascombe, the main character in this as well as in Ford's later Pulitzer Prize–winning novel Independence Day, *recalls the early period after his nine-year-old son Ralph died.*

from *The Sportswriter*

In the first six months after Ralph died, while I was in the deepest depths of my worst dreaminess, I began to order as many catalogs into the house as I could. At least forty, I'm sure, came every three months. I would, finally, have to throw a box away to let the others in. X [how he refers to his ex-wife] didn't seem to mind and, in fact, eventually became as interested as I was, so that quite a few of the catalogs came targeted for her. During that time—it was summer—we spent at least one evening a week couched in the sun room or sitting in the breakfast nook leafing through the colorful pages, making Magic Marker checks for the things we wanted, dog-earing pages, filling out order blanks with our Bankcard numbers (most of which we never mailed) and jotting down important toll-free numbers for when we might want to call. . . .

For me, though, there was something other than the mere ease of purchase in all this, in the hours spent going through pages seeking the most virtuous screwdriver or the beer bottle cap rehabilitator obtainable nowhere else but from a PO box in Nebraska. It was that the life portrayed in these catalogs seemed irresistible. Something about my frame of mind made me love the abundance of the purely ordinary and pseudo-exotic (which always turns out ordinary if you go the distance and place your order). I loved the idea of merchandise, and I loved those ordinary good American faces pictured there, people wearing their asbestos welding aprons, holding their cane fishing rods, checking their generators with their new screwdriver lights, wearing their saddle oxfords, their same wool nighties, month after month, season after season. In me it fostered an odd assurance that some things outside my life were okay still; that the same men and women standing by the familiar brick fireplaces, or by the same comfortable canopy beds, holding these same shotguns or blow poles or boot warmers or boxes of kindling sticks could see a good day before their eyes right into perpetuity. Things were knowable, safe-and-sound. Everybody with exactly what they need or could get. A perfect illustration of how the literal can become the mildly mysterious.

More than once on a given night when X and I sat with nothing to say to each other (though we weren't angry or disaffected), it proved just the thing to enter that glimpsed but perfectly commonplace life—where all that mattered was that you had that houndstooth sport coat by Halloween or owned the finest doormat money could buy, or that all your friends recognized "Jacques," your Brittany, from a long distance away at night, and could call him by the name stitched on his collar and save him from the log truck bearing down on him just over the rise.

We all take our solace where we can. And *there* seemed like a life—though we couldn't just send to Vermont or Wisconsin or Seattle for it, but a life just the same—that was better than dreaminess and silence in a big old house where unprovoked death had taken its sad toll.

ANGRY WITH SPOUSE

PATRICIA NEAL AND ROALD DAHL

Olivia, the daughter of writer Roald Dahl and actress Patricia Neal, died suddenly from complications of measles at age seven and a half—the same age at which Dahl's sister Astri had died.

from As I Am: An Autobiography by Patricia Neal

We had been thinking about what to do with Olivia's money. We had started a fund for her at birth, as we did for each child, and didn't want to just absorb it back into the family account. We wanted to do something meaningful.

At this time, a very welcome Marjorie Clipstone came into my life. I had seen Marjorie in the village. She ran the Christmas charity shop. She wrote me a most beautiful letter and I knew I had to meet this lady. She was a widow, having lost her husband only two years before, and so was particularly sensitive to the unrelenting sting death inflicts. I told Marjorie about our dilemma over Olivia's money. She suggested starting an organization to help orphans. I thought it was a fine idea and invited her to supper to discuss it further.

When dinner was over and Roald had excused himself, Marjorie and I sat and talked. She said that she believed she and her husband would be together again someday. I confided that I also believed that I would see Olivia again, but *someday* was too far away. "What do I do *now*, Marjorie? I didn't know until she was gone the treasure I had."

"Stop it! Stop it!" Roald was standing in the doorway, his face wild with anger. The anguish within me now flooded my eyes. I ran up the stairs to our bedroom. I slammed the door and the dam burst. Roald followed me, his anger gone. "I'm so sorry, Pat," he said, "but I just cannot stand such trashy sentiment. My daughter is dead. There is nothing more to be said." I looked up at him but I was not moved. "Can you hear me?" he cried. *"My daughter is dead!"*

He turned and left the room and did not hear my reply: "She is *my* daughter, too."

STAN RICE

Like the mythical sirens who by their sweet singing lured mariners to destruction, Rice's wife, novelist Anne Rice, the "illustrious one," tempts the poet time after time to the treacherous shoals of grief. The Rices lost their daughter Michele to leukemia one month short of her sixth birthday.

from Singing Yet: New and Selected Poems

Singing Death

Illustrious one, in whom death is the vagrom wound
& who wanders on the wet grasses singing, sing no more
to me. I have heard your voice plenty & I hunger for health.
Yes, though it is beautiful & seduces, Hush. Come no more
glaze-eyed to my arms asking for pity then push me aside
when the urge strikes to start singing. Transfixed
& then unhinged, crazed with the wish to die & then with the fear
the wish might be granted. I have heard your song
and it shall not drag me yet down with it on the wet grasses.

Illustrious one, in whom death goes on living season by season,
drawing its strength from your singing, lovely
& deadly, Listen: I will not make myself
dead to nourish the death
blooming within you, vagrom intensity. Rather than that I'd see
you wandering lost on the white watery lawns at midnight
singing for the police to come get you, yes, even rather

see you staring at a white wall trying to sing the shapes
out of the whiteness than continue this dying together.

Illustrious one, in whom death is no longer a solid block
but a network, sing no more to me of the waterglass & the stopped clock.
Against such songs we've crashed enough, enough.
That which was from the heart and was heart's song
has been transformed, a heartless net in which to sing
is to struggle and suffer humiliation at the hour of death.
You who sing out of the vagrom flower-mouth-wound, go back!
The white grasses will release you, bones & voice & dress
one entity, dignity regained, deathsong left where you leave
your shape on the lawn in the wet blades. Singing yet.

GETTING BEYOND DIFFERENCES

ANTONYA NELSON

*In this short story, Alan, a newspaper columnist, and his wife, Lois, are
leaving Durango, Colorado, having done what they came there to do:
visit the site on a mountain pass outside of town where five months
earlier their daughter had died in a motorcycle accident.*

from "Mud Season," in *Prairie Schooner* (1989)

When they hit the deer, Lois saw only fur and a single eye before the windshield broke. Its glass rained down on them like pebbles. The deer slid off
the hood, leaving a broad smear of blood.

"Is it a mother deer?" Lois whispered to her husband. In a flash she
thought of fawns and of full udders, the terrible ache of needing warm milk
and needing to provide it.

Her husband remained in his seat, staring straight ahead of him, his
hands bouncing lightly on the steering wheel, then harder, until the dash-
board rocked. He turned on her, his face a horror, red, monstrous. Through
his clenched teeth he spat, "Didn't you see antlers? Are you so blind and *stupid* not to have seen antlers? *Mother* deer do not have points. That's *father*
deer."

And just as suddenly he fell against her. He cried without tears, male crying. She did not know what to do at first, his head against her chest, butting into her again and again, the hard guttural sobbing. It would have been easier to handle in the dark. Even the day they'd heard of Gwen's death, he'd been late at work and she had sat on the back steps waiting for him, her arm around the dog, unwilling to enter the house. When he'd come home, they'd sat there together until it grew dark and then they'd been able to comfort one another.

She tried to soothe him now, running her hand through his hair. The worst had to be over. This would be the last bad thing. She imagined the deer, which she could not see, in front of their car. Perhaps it was alive? But she had no resources; she could not make herself leave her husband to go find out. She pictured its fur as she smoothed her palm over Alan's head. The fur would be sprouting in whorls at its haunches and throat. Its underbelly would be white. There was only so much you could do with one pair of hands, she justified.

"There can't be any more bad luck," she told Alan, in a firm whisper, using a tone of voice she'd once used to promise her children their house would not be robbed, their parents would not die. "We've reached our limits." Alan nodded adamantly into her breasts. "This trip is the end of it," she went on. "*Fin.* Goodbye."

Not a single car passed. What odds, Lois thought, Alan finally quiet on her lap. The only car on this highway and this deer could not avoid getting hit. Alan would see a column in it, but to her it seemed like a mathematical problem, the kind she used to try to help her children with. In a landscape with only two moving objects in it, how long will it take for them to collide?

Forest rangers on their way to work found them ten minutes later. One of them was young and impatient, shaking his head at their out of state license plate, angry with them for having hit the deer. Lois found herself nodding in agreement with his assessment. Careless of them, yes, traveling too fast. They should have known to expect wildlife at sunrise, in the spring, indeed. The other ranger was like Sheriff Pittman [who the day before had shown them where their daughter had died], a man who saw them through eyes screened with sympathy and recognition. Perhaps he saw that more than this accident had claimed these two people, both of whom still sat in their broken car, unable to go on.

JANE HAMILTON

Theresa and Alice, in Hamilton's novel, are neighbors and friends who watch each others' children, as young mothers do. One morning Theresa drops off her girls, Audrey and Lizzy, at Alice's. When Alice is distracted from the hubbub of children and household for a few minutes, two-year-old Lizzy wanders unnoticed to the pond and drowns. Here Theresa meets Alice unexpectedly and explains how her husband, Dan, is coping.

from A Map of the World

"Dan came home from his conference the next night. I screamed right away, the second he walked in the door, that either he had to talk to me or I would leave him. We had a fight. He accused me of breaking down everywhere I go and I yelled at him about how he is in denial the likes of which I have never seen in all my professional days, and that one of these mornings he was going to wake up and realize his heart was broken in spite of himself, that that was going to be far worse than knowing you have a broken heart and tending your hurt. I told him we wouldn't tiptoe around him anymore, that we weren't going to pretend we were fine. I said I cried to everyone else because I was scared out of my wits to even say her name, to say, 'Lizzy,' in front of him. I've been afraid that I'll make one slip and he'll break. You know that. I said it killed me to see him suffering, it hurt so much to begin with, and then with his pain on top of it. I feel sometimes, like I'm carrying everyone's pain. That's why I've had to go bawling around." She was so close to my face I could smell her. "My God," she said, "he nearly cracked up at the kitchen table. About all he'd let me do is keep ahold of his arm. Finally, finally he started to talk about it. He said he couldn't stand Lizzy being only a memory. He said he just hadn't gotten enough of her, that he hardly knew her. He has been trying to find some way he can carry her presence forward, trying to connect her with our life now. He hates the photographs because they are so flat and still."

ARCHIBALD MacLEISH

J.B. is a Pulitzer Prize–winning play in verse that retells the biblical book of Job set in modern times. J.B. and his wife, Sarah, are prosperous and happy, confident that they and their four children are secure in God's grace. Inexplicably, catastrophes strike—one after another—and J.B. and Sarah fight about God. Sarah is angry at Him; J.B. clings to his belief in divine justice. They separate but eventually reconcile. Librarian of Congress under President Franklin D. Roosevelt and later a professor at Harvard, MacLeish wrote J.B. *with his friends Gerald and Sara Murphy in mind (see p. 224). MacLeish met the Murphys in France in the 1920s when they were all part of the postwar expatriate scene. He, his wife, and their two children spent summers with the Murphy family in Antibes, and the families' friendship endured through the years. MacLeish was with the Murphys at Massachusetts General Hospital when their son Baoth died of meningitis, and MacLeish shared the Murphys' ordeal as their younger son, Patrick, unsuccessfully battled tuberculosis for seven years. When Gerald Murphy was dying in 1964, MacLeish gave him a copy of* J.B. *"hoping its message of grace under pressure would lend Murphy additional strength."*

Years later, another bereaved father, Harold Kushner, turned to J.B. *In his own* When Bad Things Happen to Good People, *Kushner reflects approvingly on the last lines of this excerpt we've chosen, one in which Sarah tells her husband to "blow on the coal of the heart." "The world," Kushner writes, "is a cold, unfair place in which everything they held precious has been destroyed. But instead of giving up on this unfair world and life, instead of looking outward, to churches or to nature, for answers, they look inward to their own capacities for loving."*

from J.B.: A Play in Verse

SARAH: *mechanically*   The Lord giveth.

J.B.:   The Lord taketh away . . .

SARAH: *flinging his hand from hers, shrieking*
                                Takes!
        Kills! Kills! Kills! Kills!

Silence.

J.B.:   Blessed be the name of the Lord.

                *   *   *

SARAH: *She moves toward the door, stops, turns.*

        I will not stay here if you lie—
        Connive in your destruction, cringe to it:

Not if you betray my children . . .

I will not stay to listen . . .

> They are
> Dead and they were innocent: I will not
> Let you sacrifice their deaths
> To make injustice justice and God good!

*   *   *

[Sarah leaves J.B. for a while, then returns.]

SARAH: You wanted justice, didn't you?
There isn't any. There's the world . . .

> Cry for justice and the stars
> Will stare until your eyes sting. Weep,
> Enormous winds will thrash the water.
> Cry in sleep for your lost children,
> Snow will fall . . .
>
>   snow will fall . . .

J.B.:   Why did you leave me alone?

SARAH: I loved you.
I couldn't help you any more.
You wanted justice and there was none—
Only love.

J.B.:   He does not love. He
Is.

SARAH: But we do. That's the wonder.

*   *   *

*They cling to each other. Then she rises, drawing him up, peering at the darkness
inside the door.*

J.B.:   It's too dark to see.

She turns, pulls his head down between her hands and kisses him.

SARAH: Then blow on the coal of the heart, my darling.

| J.B.: | The coal of the heart . . . |
| SARAH: | It's all the light now. |

Blow on the coal of the heart.
The candles in churches are out.
The lights have gone out in the sky.
Blow on the coal of the heart
And we'll see by and by . . .

ELIZABETH GLASER

In 1981 Elizabeth Glaser, hemorrhaging badly in childbirth, received HIV-tainted blood during a transfusion and unwittingly passed the virus to daughter Ariel and later to son Jake. Ariel died of AIDS at age seven; Elizabeth died in 1994, leaving as her legacy the Pediatric AIDS Foundation, a national research group she created with two friends. In this excerpt from Glaser's memoir, Ariel has already died, and Elizabeth and husband, Paul, former TV star of Starsky and Hutch, *must address the damage done to their marriage by grief, anger, and fatigue.*

from *In the Absence of Angels* by Elizabeth Glaser and Laura Palmer

A month before, Paul and I had planned a three-day trip to Santa Fe. We knew things were shaky and thought if we had some time away and alone it might help. The trip came a day after one of our worst sessions with the therapist. We barely made it to the airport. We were fighting in the car, and I was sure Paul was going to say to hell with the whole trip. But he didn't. We both got on the plane. I cried through the entire flight. I felt tired behind my eyes and my throat felt like it was closing off. My head throbbed from crying so hard and I would have done anything to end the tension between us. Our marriage felt hopeless.

Why were we fighting [now]? . . .

I think when life is terrible, when we are in a state of crisis, we block out everything to survive. Denial can be a powerful ally, and it is part of the armor we rely on when we are in an extreme situation. When the crisis is resolved, all of the feelings we've pushed aside overtake us.

Maybe Paul and I have to have one foot dangling over the abyss before we feel we can pull each other back in.

We landed in Albuquerque and Paul went to rent a car. When he came back to pick me up, I was seething. "Give me the keys," I said. "You fly back to L.A. I'm going to Santa Fe by myself and then come home. I can't spend three days with all this hatred."

Paul just looked at me and said, "Come on, let's go." He got into the car, slammed the door, and we left Albuquerque for Santa Fe. The trip took an hour.

We sat silently staring at the high desert scenery. Neither one of us dared to look at the other. I said to myself, *Elizabeth, do you want to say good-bye to this man? Do you want him out of your life?*

The answer was no. So I sat there thinking, *What can I do? How do I stop feeling so angry and sad?*

In one of the more important moments of my life, I reached out and put my hand on his. We sat like that for a while. Then Paul reached over and put his arm around me and pulled me closer. We sat quietly driving to Santa Fe, realizing that we didn't want to say good-bye. As the love slowly and softly drifted in, the anger just as gently floated away.

There is no one else in the world who can understand what Paul and I have been through except each other. We share the same trench, and like soldiers in combat, we've experienced a camaraderie no one else will ever understand. No one can offer us support like we can to each other. But when we are angry and hurt, there is no one who can make us feel more isolated than each of us to the other. When Paul and I feel estranged, it's like living on opposite sides of a wall.

All of the pain in our life can overwhelm everything else if we let it, and we certainly had by the time we got to New Mexico. Our love has had so much to overcome that sometimes we become completely severed from it. We can't find it at all.

What happened instinctively on that drive, and what I consciously realized later that weekend, was that there was no way to work back down through the pain to the love. I had to circumvent all the anger and resentment to connect with the part of me that loved Paul.

I think when Paul and I realized on that drive that we were on the verge of losing our relationship on top of everything else, we were able to defuse the tension and decide to let ourselves love.

TOGETHER IN BED

PERCY BYSSHE SHELLEY

At twenty-one, Percy Bysshe Shelley left England and his wife and children for Europe and sixteen-year-old Mary Wollstonecraft Godwin. The Romantic poet was to drown eight years later in 1822; but before that, Mary, his new wife, had had a miscarriage and given birth to four children. Her first child, born prematurely, died in eleven days. The second and third children, William and Clara, died within a year of each other at ages two and one. "I never know one moments ease from . . . wretchedness & despair . . . to loose [sic] two only & lovely children in one year— to watch their dying moments . . . I feel I am no[t] fit for anything & therefore not fit to live," she wrote to her friend Marianne Hunt. As Mary withdrew into a severe depression, Percy immersed himself in his writing, producing some of his best poetry. In a private notebook, he wrote secret poems expressing his feelings of emotional and sexual abandonment.

from *Mary Shelley: Romance and Reality* by Emily W. Sunstein

My dearest Mary, wherefore hast thou gone,
And left me in this dreary world alone?
Thy form is here indeed—a lovely one—
But thou art fled, gone down the dreary road,
That leads to Sorrow's most obscure abode;
Thou sittest on the hearth of pale despair,
        Where
For thine own sake I cannot follow thee.

    *   *   *

Ha! thy frozen pulses flutter
With a love thou darest not utter,

. . . .

Kiss me; —oh! thy lips are cold;
Round my neck thine arms enfold—
They are soft, but chill and dead;
And thy tears upon my head
Burn like points of frozen lead.

JOHN IRVING

In Irving's comically tragic novel, Garp accidentally crashes his car into his wife Helen's car, killing their younger son, Walt. Soon after, they and their surviving son, Duncan, go to Garp's mother's inn at the ocean to heal their many wounds. Their friends, the Fletchers, come for a week's visit, the husband counseling Helen to get pregnant right away. She needn't say that Garp had not slept with her since the accident; he'd noted the separate rooms.

from The World According to Garp

It was quite some time after the Fletchers left when Helen came to Garp's room in the night. She was not surprised to find him lying awake, because he was listening to what she'd heard, too. It was why she couldn't sleep.

Someone, one of Jenny's late arrivals—a new guest—was taking a bath. First the Garps had heard the tub being drawn, then they'd heard the plunking in the water—now the splashing and soapy sounds. There was even a little light singing, or the person was humming.

They remembered, of course, the years Walt had washed himself within their hearing, how they would listen for any telltale slipping sounds, or for the most frightening sound of all—which was no sound. And then they'd call, "Walt?" And Walt would say, "What?" And they would say, "Okay, just checking!" To make sure that he hadn't slipped under and drowned.

Walt liked to lie with his ears underwater, listening to his fingers climbing the walls of the tub, and often he wouldn't hear Garp or Helen calling him. He'd look up, surprised, to see their anxious faces suddenly above him, peering over the rim of the tub. "I'm all right," he'd say, sitting up.

"Just *answer*, for God's sake, Walt," Garp would tell him. "When we call you, just answer us."

"I didn't hear you," Walt said.

"Then keep your head out of the water," Helen said.

"But how can I wash my hair?" Walt asked.

"That's a lousy way to wash your hair, Walt," Garp said. "Call me. *I'll* wash your hair."

"Okay," said Walt. And when they left him alone, he'd put his head underwater again and listen to the world that way.

Helen and Garp lay beside each other on Garp's narrow bed in one of the guest rooms in one of the garrets at Dog's Head Harbor. The house had so

many bathrooms—they couldn't even be sure which bathroom they were listening to, but they listened.

"It's a woman, I think." Helen said. . . .

"I thought at first it was a child," Helen said.

"I know," Garp said.

"The humming, I guess," Helen said. "You know how he used to talk to
himself?"

"I know," Garp said.

They held each other in the bed that was always a little damp, so close to
the ocean and with so many windows open all day, and the screen doors
swinging and banging.

"I want another child," said Helen.

"Okay," Garp said.

"As soon as possible," Helen said.

"Right away," said Garp. "Of course."

"If it's a girl," Helen said, "we'll name her Jenny, because of your
mother."

"Good," said Garp.

"I don't know, if it's a boy," said Helen.

"Not Walt," Garp said.

"Okay," Helen said.

"Not *ever* another Walt," said Garp. "Although I know some people do
that."

"I wouldn't want to," Helen said.

"Some other name, if it's a boy," Garp said.

"I hope it's a girl," said Helen.

"I won't care," Garp said.

"Of course. Neither will I, really," said Helen.

"I'm so sorry," Garp said; he hugged her.

"No, *I'm* so sorry," she said.

"No, *I'm* so sorry," said Garp.

"*I* am," said Helen.

"*I* am," he said.

They made love so carefully. Helen imagined that she was Roberta
Muldoon [a transsexual], fresh out of surgery, trying out a brand-new
vagina. Garp tried not to imagine anything.

Whenever Garp began imagining, he only saw the bloody Volvo. There
were Duncan's screams, and outside he could hear Helen calling. . . .

"Where's Walt?" Helen said, trying to see into the Volvo. She stopped screaming.

"Walt!" cried Garp. He held his breath. Duncan stopped crying.

They heard nothing. And Garp knew Walt had a cold you could hear from the next room—even two rooms away, you could hear that wet rattle in the child's chest.

"Walt!" they screamed.

Both Helen and Garp would whisper to each other, later, that at that moment they imagined Walt with his ears underwater, listening intently to his fingers at play in the bathtub.

"I can still see him," Helen whispered, later.

"All the time," Garp said. "I know."

"I just shut my eyes," said Helen.

"Right," Garp said. "I know."

But Duncan said it best. Duncan said that sometimes it was as if his missing right eye was not entirely gone. "It's like I can still see out of it, sometimes," Duncan said. "But it's like memory, it's not real—what I see."

"Maybe it's become the eye you see your dreams with," Garp told him.

"Sort of," Duncan said. "But it seems so real."

"It's your *imaginary* eye," Garp said. "That can be very real."

"It's the eye I can still see Walt with," Duncan said. "You know?"

"I know," Garp said.

SHARING GRIEF THROUGH MEMORIES

CHANG-RAE LEE

In this excerpt, a father recalls happy family outings before his son Mitt died at six, suffocated while playing with friends.

from *Native Speaker*

I used to love to walk these streets of Flushing with Lelia and Mitt, bring them back here on Sunday trips during the summer. We would eat cold buckwheat noodles at a Korean restaurant near the subway station and then go browsing in the big Korean groceries, not corner vegetable stands like my father's but real supermarkets with every kind of Asian food. Mitt always marveled at the long wall of glassed-door refrigerators stacked full with gallon jars of five kinds of kimchee, and even he noticed that if a customer took one down the space was almost immediately filled with another. *The kimchee museum,* he'd say, with appropriate awe. Then, Lelia would stray off to the butcher's section, Mitt to the candies. I always went to the back, to the magazine section, and although I couldn't read the Korean well I'd pretend anyway, just as I did when I was a boy, flipping the pages from right to left, my finger scanning vertically the way my father read. Eventually I'd hear Lelia's voice, calling to both of us, calling the only English to be heard that day in the store, and we would meet again at the register with what we wanted, the three of us, looking like a family accident, gathering on the counter the most serendipitous pile. We got looks. Later, after he died, I'd try it again, ride the train with Lelia to the same restaurant and store, but in the end we would separately wander the aisles not looking for anything, except at the last moment, when we finally encountered each other, who was not him.

LIZZIE AND HERMAN MELVILLE

Lizzie and Herman Melville had marital problems and at one point, some members of the family encouraged her to leave him. She never did. In 1867, their eighteen-year-old son Malcolm was found dead in bed. He had shot himself either accidentally or, more likely, intentionally. Nineteen years later, Stanwix, their second son, died at age thirty-five.

from *Melville: A Biography* by Laurie Robertson-Lorant

Lizzie, meanwhile, had been trying to recover the tinted photograph that Herman had presented to Malcolm's regiment after his death. Although the company had been disbanded years earlier and its effects sold or stored in Albany, Herman managed to trace the portrait to the home of a newly married couple who had purchased it in a secondhand shop to place among various knickknacks expressive of the families' collective identity. It was the fashion for middle-class Victorians to display stereopticons featuring views of natural monuments, city landmarks, and Civil War battlefields alongside family photographs, reproductions of artworks, personal mementos, and photographs of men in uniform. As the young couple had no relatives in the war, they had placed an unknown soldier's picture on their mantel to symbolize their patriotism, so they readily accepted Herman's offer to exchange it for a more valuable, handsomely framed watercolor showing another unknown young soldier.

The search for Macky's photograph, which was made even more meaningful by its seeming absurdity to outsiders, drew Herman and Lizzie together.

ROBB FORMAN DEW

Dew's novel begins six years after Martin's younger son, Toby, was killed (see p. 10). Martin had just picked up both sons, Toby and David, at a soccer game and had stopped his car behind another. His thoughts elsewhere, the teenager behind them failed to brake, killing twelve-year-old Toby in the backseat. Here Martin and his wife, Dinah, are taking a walk.

from *Fortunate Lives*

"You were thinking about Toby, weren't you?" Martin asked her. "In the parking lot?"

She looked at him in surprise. "No, not really." She didn't want to talk about Toby's death. She thought that with David's recent departure [to college] they were both susceptible to opportunistic sorrow, as if a flu had been going around and their white counts were low.

"Well, you were." Martin was insistent.

"Not only Toby . . . Those two children . . . the dates on the gravestones. I'd never read them before. They were both about two and a half years old. I was wondering if it was any easier—if it was a different kind of grief, somehow—to lose such a young child."

Martin was silent. They both kept their eyes on the landscape, and Duchess came loping down the slope and sank down next to Martin, panting even in the cool weather.

Dinah said, "I don't think it would make any difference. It would be just as terrible."

Martin nodded. He thought so, too. "You know," he said, "I still keep wondering if there wasn't some way I could have avoided that wreck. I've gone over it and over it. I was so distracted. . . ."

"If you could have avoided it?" Dinah's voice rose a little in consternation. "Don't even think about that, Martin. Of course you couldn't have avoided it. That's not fair to yourself—it's not even fair to me—for you to try to . . . oh . . . take on the responsibility." Dinah knew that the wreck that killed Toby was nobody's fault, but in spite of herself she held *herself* accountable. She constantly fought off this absurd idea, but nevertheless she had been his mother.

"I know. I know. But I can't help it. If I had checked my rearview mirror . . ."

"What could you have done?" Dinah stood up and brushed the spruce needles off her slacks. "There was a car in *front* of you. You were caught. It was just bad luck. That's all."

Martin stood up, too, but Duchess lay there looking at them imploringly. "God, luck," and he bent to pick up a stick, waving it at Duchess to tempt her along. When he tossed it far ahead of them, Duchess rose and went lumbering after it. "But I *was* distracted, Dinah. Toby was so excited. He kept leaning forward, grabbing the back of my seat. It made me . . . *cross.* You remember how he sometimes would get so carried away? How he just didn't pick up on when to stop." They were walking side by side on the level ground, and Martin put his hand to his forehead and brought it down across his face, as though it were unbearable to have vision, as though he were pulling a shade. "He was so excited about scoring that goal in the scrimmage."

"What?" Dinah said, suddenly alert.

"In the soccer game. He was so excited. You know how Toby always talked with his hands? He was distracting me. I'd told him to calm down, but he wasn't paying attention."

"Martin. You never told me that Toby scored a goal in that soccer game."

"I must have. I'm sure I did . . . he was really good at soccer."

"You never even told me that he was good at soccer. He used to get so nervous about going to practice. You never told me he scored a goal that day. He hadn't scored a goal before that, had he?" They had reached the narrow path that they would have to descend single file, and Dinah reached out and detained Martin by holding on to the crook of his elbow.

"No. Well, not in Group Three soccer. He'd just been moved up that year." Martin was distracted from his brooding by this curiosity on Dinah's part. "He was pretty young for that group, but he was one of their best players. He was the youngest kid on the team. He was a good athlete."

Dinah was still for a moment. Then she pulled Martin closer to her and reached her head up to kiss him lightly on the cheek. "We'd better go ahead. I don't hear Duchess anywhere."

"She won't leave the path," Martin said, turning and preceding Dinah down the hill.

She followed him slowly, tantalized by this new way to understand Toby's death. She had always thought that the tragedy of the death of children is that they haven't had a chance to complete any of the natural cycles of their lives, and therefore it strikes a universal chord of injustice. Their lives seem incomplete to the survivors. But now she thought about the whole of Toby's life. Maybe it had been happily complete in that very instant before his death. There he had been: a hero in his own mind. He had been gesticulating and excited and pleased, and then his life had ended. Of course, she couldn't let go that easily; she would forever grieve for all that Toby hadn't had a chance to accomplish, or attempt to accomplish. But at least she could feel a certain relief at knowing that the greatest sorrow of Toby's death was for her and Martin to bear, that it had never, for an instant, weighed heavily on Toby himself. And she and Martin would be all right, the two of them. When they reached the bottom of the hill, she linked her arm through Martin's. This new bit of knowledge about the mystery of Toby's life—and his death—was something she would bring forth and examine again and again, for the rest of her life.

6

Sisters and Brothers Grieve Too

I brought Alexander home from the hospital on a sunny day in June. I laid him in his crib. Hilary, almost four, put her toy television in the crib to entertain her new brother. As the music tinkled, Allie opened his eyes. Thus began a warm and special relationship. Allie admired Hilary and was proud of her. In fact, she was at the top of a list of favorite things we found in his papers. And Hilary was always solicitous and protective of him.

Although they were four years apart, Hilary and Allie enjoyed each other's companionship. I see them together eating hamburgers in the dining room of the Hotel Dan in Tel Aviv while Peter and I went out for spaghetti on Dizengoff Street. Or riding up the chairlifts at ski resorts. Or setting off together for Allie's first day of school. So many memories shared.

I remember closing the front door one night when Peter and I were going out, and hearing Allie shout jubilantly, "They're gone!" They couldn't wait to get rid of us. This may have been my first realization that their relationship had a life of its own from which I was excluded. Although I sometimes wished I was privy to the information that they shared with each other, I felt blessed to have children who got along and supported one another.

When Hilary left Baltimore for college in New York City, Allie went to visit her. I have a picture of both of them at Earth Day 1990 in Central Park. And he stayed with her in the dorm that last spring when we went to New York for Passover with Peter's family and Easter brunch with my mother.

The last time they were together was in Baltimore. Hilary brought several of her college friends home for the Preakness. Pimlico racetrack is within walking distance of our home. I looked out my bay window with such pride and joy as Hilary, Allie, her friends and a friend's younger brother swarmed across the yard on their way to the race. They stopped en route at my friend Vicki's. She hadn't seen Allie in a while and later told me she was surprised to see how he had grown. She said he had his arm around Hilary and was laughing, delighted with life.

Hilary went back to New York to finish her junior year and three weeks later, on a Friday evening, we called to tell her her brother was dead. "Take the train home right away and bring something to wear to a funeral." She was alone at the time, and I didn't know who to call to assist her. She got the train but forgot to bring anything at all to wear.

When Hilary talks about Allie now (which is not that much or that often), it is usually to recall something cute or funny that he said or did. She rarely discusses her feelings and once said talking was too painful. But every so often, she makes a comment that reveals how close they were and how profound her loss is. She told me she wants to be buried next to him when she dies. And she says she does not want a big party at her wedding because it would be too sad without Allie.

Hilary has lost both the companion of her childhood and her innocence. I don't know that anyone will love and admire her as unconditionally as Allie did. Siblings are the only people who can truly appreciate the idiosyncrasies of growing up in a particular family. Allie and Hilary would go into gales of laughter over the time they watched me crash down a hill in a cloud of snow when we were skiing, or the time Peter and I were fighting and I slammed the door so hard the smoke detector fell apart. Hilary has no peer with whom to share the family stories now.

Not only has Hilary had to cope with losing her brother but also with losing her parents as she knew them. Overnight we were transformed into agonized zombies clinging to life by our fingernails. A few months after Allie died, Hilary reminded me that I used to beg the two of them to take care of themselves because they were so precious I wouldn't want to live without them. She was afraid that I would kill myself. She definitely thought I was too distraught to drive. And I know for a fact there were times she thought it might be better to be the one who was dead than the one who survived and had to cope with the aftermath.

I used to take Hilary and Allie shopping for their Christmas presents for us. I didn't even think about this the first time we exchanged gifts after Allie died until Hilary told me how hard it was for her to shop by herself. Hilary is now our only living child and consequently she bears the burden of all our hopes, dreams, and expectations. It is certainly not as we would have it, and we try to go easy on her, but all three of us know it is so. Someday she will also have all the filial responsibilities for elderly parents. It breaks my heart to think of her having to sort out the relics of our lives, including what we have saved of Allie's, and dispose of them by herself.

People tend to say that a parent's loss is worse than a sibling's. What is the point of comparing different degrees of tragedy? Losing someone as beloved as Allie in the prime of his life is more than any of us should have to bear. Hilary is at a different stage of life. She has a lot to look forward to in her career, as well as opportunities for new loves in a spouse and children. Peter and I know beyond any doubt that the best will always be behind us—the time when Allie was alive. But Allie is as irreplaceable for Hilary as he is for us.

MARY

After the accident that killed Jake, after I got out of the hospital, I lay in a bed in our living room for seven months. A broken bag of bones.

Those months a village did indeed raise my remaining child. Hollis, four months shy of three, spent her days at home with Shirley, a newly hired housekeeper who brought to mind words like "heaven-sent." Shirley, the neighborhood children, their mothers, the college baby-sitters, they all looked after Hollis as if she were a princess who needed and deserved the entire castle's attention. And—still asking daily, "Where's Jake?"—she did.

Nights, Hollis had her dad. From the second floor, where I couldn't go, I'd hear scuffling and giggling; later, bathtub play and more giggling. She'd come down to me to have books read, then head back upstairs to bed. But I knew she'd return.

Because every night, all those months, Hollis would appear in the living room around midnight, ostensibly to check on me. "You're all by your lone," she said the first time, by way of explanation. She'd brought her own pillow, I gave her a blanket, and she curled up on the sofa near my hospital bed and went to sleep.

Hollis was right. I *was* by my lone, but in the larger sense, so was she. And still is.

Although not by plan, Hollis has ended up an only child, and like most, she's happy. But there is a difference between being an only child from the start and becoming one by default. She has her treasured pictures of Jake, a few memories, his toys, his stuffed animals, his room. But when she plays with friends who have sisters and brothers, she sees what she doesn't have. Other single children probably yearn for siblings too, and the yearning may be every bit as strong. But Hollis had a brother who was stolen. She can put a face on her yearning, and there's the difference.

Read biographies, talk with older people, and stories of early loss are stupefyingly common. Parents die, children go blind, lose their legs, their homes, their innocence. The world throws rocks at them, yet for the most part, incredibly, children adjust. As has Hollis. Eventually she accepted that Jake would not come back. She stopped wasting her pennies on that wish. She also got used to hearing her parents cry, and from the start, surely to compensate, willed herself not to. No child avoids sad movies better than Hollis.

What she's never accepted is how precious she is to Tom and me; the more so, of course, because we now know how quickly children can be taken from us. At eleven, Hollis is old enough to understand that the accident gave her different parents than Jake had: sadder, yes, but also more protective. She hates that, and I don't blame her. Hollis wants normal parents who can assume she'll take risks, learn from her youthful mistakes, and survive. What she doesn't realize is how much I'd love to *be* that parent again. I just can't.

In fourth grade, Hollis came home from school with a Mother's Day "memory" gift. Her drawing had me, a black abstract figure, sitting in a lavender field of pink and blue flowers. Inside the card, she wrote:

> *I am lying on my soft bed, you in a hospital bed sound asleep. You wake up hearing the "bump, bump" of my stuffed dog bouncing down the stairs like a ball. I walk into the living room, my pillow and green blanket already laid out. I bend over to you and ask, "Are you all by your lone?" Then I climb onto the couch, and I sink in like cotton into water. Love, Hollis*

It is, of course, her memory *and* mine. And when I hold it to the light, I see more than a little blond-haired girl in a pink robe bumping her favorite stuffed animal, Floppie, down the stairs. I see a memory that became a metaphor for what she learned in the aftermath of the accident and Jake's death. Hollis saw us suffering, our hearts broken, and thought comforting her parents was her job. It wasn't, and shouldn't have been. But did trying hurt her? By her lone too, Hollis also learned to look out for herself, to stave off her own fear and loneliness any way she could. Even if it meant midnight trips to a sofa in the living room.

In those normal families Hollis wants to be part of, other children probably handed their mothers memory gifts of especially happy days spent at the beach or Disney World. By now, my daughter has plenty of good memories too, but she chose this one for me. And like a therapist, I see reasons. The qualities she developed early on, compassion and self-reliance, are good ones. Both will serve Hollis well in life. I'm just sorry she had to learn their value so early. And so deep in the bone.

ANNE

"O HOW LONESOME"

JILL KER CONWAY

Historian Jill Ker Conway was the first woman president of Smith College. Her autobiography, The Road from Coorain, *chronicles her childhood on a sheep ranch in New South Wales, Australia, and her coming of age in Sydney, where she moved with her mother and two brothers after her father drowned. She was the one to answer the door when the police arrived in the middle of the night to tell the family that her older brother, Bob, had been killed in a car accident.*

from *The Road from Coorain*

After he left, I was overcome by the need to do my grieving privately for a while. I wanted to sit alone and take it in. I also knew it would be a long time before my mother slept peacefully again, and thought she would need her rest for what was awaiting her tomorrow. . . . I was literally glad to have time to take in his death alone. It meant that in my incestuous way I could hold on a little longer to something about him which for the moment was mine alone. He had been like the sun in my universe, and most of my aspirations at school and in my daily life had centered on winning his approval. Now there were not just my father's wishes to be carried out in his absence, but Bob's too. I realized I would always be trying to live out his life for him.

As the cold night wore on, I began to gather my wits and worry about Barry [her other brother]. I hadn't heard him come in, and I dreaded the thought of giving this news to my mother alone. Finally, looking at the time, I understood that he must have come in hours ago. I stumbled frantically into his room to waken him and whisper the news. Downstairs, we sat together again, waiting out the night, just as we had waited out the day of our father's death together. As the first light came in, it struck me like a blow that the sun would soon rise on a world without Bob. With the light we stirred ourselves and agreed upon a plan. As soon as dawn arrived, Barry would go out to a phone box and call our uncle. He would then borrow a neighbor's car, collect our uncle, and bring him to our house in time to help tell my mother. There need be no waiting then. They could set out at once for the hospital and the police. While Barry went to make his phone call, I crept about the kitchen to make us hot tea. When he returned we drank it, our teeth chattering against the cups from cold and shock. After he left I settled in to wait, watching the sun rise, staring at the new day in frozen sorrow. We had thought there could be no greater grief than the loss of our father, but there was and it was upon us. I knew with foreboding how it would affect our mother.

Barry and our wonderful, reliable uncle arrived almost before it seemed possible that they could be at the door. I gave them hot tea while we talked in low voices, each of us putting off the time when she must be told. Finally he went upstairs. There was a long silence. Then he returned despondently, saying, "I hope I never have to do something so hard again. She'll be down soon. Treat her gently. She's in shock."

Shortly my mother appeared, dressed and ready to leave. She looked like a character in a fairy story on whom a sudden spell had been cast. She said in an incredulous voice to no one in particular, "But he was my *first* baby." We nodded and then they set out.

After my brother Bob's death, it seemed as though I had lost the capacity for emotional response. Daily life was in black and white, like a badly made film. My trancelike state excluded music, feeling, color, desire. Although on the surface I was doing well, I was actually going through each day like an automaton. I was vice-captain of my class at school and I mastered intellectual tasks with the same ease as in the past, but they gave little pleasure. I knew that I would win several academic prizes at the end of the year, but they didn't seem to matter very much. I gave up athletic competition because during the practice hours after school I was haunted by the knowledge of my mother, alone at home. I often came in to find her just sitting gazing into space.

I never touched the keys of a piano again, nor could I listen to music. When I heard something Bob had played or that we had listened to together I could not manage the feelings of grief that swept over me. Just as with our departure from Coorain, my consciousness had retreated to a great distance. It was hard to bring it back to earth unless I was concentrating every energy on some difficult intellectual effort. I came to love my hours of homework because when I finally sat down alone in my room with my books, I could get my mind and body together again, and escape the discomfort of watching the world from the other side of some transparent but impenetrable window. At school I laughed when people told jokes and listened to the detailed descriptions offered by my classmates of the dresses to be worn at dances, or tales about the sweetheart of the moment, but I could not really participate.

When we went to the theater, I sat physically in the stalls but was emotionally somewhere up with the lighting tracks and girders of the building. Well-meaning family friends tried to jolly me along, but it was no use.

Each weekend my brother and I would feign interest in some expedition or diversion so we could get our mother out of the house, talking to people, seeing scenery, doing anything but sitting alone, or attending the séances which had become her obsessive interest. If we were sad, she was distraught. I often wondered if it would be better to rend one's garments and tear one's hair to express grief. My mother was quiet, but frozen.

My brother and I had to contend with the fact that our anxiety-crazed mother now confidently expected that our lives would also be cut short by accidental death. A missed train or a miscalculation about how long an errand or a weekend trip to the school library would take brought us home to a trembling, white-faced woman who had been steeling herself for the inevitable disaster. We learned to exaggerate how long the simplest journey would take, and ourselves swung between sharing her foreboding and laughing nervously about it to one another.

WALLACE STEGNER

Wallace Stegner said that he wrote in order to make sense out of life, so it is not surprising that the loss of a child is a theme that runs throughout his books. His mother's first child was stillborn and his older brother, Cecil, died of pneumonia when he was twenty-three. Stegner, twenty-two at the time, had recently left their hometown, Salt Lake City, for the State University of Iowa. This selection from Stegner's autobiographical novel The Big Rock Candy Mountain *describes the train ride his fictitious character Bruce Mason takes back to Salt Lake City when his older brother Chet dies.*

from *The Big Rock Candy Mountain*

He opened his eyes and saw the row of green chair backs, the blue night lights, the sprawling figures of sleepers, the pale gleam of bunched pillows half falling off the arms into the aisle. Outside there was a thin and watery light, not yet strong enough to be called daylight, but not quite darkness. His mouth was bitter with the taste of coal smoke, and his throat was sore.

In the curious unreality of the chair car, less real than the dream he had just awakened from, he straightened himself, lifted his aching shoulder from its cramped position. Half stupefied, he rose and rocked back between the sleepers to the men's room, rinsed his mouth, washed his face and hands, looked at himself in the mirror. His face was pale and floating, his tie twisted, and for a long time he stood stupidly wondering where he'd got the overcoat. It wasn't his. He didn't own one. He had got around to combing his hair before the realization came to him, not suddenly, but as a dull transition from not-knowing to knowing. Brucker's coat. He remembered Brucker [a school friend], solicitous, almost anguished, and himself wandering down the hall, shaking off Brucker's hands, standing with his back to the top of the stairs while the messenger boy's scared face went on down and the fact of death lay in the hall like a heavy foul smell. Then Brucker putting him on the twelve-fifteen later, pressing his overcoat on him, shaking his hand hard, wringing it, his face stiff with sympathy. A good guy, a good friend.

He moved a spittoon with his foot so that he could sit down on the leather bench by the window. The pane was so streaked that he could barely see out. What he could see looked like Nebraska. Farms, windmills, occasional trees, fields and fences, a strip of ghostly highway and a car on it, its lights still on. He put his hand in his overcoat pocket, felt the paper, drew it out yellow and crumpled, read it again.

"Chester passed away this morning wiring you train fare love. Harry Mason."

Harry Mason, Bruce thought. Not "Dad." Not "Father." Harry Mason. As if he didn't dare use any familiar word, or were so confused he didn't know quite what he was doing. Or as if the loss of his one son had made him realize what a bottomless gulf lay between himself and the other. A stiff and formal telegram. Chester passed away this morning . . .

Oh Jesus, Bruce said, poor mother!

Tears squeezed between his lids, and at the sound of a step in the aisle he rose quickly and washed his face again. The brakeman looked through the curtain, nodded, and went on. Bruce went back to his seat and lay down, his eyes close to the the smeared window, staring out across the flat land. It couldn't be Nebraska. It had to be Minnesota or Iowa. They weren't due in Omaha till sometime around six. Then a thousand miles of Nebraska and Wyoming and Utah. He'd get into Salt Lake at the worst possible time, two or three in the morning.

Chet is dead, he said. Your brother has died suddenly, and you are on your way back to his funeral. Your father has sent you a telegram and a money order. You change at Omaha to the Union Pacific and you will arrive very early in the morning in Salt Lake. You will see your mother with the knife in her. You will see Chet's wife, whom you do not much like, parading her grief, and his little girl bewildered and whimpering. You will also see your father, whom you hate, and how will he be taking it? He always liked Chet better than you, even though he treated him harder.

And Chet, he said, is dead. His life is finished at twenty-three, before it had a chance to begin. Never, he said. Not ever. He was, and now is not.

Suddenly he was flooded by memories of terrifying clarity, he and Chet trapping muskrats together on the river in Canada, playing soldier down in the burnouts on the homestead, singing together in school cantatas, getting into fights over the Erector set, swimming in the bare-naked hole down by where Doctor O'Malley's tent used to be pitched, playing map games on the long ride down from the Canadian border to Utah. The smell of gasoline from the auxiliary can in the hot grove near Casper, the mourning doves that cooed all that morning from the cottonwoods, and the ledge up behind, where they killed the rattlesnake. The pride he had felt, the tremendous exuberant exultation, when Chet caught the pass in the last quarter to beat Provo, and himself running out on the field hysterical with "school spirit," pushing through players slimed with black mud from head to foot, only their eyes unmuddied, to grab Chet's hand and pound him on the back, and the way Chet had grinned almost in embarrassment behind his mask of mud, still holding the ball in his big muddy hands . . .

It had never seemed that he and Chet had much in common, that they had ever run together much. Chet had been above and beyond him, with the big gang. But there were thousands of ties, millions, so many that he was amazed and saddened. They were brothers, something he had never really considered before.

Had been, he said. Had been brothers. That was all gone. Everything that had force to make them brothers was already done. If he wanted to find a brother now he had to find him in the past, in recollections that he hadn't even known were there.

He bit his lips together and bent his forehead against the cold windowpane. But he did not cry much. His eyes were dry when they ran through the shacktowns and suburbs of Council Bluffs and across the river and into Omaha.

For two hundred miles across Nebraska he thought of nothing except how clean the Union Pacific kept its trains. At Kearney he bought a newspaper and read it through painstakingly, knowing what he was looking for and completely aware that it was not there. People died everywhere, all the time. Why should anyone in Omaha take note that Chet Mason had died suddenly in Salt Lake City? Who was Chet Mason that anyone should mark his death? Yet the strange lethargy that held him, the torpor waiting on complete realization, did not believe that slip of yellow paper in his overcoat pocket, and the absence of any notice in the paper was almost comforting. He knew he would not believe Chet was dead until he had more proof than the telegram.

At North Platte he bought another paper. At Cheyenne he bought another. From Cheyenne clear on across the plateau to Rock Springs he sat in the club car playing poker with three drummers, and won eighty cents. When they hiked the ante he left the game and went back to his seat to try to sleep. Out past the panes of double glass the moon silvered the empty waste of the Wyoming Plateau, and the telegraph poles were like the ticking second-hand of a watch, the muted racket of the wheels, the grinding of a remorseless mechanism carrying him closer and closer to the time when he had to wake up.

When the train swung out of the canyon in a long curve and backed into the yards at Ogden he roused himself and got off for a cup of coffee. Forty miles to go. In the station washroom he washed and combed his hair, and at the newsstand he bought a Salt Lake paper.

He didn't look into it until the train started again. Then he went back to the men's room and sat down. He found it immediately, a little three-inch story on the local page, and the fact that Chet was not stuck away in a column of nameless and unimportant deaths brought him an instant of fierce pride. "Former High School Athlete Dies," it said. So Chet was not entirely unknown. Some of the people reading that three-inch notice would recall games he had starred in, plays he had made spectacularly.

Why try to fool yourself? he said. Why pretend that Chet was anything, amounted to anything? Why back up your grief by making believe Chet mattered to anyone outside his family? He mattered to you, isn't that enough? Does he have to be important to other people before you'll think him worth a tear?

But those three inches of type helped, nevertheless. He was more calm when he stepped off the train than he had been all day, and when he saw his mother, alone, coming toward him with her face twisting toward tears, he did not break down. He spread his arms and she came into them.

SARAH DAVENPORT

These diary entries were made by twelve-year-old Sarah who lived on a farm in New Canaan, Connecticut.

from A Book of Your Own: Keeping a Diary or Journal by Carla Stevens

Saturday, June 15, 1850
It rained in the morning but it cleared off about noon. My brother was taken very sick this afternoon about one o'clock. Dr. Teller, Dr. Roberts and a few of our neighbors were assembled here. The doctors could do no good he died a little after three o'clock he has not been very well although almost always with red cheeks and playful countenance the Drs. pronounced the disease to be the Croup the funeral will be tomorrow afternoon at one o'clock.

Sunday, June 16, 1850
The funeral of my dear little brother was appointed to be at one o'clock this afternoon at the church. We followed him to the grave and there his earthly remains was laid side by side with my other brother and sister and I alone remain.

Monday, June 17, 1850
Warm and pleasant. O how lonesome it is without Burrell everything seems to be so desolate to me without him I wander from one room to another but I cannot find him . . .

Tuesday, June 18, 1850
I have worked a little and read some. But O how lonesome.

LIVING WITH LOSS: SOME DO BETTER THAN OTHERS

J. M. BARRIE

Generations of children and grown-ups have been enchanted by the story of Peter Pan, the boy who never grows up, and his band of lost boys. But the inspiration for this seemingly whimsical tale derived from a family tragedy—the sudden death of Barrie's older brother David from a head injury. The replacement child for "the son who by dying had remained

*ever young," Barrie wrote about childhood all of his life: he even called
his last play* The Boy David.

from *The Worst Loss: How Families Heal from the Death of a Child* by Barbara D. Rosof

J. M. Barrie, the English playwright who wrote *Peter Pan,* was six when his
brother David, thirteen and his mother's favorite, died in a skating accident.
His mother stayed in her darkened bedroom, clutching David's christening
robe, refusing food or company. Young James was sent by his older sister to
console their mother.

> [My sister] told me not to sulk when my mother lay thinking of him,
> but to try instead to get her to talk about him. . . . At first I was often
> jealous, stopping her fond memories with the cry, "Do you mind noth-
> ing about me?" but that did not last; its place was taken by an intense
> desire to become so like him that even my mother should not see the
> difference, and many and artful were the questions I put to that
> end. . . . He had a cheery way of whistling, she had told me; it always
> brightened her at her work to hear him whistling, and when he whis-
> tled he stood with his legs apart, and his hands in the pockets of his
> knickerbockers. I decided to trust to this, so one day . . . I secretly put
> on a suit of his clothes, and thus disguised, I slipped, unknown to oth-
> ers, into my mother's room. Quaking, yet so pleased, I stood still until
> she saw me, and then—how it must have hurt her! "Listen!" I cried in
> a glow of triumph, and I stretched my legs wide apart and plunged my
> hands into the pockets of my knickerbockers and began to whistle.

Here the child himself has taken on the task of replacing his dead sibling.
What evolved was an intensely close attachment, in which, for both mother
and son, the boundaries between the dead boy and the living one blurred.
Barrie attributed the growth of his imaginative capacity to this unusual relationship with his mother. For that, generations of fans of *Peter Pan* must
be grateful. But Barrie's personal life was plagued by significant difficulty in
forming any other close attachments, especially with women. The task of
standing in for his lost brother left him forever a Lost Boy.

PATRICIA NEAL

*The night before, Broadway and movie actress Patricia Neal had assured
her young daughter Tessa that despite the frightening sight of a wailing*

ambulance taking her sister away, Olivia would be all right. Now she must tell her otherwise.

from As I Am: An Autobiography

When Tessa woke up, I sat with her on the bed. How do you tell a five-year-old that her sister has died, when just hours before you assured her that she was only asleep and would be able to play in a few days? I pulled her up onto my lap. "My darling Tessa, our Olivia is dead." She looked up at me with disbelief. "God decided to take her to heaven to live with Him," I told her, holding her close. She didn't say a word for several moments. Then she gazed around the room.

"Does that mean everything in here is mine?" she asked. She squirmed off my lap and ran over to the toy chest and opened it. I was utterly horrified. I watched her pull out things that belonged to her sister. My mind told me that she really didn't understand. What else could a five-year-old do? But as I left the room, I was in such pain that I could not speak.

JOHN O'HARA

Death fascinates most children with its mystery. But answering their questions about death—especially young children's questions—is hard. Few of us are prepared with well-thought-out answers, so instead we give them clichés so unsatisfactory, so downright goofy sometimes, it's no wonder children keep pressing for more explanations, as in this O'Hara novel. "Things were different now, with no William, and there must be some things his mother and father wanted to tell him. It was not clear in his mind what kind of things, but they must want to talk to him," eleven-year-old Alfred muses after his older brother dies. Here Alfred is at the breakfast table with his mother, Martha, and his younger siblings.

from From the Terrace

"Won't Billy *ever* come back? *Ever?*" said Constance. . . .

"No, he's in heaven with the little Lord Jesus," said Martha.

"He doesn't know the little Lord Jesus," said Constance.

"But the little Lord Jesus knows him," said Martha. "They're very happy together."

"How do you know?" said Constance.

"Because everybody is happy with the little Lord Jesus."

"I'm not. I don't know Him. I never saw Him," said Constance.

"Well, you know what He looks like," said Sally. "You've seen pictures of Him."

"They're all different," said Constance.

"It's religion," said Alfred. "Don't you go to Sunday School?"

"Yes, but . . ." Constance paused to think.

"But what?" said Alfred.

"I don't understand it," said Constance.

"What don't you understand, dear?" said Martha.

"The whole thing."

"Well, there's a lot to learn and you can't learn it all at once. The little Lord Jesus sent for Billy, and so Billy went to heaven."

"But I don't think that was nice of the little Lord Jesus to make him so sick. Billy had to throw up—"

"Not at the table, " said Sally.

"And why did He send for Billy? Why didn't He send for Alfred?"

The boy looked at his mother.

"Because—" she began.

"He wanted Billy," said Alfred.

"No," said Martha. "Not because he *preferred* Billy, but perhaps because, you see we don't always understand what God does, and the little Lord Jesus—*I* know! At least I think He wanted Alfred to stay here and take care of all of us. And that's what Alfred will do, too, won't you, dear?"

"I guess so. I don't know," said the boy.

JACQUELYN MITCHARD

This excerpt from Mitchard's novel occurs on Christmas Eve when seven-year-old Vincent eavesdrops on his father's conversation with Vincent's aunt. The two adults are talking despairingly about Vincent's mother, Beth, who has gone to bed early as usual. Months after the kidnapping loss of Vincent's three-year-old brother Ben, Beth—once a dynamic photojournalist—has all but resigned from life.

from *The Deep End of the Ocean*

He heard his dad say to his aunt, ". . . the amount of stress. And she doesn't answer it because she thinks half the time it's going to be the police saying they've found another kid or some nut trying to tell her we killed him."

"But even given all that, Paddy, she needs professional help. She really needs professional help."

"Maybe," said his dad. "Yeah."

Then they started to talk about Monica being stuck up and all kinds of stuff Vincent didn't even care about.

But professional help. That, thought Vincent, was a great idea. He hoped his dad really meant it. If his mom had a professional helper, someone who did helping for a job, right in the house all the time, she would have to wash and change her clothes every day, because the helper would make her. She would have to change [his baby sister] Kerry more often, so that Kerry didn't soak through the front of her little sleepers every day before Jill [the baby-sitter] got home. Vincent couldn't change diapers, because Kerry was too wiggly; he'd tried, and she just rolled over and over until she was away from him. His mom had to do it. If the helper could get his mom moving, so she did more things without taking forever, she would have more time, because as far as Vincent could tell, she wasn't doing her picture work anymore at all. They could maybe take walks. Maybe make a mobile; she used to like to make mobiles out of wire hangers and cut-out stars. He might be too big for that now, but he didn't care. He'd do it if his mom wanted to. And after a while of doing normal things again, she would start to realize that even if Ben was gone right now, she still had even more kids than she'd lost. She had double the number of kids she'd lost.

And he was pretty sure he and Kerry together made up for one Ben. Maybe even one and a half.

URSULA HEGI

Children's lives are affected by the death of a brother or sister, even when it occurred before they were born or were old enough to remember the child. In the novel Floating in My Mother's Palm, *a twelve-year-old German girl mourns her younger brother whom she cannot remember. She only knows where he is buried and the circumstances of his death. She creates a posthumous relationship with her brother by stealing flowers for his grave and imagining a sleigh ride they might have shared.*

from Floating in My Mother's Palm

Once I was almost caught stealing flowers for my brother's grave. I'd done it before, making sure to check the paths of the Burgdorf cemetery before I took flowers from other graves, but I never took more than one. I'd gather them in my hands until Joachim got a bigger bouquet than anyone else, and I'd try to feel the sadness I read about in our housekeeper's romances.

In those books there was always the single tear that slid down the heroine's cheek without blemishing her complexion or dignity. I can still see myself at twelve, trying to squeeze out that one significant tear. But I simply wasn't skilled at producing tears; I cried too seldom. . . .

How I yearned for real tragedy. But the most tragic thing in my life—my brother's death—had happened when I was two, and I couldn't even remember his face, or touching him. He was just a sequence of letters on the family headstone below the names of my mother's parents; still, he was my only link to real tragedy, and I kept returning to the cemetery, trying to feel his loss.

I badgered my parents with questions about his death, and I took their words and filled in the spaces until I could evoke the afternoon he'd died and watch it on an inner screen like a film I could rewind or stop at will. Since we had no photos of Joachim, his features kept changing for me, but he always had reddish hair like my father.

My mother rocked my brother for three hours after he died. He was only nine days old. Sitting on a wooden chair inside the hospital room, she held him in her arms, rocking her upper body back and forth though her chair stayed motionless. . . .

At first my father tried to have her relinquish the dead infant to the nurse who spoke to my mother in soothing words. He felt powerless as she sat there, staring straight ahead, her body rigid, their child in her arms, rocking. Rocking. Finally, allowing his grief to match hers, my father knelt beside her, his arms around her and his son, his body a shadow of her rocking motion.

And so my mother sat there for hours, her arms around my brother, encircled by my father's arms. From time to time the doctor entered the room, and my father told him, "Not yet." By now he felt the soothing rocking himself, felt the thread of his grieving woven into that of my mother's.

The muted light of the winter afternoon gave way to dusk that stripped the white from the walls and made all sounds in the street seem to come from far away. My father laid one finger against the cheek of his child. Only a few hours earlier his son was still breathing, a sound as if he were blowing bubbles from a place deep within his narrow chest. His face was flushed, but slowly it turned ashen. Though his cheeks stayed red for a while, they soon faded until his skin became translucent and his lips took on a bluish tinge.

And his rattly breathing—it made the room seem small and opened up a wish in my father, the wish for it to end, the wish to spare Joachim the struggle as his lungs filled with fluid.

Gradually my mother's body lost some of the rigidity that first made her cling to the child while others tried to take him from her. My father knew she'd be able to let go—not yet, though—but with each moment it seemed more possible. He knew this child, knew the way his hands had formed fists, then released themselves into curled fingers as he nursed. He knew the way his son's eyes had resisted closing when he fell asleep as if he sensed how brief his life would be and felt reluctant to miss one single moment.

And what my father had to do now was know his son in this new, silent form. Remember his changed face, longer somehow and solemn, his still hands. Remember him like this to carry himself and my mother through mourning. . . .

I pushed the vase deeper into the earth [vase of flowers at the grave]. That's where Joachim was. What was left of him. We'd never unhinge garden doors together and hide them around the corner. We'd never swim in the Rhein together or ride our bikes or play ball or—I caught my arms against my stomach, tight. Rocked myself back and forth. All at once I saw Joachim and myself, sitting on my wooden sled on top of the dike, our faces red from the cold. *"Hold on!" I shout out to him as I push off. Joachim sits in front of me. My feet are on the metal runners, my arms around my brother's chest. I'm the one holding on; yet, I keep shouting, "Hold on, Joachim!"*

My breath is a white lace scarf that touches his neck and reddish hair. Joachim is almost as tall as I. Sitting straight, I hold on to him as our sled hurtles down a slope that doesn't end. But he is getting smaller in my arms. At first my hands barely meet in front of his jacket, but now I can cross my wrists, then my arms as if I were hugging myself. "Hold on, Joachim," I shout once more, frozen tears on my face. My arms around myself, I know for the first time what it feels like to have lost him, to be without him not only this moment but millions of moments like this, linked and stretching into all my tomorrows. I see myself grown up, my newborn son in my arms, pouring a trickle of holy water over his head, forming the sign of the cross on his forehead, chest, and shoulders, whispering fragile words of insurance against purgatory:"Im Namen des Vaters und des Sohnes und des Heiligen Geistes . . ."

But suddenly my brother is here again, solid in my arms, snow coating his shoulders and swirling around us as the sled races down the white bank. The

Rhein is frozen, and as we glide across it, huge turtles and tropical fish swim be-
low the clear ice. On the other side of the river two riders gallop along the bank
on blue horses.

STEPHEN DIXON

Margo, now a married adult, was sitting beside her six-year-old sister,
Julie, in the family car years earlier when a stranger in another car pulled
out a gun and killed her. As this excerpt from Dixon's novel illustrates, the
repercussions of such horror run deep.

from *Interstate*

I mean we slept in side-by-side beds once she was out of her crib and on va-
cations sometimes in the same bed for a week and had our birthday parties
together though our birthdates were a month apart—my God, we used to
play together eight hours a day straight some days, drawing and cutting out
fifty or so paper figures and acting them all out in different voices till we
were hoarse, starting from scratch whole puppet shows, meaning not only
making the papier-mâché characters but the scenery and stage and thinking
up the play—I wouldn't—what'd I say, five? maybe it wasn't even to you, but
she died at six—but I wouldn't—six years old, of course—I could barely
stand sleeping in our old bedroom but it was the only other one we had—in
fact I had to have not only her bed removed but mine too because they were
twins and a new one put in for me—my dad wasn't even aware of it he was
so into his own world looking for the this and that . . . but I wouldn't, what
I started out saying, even look at the framed photograph my mother had of
her by her bedside—Julie, at a beach in a bathing suit, bangs being blown
back above her head, whopping smile, fingers entwined beneath her chin,
her eyes, I forgot to mention, dark black to my green—"Turn it around
first," I used to say and frequently scream at my mother if she summoned
me into her room for something or sent me there to get her necklace from
the dresser, let's say, and years later, long after she'd remarried and had another child and I not only had a different house and time zone to live in but
another new bed and I was still doing this, she suddenly said, "What're you,
crazy?—it's just a picture, a beautiful picture, there for our pleasure, your
dearest sister, my darling treasure, get over it already, at least that aspect,"
and I swear slapped the photo smack into or maybe just up to my face—

must have been up to it or maybe even a foot or two away but facing me face to face, and I could look at it even less after that and maybe I couldn't even look at that one today.

DEBRA SPARK

"Cyndy is dead, of course. . . . She died of breast cancer at age twenty-six, a fact which I find unbelievable, a fact that is (virtually) statistically impossible." So begins Debra Spark's memoir, from which the following excerpt is taken, of the five-year decline and death of her youngest sister.

from "Last Things," in *Ploughshares*, fall 1994

One trip out to my parents that stands in my mind: Cyndy had the shingles, an enormously painful viral infection that runs along the nerve path on one side of the body. Just getting her down the staircase into my car was horrible. Cyndy was sobbing and sobbing, and ordinarily she didn't cry. I put her in the passenger's seat and cursed myself for having the kind of life that made me buy such an inexpensive and uncomfortable car. The requirement of bending was too much, and Cyndy wept and wept. I drove as fast as I could and neither of us talked. I thought, I'll just get her home and it will be all right. My father, the doctor, would know what to do. My mother would be, as she could be, the most comforting person in the world. When we got there, I said, "It's okay, it's going to be okay," as Cyndy walked, with tiny paces, from the car to the front steps. My parents were at the front door and it was night. My mother brought a kitchen chair to the front hall so as soon as Cyndy got up the stairs, she could sit down. I stood behind her, and my parents stood at the top of the six stairs that lead to our front door. My mother (blue turtleneck and jeans); my father (stooped). Both of them had their hands out and were reaching for Cyndy but they couldn't get her up the stairs. She had to do that herself. And I thought, looking at them in the light, and Cyndy still forcing herself up through the night— *Oh, my God. All this love, all this love can't do a thing.*

But that wasn't completely true. The love did do something. It just didn't save her.

SAPPHIRE

Sapphire is a novelist and poet who writes about social problems affecting the black community. One of these problems is the high rate of death among young African American males, which leaves many families bereft. In this poem, a younger sibling is speaking to a dead older brother.

from American Dreams

where jimi is

go now.
I used to follow you
you never could get rid of me.
now since you're dead
it's you
following me,
trying to escape that last exit—
the obsessive smelly
wet lips of death.
go now,
this is too long to wander.
1986 was your time.
go now.
it's not a devouring
void forever
black.
it's not gonna be like that, Michael
i promise.
death is where
jimi hendrix is,
where our revolution
ended up.
death—why mommy's there
and she has time
for you
now.

LAURA WEXLER

Writer and assistant editor for Georgia Magazine, *Laura Wexler was seventeen and leaving for college in a week when her sister Rachel, eighteen, was killed in a freak boating accident at a summer camp where they were both counselors. The following are excerpts taken from the senior thesis Laura wrote four years later.*

from "I'm Still Here"

At first, *I'm still here* was the mantra I chanted inside my head, chiding myself for sadness, urging myself that, unlike Rachel, I was still living and must not be sad, must not miss a moment of time or anything else precious. Months later, unable to contain my grief, I said *I'm still here* as if I were the only one of my tribe to escape slaughter and wandering plains alone. I wanted to die. Not because I hated life, but because I wanted to see Rachel.

Many times my parents, washed in grief, looked at me through saltwater, saying, *You're still here. You're all we have left.* Those words weighed heavily upon me, made me feel too loved, too lucky. And they made Rachel feel too gone. But, just as many times I've wanted to shake my parents out of depression and back into the life before Rachel's death, saying *I'm still here. Don't you leave me, too. . . .*

I felt strange rummaging through Rachel's stuff that first week, scavenging for pickings. I had picked through her clothes and jewelry when she was alive, but not openly, legally. It was always furtive, my heart racing, expecting to hear Rachel slam in the front door and bolt upstairs before I'd covered my tracks. Without the risk of Rachel coming home, saying, "No way in hell I'm letting *you* borrow *that,*" it seemed all screwed up, an unfair fight. I don't know, maybe that's something unique to sibling relationships. Always there's competition—for stuff from parents, for attention, for whatever—but there's also the sense that the competition is fairly even. I was a sister before I was a woman or an individual, and I shared my mother's milk and attention, the smeared chocolate icing on my birthday cake, a wobbly stroller before I knew I was doing it. At seventeen, to become an only child made me uncomfortable, as did the extra money my parents would later send to me at college. I never wanted to benefit. . . .

For almost a year after Rachel died, I didn't say her name out loud. The sound of the R and the A and the ending L felt foreign on my tongue. Later, when I joined a support group, the facilitator noted that I never said

Rachel's name. It just hurt too much. And if I'd had my choice, I would have asked my parents not to say Rachel's name either. Any instance we now used her name was unhappy. My mother, who had stood at the bottom of the stairs and yelled "Rachel—telephone!" now said her name as if she were standing in front of the pile of eyeglasses in a room at Auschwitz. It seemed to me that Rachel's name was too much hers to be spoken without her around.

Talking about families or home or anything in my past was terrifying for me. Sometimes, as I told a story or recounted a memory, I said "we" instead of "I." Pretty soon, though, I got the hang of checking over everything in my head before I opened my mouth. The thing is, though, if you tell a lie enough times, you start to forget the truth you're trying to cover up in the first place. I started to feel my memory blurring and that frightened me. Memory was my only link to Rachel.

And though my friends confided in me, I couldn't (and still really can't) reciprocate. One night I was driving around in Baltimore with my friend. He talked for a half-hour about his parents' divorce and how he felt deserted now that his sister was moving away and I listened but I felt so embarrassed that I couldn't talk about my family. When I looked through the comments various therapists made throughout the two years after Rachel died, the same issue of telling people about Rachel's death recurs.

I ask myself why I have such trouble talking about Rachel's death or even her life, and come up with a couple of things. I really believe no one understands my particular pain, the things that I've lost, tangible and intangible, since Rachel's death. As Holden [*Catcher in the Rye*] said, *You didn't know Allie.* That's not anybody's fault. The only person who knows exactly how I feel is dead. And yes, I desperately want people to understand my loss. I feel like no one will ever really know me unless they do. But I just don't see it happening. . . .

It's hard to worry about your own grief when your parents are not parental anymore. My mother, who probably told me when to take my first breath and how long it would last, abruptly withdrew from being an overbearing presence in my life. She never left me completely, but there were enough times when she'd look down at her feet and say quietly—not in the abrasive voice I'd grown up hearing—"Laura I just can't take this right now. I'm lucky if I can get up in the morning." Just as I wanted my old self, my old world back, I wanted a mother I could fight with.

"I think I felt more grief at losing my mother than losing my brother," my friend Michael said. "Her hair went from jet black to gray in one month. It's been twelve years since my brother died and my mother is just coming back."

My father stands in the driveway of my old house yelling for me to come in, it's time for bed. My father paces the sidelines in a dank gym on a Saturday afternoon, yelling "Don't hog the ball, Laura!" My father spreads the *Wall Street Journal* over the kitchen table, scolding Rachel and me for dropping cereal on the front page. My father comes to bail me out when I'd parked the flesh-colored '79 LeMans in the fire lane at the library and couldn't start it. My father sits at the head of that kitchen table, head bent to his chest, and pulls his glasses off to sob freely. . . .

This idea that you should be able to protect and comfort and be there for your parents even more than for yourself is particular to people on the brink of adulthood. Like me. In other words, if I were twelve or thirteen, few people would expect me to assume a parental role. But as I was almost eighteen, it was apparently okay for people to continually ask, "How are your parents doing? Are you helping them as much as you can?" I felt guilty enough about being alive. And then to have people insinuate that my main function in life thereafter was to be a comfort for my parents made me feel worse. Because I honestly didn't see that my parents were remarkably comforted by me. They were sad when I was there and when I wasn't. I couldn't do a thing about it. . . .

. . . I guess I fear my friends will die, and this fear, at times, makes me feel old, neurotic, un-carefree. I also fear that, having experienced a tragedy at a relatively young age, I am somehow marked for misery throughout life. I fear that I will have the look of the woman squatting in a bombed-out basement, waiting for the next wave of destruction that, this time, is sure to destroy her. . . .

I think of Rachel on Indian Summer days, in winter rain, at dusk, and in the morning when I run my feet over the sheets making imaginary snow angels. Some days I do not think of Rachel at all—times when I am so immersed in the present that I do not stop to think *how would it have been different? Who would we have been had she not died?* My friend Hilary, whose brother was sixteen when he was killed in a car accident, said, "I have a hard time remembering what I was like before . . . who was I?" I can't answer that question.

MAXINE KUMIN

Maxine Kumin's poem about her older brother gives a sense of what it is like to watch a sibling die from a progressive, debilitating disease.

from *Our Ground Time Here Will Be Brief*

Man of Many L's

My whole childhood I feared cripples
and how they got that way: the one-
legged Lavender Man who sold
his sachets by St. Mary's steeple,
the blind who tapped past humming what they knew,
even the hunchback seamstress, a ragdoll
who further sagged to pin my mother's hems,
had once been sturdy, had once been whole.
Something entered people, something chopped,
pressed, punctured, had its way with them
and if you looked, bad child, it entered you.

When we found out what the disease would do,
lying, like any council's stalwarts,
all of us swore to play our parts
in the final act at your command.

The first was easy. You gave up your left hand
and the right grew wiser, a juggler for its king.
When the poor dumb leg began to falter
you took up an alpenstick for walking
once flourished Sundays by our dead father.
Month by month the battleground grew thinner.
When you could no longer swallow meat
we steamed and mashed your dinner
and bent your straw to chocolate soda treats.

And when you could not talk, still you could write
questions and answers on a magic slate,
then lift the page, like laundry to the wind.
I plucked the memory splinter from your spine
as we played at being normal, who

had eased each other in the cold zoo
of childhood. Three months before
you died I wheeled you through the streets
of placid Palo Alto to catch
spring in its flamboyant tracks.
You wrote the name of every idiot flower
I did not know. Yucca rained.
Mimosa shone. The bottlebrush took fire
as you fought to hold your great head on its stem.
Lillac, you wrote, *Magnollia. Lilly.*
And further, *olleander. Dellphinium.*

O man of many L's, brother, my wily
resident ghost, may I never spell
these crowfoot dogbane words again
those showy florid words again
except I name them under your spell.

SIEGFRIED SASSOON

*Although English poet Siegfried Sassoon was honored for his bravery in
World War I, he was so appalled by the suffering he saw that he risked his
reputation to publicly protest its continuation. His war poems, for which
he is best known, are read to this day. Sassoon lost his younger brother in
the Battle of Gallipoli in 1915, and he was still serving in the military
when he wrote the following entry in his diary.*

from *Siegfried Sassoon Diaries, 1915–1918*, edited by Rupert Hart-Davis

The rain has ceased. Broken clouds drift slowly from the west, glorious with
fringes of evening colour. On a hillside I am alone with my happiness, hearing everywhere the faint drip and rustle of summer green: there is a stirring
in the grass; each flower has a message to give me. All sounds are small and
distinct, as though they expressed the liquid clarity of the air. The country
is now properly arrayed in a sort of rich calm, shining and yet subdued and
gracious.

The roofs and stacks of the farm among its trees below the hill, the farm-
house chimney with its wisp of smoke, a bird winging out across the valley-
orchards, and the sound of a train going steadily on, miles away—all are as

I would have them, as I would keep them remembered. I am back in child-hood; home with my kind dreams; soon I shall hear my brother's voice along the garden, where moths will be fluttering like flowers that are free from their hot parades in sunshine, free to go where they will among the dimness of quiet alleys. O brother, tell me what you have seen to-day, what have you done?

He will not answer, for he is dead. And I am far from the garden, far from the summer that is past. I am alone in this bitter winter of unend-ing war.

DAVID MASON

In his poem about mourning a brother, Mason touches on the ambiva-lence some of us feel about returning to the spot where we left precious ashes.

from *The Country I Remember: Poems*

A Motion We Cannot See

We found the path somewhat as it had been:
heather and rock of an alpine meadow
ringed by peaks like giants in a myth
we never learned; all our lives
we had played among them, and perhaps
our grief was payment of an unknown debt.

Perhaps the strange mist
caused us to question the path,
but our boots made a familiar sound
on the dirt runnel; the gray rocks
and stunted firs were congregated
as before.

We couldn't say why we had come,
two living brothers and our father
whose hands were like ours
and like our brother's hands,
bones and hair so much like ours,
flesh of our silent flesh.

I saw the place where we had cupped
the ashes, letting them blow
and drift over the heather.
A year of snow and snowmelt later
what could be left of him,
so utterly possessed by mountains?

Yet after the year of weather
tiny pieces of my brother's bone
still lay in clefts of rock.
We found them under our hands,
cupping them once again in wonder
at what the giants left us.

Since then I have not gone back
to hold my brother's bones. The prayers
of blizzard and snowmelt have him now,
and time flows down the mountain like the ice,
a motion we cannot see,
though it bears our blood almost forever.

BARBARA KINGSOLVER

*Codi is still digesting the fact that her younger sister Hallie, in Nicaragua
to teach farmers about crop disease control, has been murdered. Single,
Codi decides she can now no longer live in the town where she and Hallie
grew up. She's lined up a job in another city, and she's set to leave the next
day. Here Codi says good-bye to her Native American boyfriend, Loyd,
who himself lost a brother years before. (Hallie's life and death are loosely
modeled, as Kingsolver's dedication of her novel indicates, on that of Ben
Linder, a twenty-seven-year-old American who likewise died in
Nicaragua. Working without pay to improve the living conditions of the
poor, Linder was murdered in 1987 by United States–sponsored contra
rebels who fired a bullet through his head at point-blank range.)*

from *Animal Dreams*

"Where do you think people go when they die?" Loyd asked, the day before
I left. He was on his way out to take a westbound into Tucson; the next day
he would fetch home the Amtrak. We stood in my front door, unwilling to

go in or out, like awkward beginners trying to end a date. Except it wasn't a beginners' conversation.

"Nowhere," I said. "I think when people die they're just dead."

"Not heaven?"

I looked up at the sky. It looked quite empty. "No."

"The Pueblo story is that everybody started out underground. People and animals, everything. And then the badger dug a hole and let everybody out. They climbed out the hole and from then on they lived on top of the ground. When they die they go back under."

I thought of the kivas, the ladders, and the thousand mud walls of Santa Rosalia. I could hear the dry rattle of the corn dancers' shell bells: the exact sound of locusts rising up from the grass. I understood that Loyd was one of the most blessed people I knew.

"I always try to think of it that way," he said, after a minute. "He had a big adventure up here, and then went home." . . .

"I'm sorry about everything, Loyd."

"Listen, I know how this is. You don't think you'll live past it. And you don't, really. The person you were is gone. But the half of you that's still alive wakes up one day and takes over again."

"Why should I look forward to that?"

He turned my hand over. "I can't answer that."

RICHARD HOFFMAN

The ramifications of sibling loss extend to the next generation. Hoffman, who lost two of three brothers to muscular dystrophy, gained deeper insight into his parents' grief when he had a child of his own.

from *Half the House: A Memoir*

Between 1970 and 1972, my mother lost her mother and two of her sons: first Mike, then Mammy Etta, then Bob. Careful to hide her bitterness, she went deep inside herself and stayed there, at the same time constructing some other person to present to us, someone who was cheerfully busy, brimming with jokes, gossip, idle chatter. It was as if she herself were absent, but had created some rough replica through which she attempted to go on with her life. I pretended not to see this, played along with it; I believe we all did. She'd tell the same jokes over and over, sometimes within the same conversation. She'd talk about the rising price of peas or lettuce, and if the conversation lagged, she'd repeat herself, sometimes in exactly the same words. . . .

One morning, when Robert [Hoffman's son] was small enough to hold in the crook of my arm, my lips against his silky head, I dozed and dreamed that he and I were at an outdoor celebration. There was a big yellow-and-white-striped tent like the one Kathi and I had at our wedding. I was holding Robert proudly. People bent to him and touched and patted me, nodding and smiling. We were seated at a very long table, across from a radiant old man. I asked him why we were celebrating, and he said there was no occasion, that he and all the others were always there; didn't I know that? I suddenly felt that I did. I propped Robert in his little plastic seat on the table. "We're always here; we're family," the old man said, touching Robert and smiling at me.

The food was delicious. The baked beans were my mother's. She used to make them for picnics when I was a boy. I wanted more. The food was under the yellow-and-white-striped tent. I heaped the plate high and ate some right away, on my way back to the table.

They were gone, all of them. Robert's yellow seat was on the table, empty. Oh no. Oh no no no no no. Again I felt that I knew what had happened. I saw the old man, in the distance, walking away. "Wait!" I called, and ran to catch up to him.

He turned and said, coldly, what I fully expected to hear. "You didn't take care of him, so he's been taken from you." I tried to grab the old man, but I fell, helpless, and lay on the ground.

I woke, and Robert stirred in the hollow underneath my chin but remained asleep, his tiny mouth making sucking movements. He had given me the dream as a gift: without the small warmth of him to wake to, reassured, I would never have let myself have that dream. I would never have been able to feel, if only briefly, the horror and despair and shame of losing him. For the first time, I touched, for merely a dreaming moment, the kind of pain my parents must have felt, grieving for my brothers. . . .

We always stand beside the graves, or at the foot, and we walk around them as if the mounded earth had never settled or the torn sod healed. So I stood at the foot of the graves, and my father stood beside them with his head bowed. He appeared to be praying.

I was trying to feel my mother's presence. I figured that here at her grave I should be able to talk to her. From time to time since her death I had spoken to her, bringing her up to date about my life. It was more rhetoric than necromancy, like writing a letter to someone who you know will never read it. On occasion I had found myself talking to my brothers in the same way. I always spoke to Mike as if he were thirteen, his age when he died. When I spoke to Bob, he was in his late teens, the age I left him for New York, for college, and I always spoke of the places I'd been and things I'd seen just as I had during those years when, visiting home, I tried to bring back some of the world for him. Now I couldn't address them, and I felt empty.

"Room for one more here," my father said.

I didn't know what to say. I wasn't sure what he meant. There is a space on the headstone for a fourth name, I thought; that must be it.

"That's my spot, right there," he said. "That's where you're to plant me, you hear? Right there. It's already paid for. I'll show you when we get home. The papers are in a special place, in a steel box, with the insurance stuff and my will and other things you'll need to take care of. I'll show you where it is when we get home. It's important you remember where it is. It's all taken care of ahead of time, so you shouldn't have any trouble when the time comes."

I felt annoyed. I had thought we'd come here to grieve together, and here he was, juggling self-pity with fatherly instructions. I knew the gray steel box he meant.

But I had also heard the sardonic note of the verb "plant," and, looking at his face, I suddenly heard, loud and clear, his desperate wish to be the next to die. It frightened me.

"What do you mean, 'when the time comes'?"

"Just what I said. Oh. No, no, no, relax. I'm feeling good. Oh, hell, I plan to be around another twenty-five or thirty years. No. Don't you worry. You and your brother will be cursing the old bastard for being such a stubborn son of a bitch." He took out a handkerchief, blew his nose, and smiled.

And I heard what he said, all of it, as if it were a prayer: that he should be buried here, that he should not die soon, and that Joe and I should survive him—that above all: that he should not have to bury another of his children.

7

Especially Bad Days

I avoided thinking much about the second Thanksgiving after Allie's death until five-thirty or so on Thanksgiving Eve, when I had to do some shopping. The radio reported news for travelers about highways, trains, and planes. Local streets were congested, parking lots full, and shoppers looked hassled as they picked up last-minute items. In spite of the inconvenience, there was a hum of excitement. People were looking forward to travelers arriving safely and to gathering together with their loved ones to feast during Thanksgiving Day. Complaints about traffic and too much work were just part of the ritual.

In the liquor store, I stood behind a handsome, blond man in his forties buying champagne. He looked successful and content as he joked with the clerk behind the register. I imagined a big house, pretty wife, healthy children, and loving grandparents sitting at the table where this champagne would be served the next day.

Coming out to the dark parking lot, I finally confronted the hard, cold fact that there is no excitement or joy in our house: instead, there is grief and despair. Allie should be coming home for his first college vacation. He should be one of the millions crowding the roads, train stations, and airports. We should be anticipating welcoming him with hugs and kisses, our hearts swelling with love. But Allie is dead, not away at school as I sometimes pretend. He won't be coming home this Thanksgiving or ever. Our Thanksgiving is a day to get through, not celebrate.

Our friends Nancy and Dave have invited us to Monkton for the Blessing of the Hounds at an Episcopalian church on Thanksgiving morning. It's a way for us to get away from the house and our own sad company. Also, there are Bloody Marys served tailgate-style, so we can drink early and numb our pain.

Both of Dave's sons from his first marriage are home for Thanksgiving. Andy, now twenty-three, flew in from San Francisco with his girlfriend

Melissa. They look good. Jeff, eighteen, was born three months before Allie. They were best friends until they were about eleven. Jeff sports a Hare Krishna hairdo, earrings, a nose ring, and tattoos. Rachel, Nancy's twenty-eight-year-old daughter, is there too, bubbling with stories about her two little daughters.

Even in fog and drizzle, the Blessing of the Hounds is quaint and picturesque. The hunters, who range in age from little girls to elderly men and women, wear dark, fitted riding jackets and black velvet helmets. The hunt officials have on traditional red jackets and black hats. The horses, with their curried coats and glossy tails, are beautifully groomed. The spectators are, for the most part, ordinary suburban families. But there is also a smattering of country gentry with smart felt hats and Abercrombie and Fitch clothing. Jeff looks funny in this crowd. The priest and his acolytes, dressed in red and white vestments, come out of the church to give the blessing on a hill overlooking the riders and beagle hounds. With two Bloody Marys under my belt, I am able to appreciate the beauty of the scene and the conviviality of the crowd. I could be in nineteenth-century England.

Afterwards we all go back to the house. We hang out in the country kitchen. Nancy is making piecrusts for dinner. Dave takes Peter for a walk around the pond and confides his worries about Jeff. Rachel talks to Jim, another guest. My daughter, Hilary, chatters with Andy and Melissa while they make soup. She and Allie grew up with these kids, they were like cousins. They haven't seen each other in a couple of years, and I enjoy listening to them reconnect. No one mentions Allie, though I'm sure everyone thinks about him. I drink another Bloody Mary and for a while I have a feeling of well-being, as if I really belong here. But it's an illusion. This is a borrowed family. It isn't mine.

The scenario is exactly what I had envisioned for us. After all, isn't it what having a family is all about? You put in about twenty years of hard work, giving the best of your energy, time, money, and love, and then the kids are raised. You can relax and enjoy the fruits of your labor. I anticipated that holidays would give me my greatest pleasure. My children would come home to a warm house filled with good food and love. They would bring lovers, spouses, and eventually grandchildren, whom we would welcome.

We were almost there. We were in the homestretch. Then Allie crashed into that tree on Old Court Road, and this dream crashed too. I won't ever gather my whole family into my home on a holiday. Somewhere out there are lovers and a spouse who will never cross my threshold.

I am fond of Nancy and Dave. They are good-natured and generous with their friends. Knowing that today would be hard for us, they reached out and invited us to share their family with them. So I stand in their kitchen this Thanksgiving. Their house is warm and festive; their children are home. And my son is in his grave; my house is filled with gloom.

I am thankful for Hilary and Peter. I am grateful to Dave and Nancy for their hospitality. We are fortunate to have them and other thoughtful friends. But I miss Allie, and I'm jealous. I was cheated. I did my job as well as I could, and I deserve a Thanksgiving I can truly *celebrate*. Standing in someone else's kitchen with borrowed family falls so far short of my dreams.

MARY

NICHOLAS WOLTERSTORFF

"Still five children, but one always gone," Wolterstorff writes in his memoir (see pp. 56 and 107). "When we're all together, we're not all together." And holidays especially drive that home.

from Lament for a Son

The worst days now are holidays: Thanksgiving, Christmas, Easter, Pentecost, birthdays, weddings, January 31—days meant as festivals of happiness and joy now are days of tears. The gap is too great between day and heart. Days of routine I can manage; no songs are expected. But how am I to sing in this desolate land, when there's always one too few?

Innocent questions make me wince.

"Will the family all be home for Christmas?" What am I to say? "Yes," I say, "we'll all be home."

"What are your children doing now?" I go down the list: Amy, Robert, Klaas, Christopher. But I omit one. Do I call attention to the omission or do I let it pass?

"How many children do you have?" What do I say, "four" or "five"? "Five" I usually say. Sometimes I explain, sometimes I do not.

GWENDOLYN PARKER

In this novel, Aileen is in early grieving for her only child, Mattie, who died in their backyard from a fall from her slide (see p. 107). It isn't a special day, a birthday or death anniversary, but still, Aileen instinctively feels it's going to be a bad one.

from *These Same Long Bones*

So far, it had not been a good day. Good days did not start out this way. On a good day her mind was filled to the edges so that there was no room for Mattie to sneak in. On a good day, she was fast and alert and could veer away from the things that would hurt. On a good day, she could get from the back stairs to the stove in the kitchen without looking out into the backyard. On a good day, she didn't hear muffled giggles coming from under the stairs. On a good day, she didn't smell the lilacs or the honeysuckle or the roses, or any of Mattie's favorite flowers. But today was not a good day, and she'd been caught before she'd even made it out of her room.

Today, it happened when she put on her slip. She had her arms up over her head, and as the material slipped down over her body, just the feel of it passing over her head and her shoulders and her hips made her remember that night, right after Sirus's dinner, when everything had still been wonderful. She and Mattie had both been here in the kitchen in their slips. It was a hot night and they were excited, and neither of them had wanted to go upstairs. So she told Mattie that they could do something she and her sisters used to sneak and do. They took off their fancy dresses, laid them carefully over a chair, and had ice cream out on the back porch, just in their slips. She knew it felt to Mattie the way it had to her when she was that age, daring and free, to be outside, and a little undressed, with the cool night air resting on her skin. She remembered too the glow they both had, that shiny white of their slips, reflecting all the moonlight, and also how skinny Mattie was in her slip, no difference between her body and that of a young boy, except how delicately thin she was, with maybe a promise of something to come. But this morning, as she'd put on her slip, Aileen was forced to remember how nothing else would be coming . She felt her own body under her hands and she smoothed her slip, and her body felt like a curse. Feel how full my body is, she cried to herself; look at these hips and these breasts, Mattie will never run her hands along her own body like this; nor would she know the rest of it—the boys who would admire it, the pleasure it could give her, the husband, the children, damn it, just the weight of being a woman; how that felt, standing, walking, lying down in bed at night.

Aileen stirred sugar into her coffee. That was how things went on a bad day. Reminders were everywhere. Sometimes, when they got too bad, she drove over to the white part of town, to one particular schoolyard where she knew the schedule, and she'd wait for recess. A door would open and forty or fifty children would tumble out. The playground would go, in an instant, from empty to full, and the children were all pink and happy. She could hardly stand to see a colored child of Mattie's age, but she could watch these pink and white children.

STAN RICE

"Dont look backwards the blackness will blind you . . ." Some days you just will yourself through (see pp. 5 and 118).

from *Singing Yet: New and Selected Poems*

First Xmas after Daughterdeath, 1972

Christmas Day . . .
The Morning Star closes its lips in the gum trees . . .
My niece turns the handle of the pencil sharpener . . .
Her cinnamon-roll shines in the sun . . .
Where the gnats fly.

Now theyre gone to her Grandmother's . . .
The candles stick up their wicks . . .
The coffee can full of pot; ah! he left it . . .
The rubber head of the rooster-puppet continuously crowing . . .
Yet things are not ok.

In a deep lake gloom not of my making . . .
Pressure in the head . . .
Playing with my niece, beside whom milk would look yellow . . .
Growing my beard so that my face will look fatter . . .
Where death holds me by the ankles.

Dont look backwards the blackness will blind you . . .
Christmas . . .
The unbought trees lying on their sides by the Bank . . .
Anne wakes up walks in opens a beer stares at the window . . .
We dont speak.

JOHN EDGAR WIDEMAN

The grieving mother in this short story (see p. 94) can neither celebrate nor ignore her daughter's birthday.

(see p. 94)

from "Welcome," in *The Stories of John Edgar Wideman*

She would be twelve now. A dozen candles on the cake to count. 1—2—3—4—5 . . . and her chipmunk cheeks bell to puff them all out in a single breath. No one had said one word last birthday. She'd waited for her mother to call and when she finally did neither of them mentioned the day, the day Njeri had come here or the day one year plus eleven days more when she'd left. She tried to remember what they did say. What else could they have talked about? Her mother knew the birth day, the death day. How in this season those days would drop like something heavy shot from the sky. A soundless explosion, the sky screams, the earth buckles as something that had been flying lands with all the weight of things broken that will not rise again. Perhaps they'd talked about the grandkids, what each one wanted, what they were going to get and not get. Lines in the stores. Layaways. Snapshots with tacky Santas the wrong color. Dolls that pee. Machines that talk and count and shoot and how many batteries needed to make them run. How much it cost and how in God's name was anybody ever going to pay for it all in January when the bills came due. What else could they have talked about? And had her mother sighed after she hung up the phone, happy or not happy she'd avoided mentioning Njeri? Had her mother been trying to take all the weight upon herself the way she decided sometimes to spare her children and be the strong one, the one who could bear the suffering meant for all of them, willing herself to stand alone in the rain, as if she could will the rain to fall on her and no one else? How much had her mother wanted to say Njeri's name? How many times did her mother need to say it to herself as she gripped the phone and said other words into it? She had not said Njeri either.

RICHARD FORD

In Ford's novel, Frank Bascombe and X, his ex-wife, meet at the cemetery on their son Ralph's birthday. Like many couples who divorce after they lose a child, Frank and X had a troubled marriage before their son died. But they put aside their continued grievances on days like this—because who more than the other parent feels the same pain?

from *The Sportswriter*

I have climbed over the metal fence to the cemetery directly behind my house. It is five o'clock on Good Friday morning, April 20. All other houses in the neighborhood are shadowed, and I am waiting for my ex-wife. Today is my son Ralph's birthday. He would be thirteen and starting manhood. We have met here these last two years, early, before the day is started, to pay our respects to him. Before that we would simply come over together as man and wife. . . .

These pre-dawn meetings were my idea, and in the abstract they seem like a good way for two people like us to share a remaining intimacy. In practice they are as uncomfortable as a hanging, and it's conceivable we will just forgo it next year, though we felt the same way last year. It is simply that I don't know how to mourn and neither does X. Neither of us has the vocabulary or temperament for it, and so we are more prone to pass the time chatting, which isn't always wise. . . .

"Do you think you laugh enough these days?" She finishes peeling her egg and puts the sack down deep in her coat pocket. She knows about Vicki, and I've had one or two other girlfriends since our divorce that I'm sure the children have told her about. But I do not think she thinks they have turned my basic situation around much. And maybe she's right. In any case I am happy to have this apparently intimate, truth-telling conversation, something I do not have very often, and that a marriage can really be good for.

"You bet I do," I say. "I think I'm doing all right, if that's what you mean."

"I suppose it is," X says, looking at her boiled egg as if it posed a small but intriguing problem. "I'm not really worried about you." She raises her eyes at me in an appraising way. It's possible my talk with [their son] Paul last night has made her think I've gone off my bearings or started drinking.

"I watch Johnny. He's good for a laugh," I say. "I think he gets funnier as I get older. But thanks for asking." All this makes me feel stupid. I smile at her.

X takes a tiny mouse bite out of her white egg. "I apologize for prying into your life."

"It's fine."

X breathes out audibly and speaks softly. "I woke up this morning in the dark, and I suddenly got this idea in my head about Ralph laughing. It made me cry, in fact. But I thought to myself that you have to strive to live your life to the ultimate. Ralph lived his whole life in nine years, and I remember him laughing. I just wanted to be sure you did. You have a lot longer to live."

"My birthday's in two weeks."

"Do you think you'll get married again?" X says with extreme formality, looking up at me.

They talk in and around this, Frank eventually asking her the same question. X ends up crying.

She has almost stopped crying, though I have not tried to comfort her (a privilege I no longer hold). She raises her eyes up to the milky sky and sniffs again. She is still holding the nibbled egg. "When I cried in the dark, I thought about what a big nice boy Ralph Bascombe should be right now, and that I was thirty-seven no matter what. I wondered about what we should all be doing." She shakes her head and squeezes her arms tight against her stomach in a way I have not seen her do in a long time. "It's not your fault, Frank. I just thought it would be all right if you saw me cry. That's my idea of grief. Isn't that womanish?"

She is waiting for me to say a word now, to liberate us from that old misery of memory and life. It's pretty obvious she feels something is odd today, some freshening in the air to augur a permanent change in things. And I am her boy, happy to do that very thing—let my optimism win back a day or at least the morning or a moment when it all seems lost to grief. My one redeeming strength of character may be that I am good when the chips are down. With success I am worse. . . .

"Well, that's okay," I say and go down into my pants pockets for the poem I have Xeroxed at the office and brought along in case X forgot. Last year I brought Housman's "To An Athlete Dying Young" and made the mistake of not reading it over beforehand. I had not read it since I was in college, but the title made me remember it as something that would be good to read. Which it wasn't. If anything, it was much too literal and dreamily so about real athletes, a subject I have strong feelings about. Ralph in fact had not been much of an athlete. I barely got past "townsman of a stiller town," before I had to stop and just sit staring at the little headstone of red marble, incised with the little words RALPH BASCOMBE.

"Housman hated women, you know," X had said into the awful silence while I sat. "That's nothing against you. I just remembered it from some class. I think he was an old pederast who would've loved Ralph and hated us. Next year I'll bring a poem if that's okay."

"Fine," I had answered miserably. . . .

"Did you bring another Housman poem?" she says now and smirks at me, then turns and throws her nibbled egg as far as she can off into the gravestones and elms of the old part, where it hits soundlessly. She throws as a catcher would, snapping it by her ear in a gainly way, on a tape-line into the shadows. I admire her positive form. To mourn the loss of one child when you have two others is a hard business. And we are not very practiced, though we treat it as a matter of personal dignity and affection so that Ralph's death and our loss will not get entrapped by time and events and ruin our lives in a secret way. In a sense, we can do no wrong here. . . .

"No Housman today," I say.

"Well," X says and smiles, and seats herself on [a nearby] stone to listen. "If you say so." Lights are numerous and growing dim with the daylight along the backs of houses on my street. I feel warmer.

It is a "Meditation" by Theodore Roethke, who also attended the University of Michigan, something X will be wise to, and I start it in my best, most plausible voice, as if my dead son could hear it down below:

"I have gone into the waste lonely places behind the eye. . . ."

X has already begun to shake her head before I am to the second line, and I stop and look to her to see where the trouble is.

She puches out her lower lip and sits her stone. "I don't like that poem," she says matter-of-factly.

I knew she would know it and have a strong opinion about it. She is still an opinionated Michigan girl, who thinks about things with certainty and is disappointed when the rest of the world doesn't. Such a big strapping things-in-order girl should be in every man's life. They alone are reason enough for the midwest's existence, since that's where most of them thrive. I feel tension rising off me like a fever now. It is possible that reading a poem over a little boy who never cared about poems is not a good idea.

"I thought you'd know it," I say in a congenial voice.

"I shouldn't really say I don't like it," X says coldly. "I just don't believe it, is all."

It is a poem about letting the everyday make you happy—insects, shadows, the color of a woman's hair—something else I have some strong beliefs about. "When I read it, I always think it's me talking," I say.

"I don't think those things in that poem would make anybody happy. They might not make you miserable. But that's all," X says and slips down off the stone. She smiles at me in a manner I do not like, tight-lipped and disparaging, as if she believes I'm wrong about everything and finds it amusing. "Sometimes I don't think anyone can be happy anymore.". . .

"I think we're all released to the rest of our lives, is my way of looking at it," I say hopefully. "Isn't that true?"

She stares at our son's grave as if he were listening and would be embarrassed to hear us. "I guess."

8

Complicated Loss

CONGENITAL ILLNESS

JOHN CONRAD SR.

John Conrad Jr. was born with tuberous sclerosis, a progressive genetic disease. He spent much of his life in institutions. His father describes visiting John on the first of five "horrible" Christmas Eves in padded cells: "John was the only child in the entire children's hospital. I found him locked in a padded cell, in a straitjacket, asleep and exhausted from his self-injurious behavior. When I took John in my arms and woke him up, he looked up at me with his hands tied to his back and said, 'Daddy, I want to be good. I just want to be good.' It was John's ability to bounce back from his hopeless life with this undying spirit of hopefulness that inspired my wife, Kathy, and me." When John died in 1993 at age fourteen, his father delivered this eulogy.

from The Book of Eulogies: A Collection of Memorial Tributes, Poetry, Essays, and Letters of Condolence, edited by Phyllis Theroux

John Conrad Jr. (1979–1993)

How do you celebrate a life like John's? How do you celebrate a tragic life and death? How do you find any redeeming value to the life of a retarded boy who suffered from severe and bizarre emotional problems? How do you celebrate a life of dead expectations?

When John was born, we were ecstatic to have two bouncing twin babies. We had all the arrogant expectations of the best and the brightest. Then we learned that John was a victim of tuberous sclerosis. Tuberous sclerosis is a genetic disease which affects one in ten to fifteen thousand people. Eighty-five percent of the cases are new mutations, like John. TS causes a dysfunction in the cells that exist in virtually every tissue of your body: your skin, brain, heart, lungs, kidneys, and eyes. These cells become sclerotic, or hard, and cease to operate normally. John had these tumors throughout his brain, skin, and in his heart.

At first Kathy and I hoped that John would have a mild case. We hoped at one point that John could go to St. Christopher's. We hoped that he would run and play. We hoped that he could continue to live at home with us. But over the years, gradually it became apparent that he had a full-blown case. His was one of the worst-case scenarios. As John grew, so did the tumors and dysfunctions. He got progressively worse.

No one writes a book that describes or defines the parameters of normality in terms of psychiatric behavior, but after five years of sleepless nights, and three more years of bizarre, violent behavior, we learned that we simply could not handle John at home. And so our deepest expectation, that John could live at home, was dead. We committed John, through the legal system, at age eight, to a life of five years of institutionalization, first at a state psychiatric hospital, then at a residential school, and finally at a private hospital in Florida. Taking your eight-year-old child to the locked ward of a psychiatric facility, notwithstanding his sobbing pleas to the contrary, is like death, too.

So how do you celebrate a life like John's? They say that expectations die hard. John's life was full of expectations which died hard, but John taught us many lessons. They have certainly been expensive lessons, and we would never have voluntarily paid this dear price, but the value of these lessons and John's life, to us, is very profound.

We learned to live life after death; after the death of our expectations. We learned to love our child, the child we sometimes had thought would be better off dead. We learned to love our child although he was perceived to be of no value. We found that John had great value. We learned to accept him on his terms. We learned not to discount his life because he was handicapped. We learned to respect John's right to live.

John loved his life after he returned to a group home here in Richmond in May 1992. He loved his freedom. He loved the freedom of living in an unlocked building. He loved to go out in public: to the malls, the movies, the Braves games and the batting cage. He loved to go up to strangers and introduce himself. He loved to come home every Sunday for dinner at five o'clock. When I brought him home, he loved to burst through the door and call his mother's, sister's, and brother's names. He loved eating dinner with us and having his father give him a shave afterwards. And for the first time in five years, we saw John smile and laugh and sing again.

And so despite the Christmases which John spent in padded cells, injuring himself, and our thoughts that he would be better off dead, we learned to respect his right to live and gave him all the love and support humanly possible. We learned to respect the differences in people. We learned to respect people of lower functioning. We learned there is life after the death of a "normal" life. We learned that once a tragedy occurs, it redefines your life and that your life before that tragedy is no longer possible. We learned we had to build a new life with different expectations. We learned to develop positive responses to overcome tragedy. We learned to build a new life based on love, faith, and hope. We learned to live life a week at a time. We learned to find redeeming value in life. We learned to appreciate the daily beauty and joys of life. And we do. We learned to be as healthy and happy as possible and to have fun and limit our grief. And so, in the end, we got nothing we wanted in our child John and everything we could have ever needed. John gave us love that gives life a new meaning, that gives us an agenda, that gives us courage and strength and never leaves us alone.

John had his good days and his bad days. When his behavior was bad, he was very violent and abusive to his staff. When he had good days and his behavior was good, he always said he was having a "thumbs-up" day. On the last day of his life, as he sat in his bed with his shaved head, an IV in each arm, and his hands tied to the bed by restraints, when asked how he felt, John told his doctors he was having a "thumbs-up" day. He told his mother, "Mom, do you know what I like?" She said, "No, John," and he said, "You!"

Today our hearts are broken, but we have learned to live life with a broken heart and to enjoy life anyway. We have been inspired by John's love and positive, persevering spirit. And we will live our lives with as many thumbs-up days as possible.

DANIEL SPURR

When Daniel Spurr, the editor of Practical Sailor *magazine, began a long-planned sailing voyage in the summer of 1987 with his new wife, his two children from his previous marriage, Adria and Peter, joined him for the first leg of the trip. Twelve-year-old Peter's cerebral palsy rendered him as "tipsy as a drunk," but he had a "stoic" attitude about his frequent falls. Peter and his sister returned to their home in Michigan, while their father continued to sail. Two months later, Spurr received a call telling him that Peter was dead. Some rationalized Peter's death with the thought that his life would have been hard because of his disability. Clearly, his father doesn't agree.*

from Steered by the Falling Stars: A Father's Journey

He was hit by a train, knocked off a trestle onto the banks of the Huron River. Seven miles west of Ann Arbor, across the drive from his country home. Two other boys were with him, and I imagine them throwing stones, as I often did, playing on those same tracks when I was a kid. Or heaving sticks into the current, then racing to the other side of the trestle to watch their makeshift boats fly past, bound for Lake Erie.

The train rounded the curve. There wasn't much time, but there was enough. As the locomotive swung around, it first seemed to be on the outer tracks, and the boys jumped to the inside set. The red Amtrak stripes straightened, and now it was obvious it ran on the inside. The other two boys jumped back, one even making it off the trestle to the embankment. Peter didn't. He tripped and fell, his legs impossibly tangled, unable to bounce up like any regular kid. The engineer saw him and blew the whistle. Air brakes were applied, but the distance was short. Pete waved him off. I can see his arm, the elbow twisted inward, his fingers splayed, plying back and forth in a frantic, spastic motion.

The other boys saw him. One instant he was there, the next he wasn't. It was quick, save for those interminable minutes waiting for the train to stop.

When it had passed, finally stopped half a mile down, the boys looked. Pete lay in a cluster of saplings, half in the water, half out. I would like to say like Moses, saved by a basket of reeds and borne to safety on the stream.

My Pete, my Tiny Tim. So many times when his legs gave out, I hoisted him onto my shoulders and carried him. . . .

[A friend, Lennie, tells Spurr his mother's comment on Pete's death.] "I went to visit her after Pete died. I wanted to see what she thought. And you know what she told me, Danny? She said, 'That boy had tough times ahead, what with girls and all that.'"

People, it seemed, were always trying to justify Pete's death, but I would rather have had him crippled and alive than dead and "free.". . .

. . . On Pete's birthday, Adria and I throw a few flowers into the surf from the rocks at Purgatory Chasm. There, in what a French poet called the hour between the wolf and the dog, Adria and I talk about what she's doing—her sculpture, her mother, Aku, the future. Sometimes Pete's name comes up. It's not something either of us is ready for every day. Beyond the quick aside—"Pete would have liked this"—it is still too big for us. If you grasp him, you've got to hold him, and when you're trying to stay on track with the rest of your life, the weight can be too much. But every so often we let ourselves in to him, open our breasts and talk . . . about the way he smiled, the things he said ("So I was wrong!"), and how much we wish he were here with us, running into the surf with that awkward lope, kicking the waves with no more worries than Tango [a pet wolf hybrid] as she gallops after the sandpipers flying above the foam. I cannot imagine Pete without cerebral palsy. If he hadn't had CP, he wouldn't have been Peter. To wish otherwise would be to reject him.

CRIMINAL BEHAVIOR

ALFRED, LORD TENNYSON

Parents whose children were wild or troublesome grieve just as intensely as any others. In this poem, Rizpah, a dying mother, proclaims her love for her son Willy, who was hanged for thievery, and her belief that she will soon be reunited with him. She addresses an unknown lady who has come to pray with her for the salvation of her soul.

When Tennyson and his wife Emily's first child was stillborn, he wrote to a friend, "I have suffered more than ever I thought I could have done for a child still born: I fancy I should not have cared so much if he had been a seven months spindling, but he was the grandest looking child I have ever seen."

from "Rizpah," in *Poems of Tennyson*, edited by Jerome Hamilton Buckley

VI

Nay—for it 's kind of you, madam, to sit by an old dying wife.
But say nothing hard of my boy, I have only an hour of life.
I kiss'd my boy in the prison, before he went out to die.
"They dared me to do it," he said, and he never has told me a lie.
I whipt him for robbing an orchard once when he was but a child—
"The farmer dared me to do it," he said; he was always so wild—
And idle—and could n't be idle—my Willy—he never could rest.

The King should have made him a soldier, he would have been
   one of his best.

VII

But he lived with a lot of wild mates, and they never would let him
   be good;
They swore that he dare not rob the mail, and he swore that he
   would;
And he took no life, but he took one purse, and when all was done
He flung it among his fellows—"I 'll none of it," said my son.

VIII

I came into court to the judge and the lawyers. I told them my tale,
God's own truth—but they kill'd him, they kill'd him for robbing
   the mail.
They hang'd him in chains for a show—we had always borne a
   good name—
To be hang'd for a thief—and then put away—is n't that enough
   shame?
Dust to dust—low down—let us hide! but they set him so high
That all the ships of the world could stare at him, passing by.
God 'ill pardon the hell-black raven and horrible fowls of the air,
But not the black heart of the lawyer who kill'd him and hang'd
   him there.

IX

And the jailer forced me away. I had bid him my last good-bye;
They had fasten'd the door of his cell. "O mother!" I heard him cry.
I could n't get back tho' I tried, he had something further to say,
And now I never shall know it. The jailer forced me away.

X

Then since I could n't but hear that cry of my boy that was dead,
They seized me and shut me up: they fasten'd me down on my bed.
"Mother, O mother!"—he call'd in the dark to me year after year—
They beat me for that, they beat me—you know that I could n't but
   hear;

And then at the last they found I had grown so stupid and still
They let me abroad again—but the creatures had worked their will.

XI
Flesh of my flesh was gone, but bone of my bone was left—
I stole them all from the lawyers—and you, will you call it a theft?—
My baby, the bones that had suck'd me, the bones that had laughed
    and had cried—
Theirs? O, no! they are mine—not theirs—they had moved in
    my side.

XII
Do you think I was scared by the bones? I kiss'd em, I buried
    'em all—
I can't dig deep, I am old—in the night by the churchyard wall.
My Willy 'ill rise up whole when the trumpet of judgment 'ill sound,
But I charge you never to say that I laid him in holy ground.

XIII
They would scratch him up—they would hang him again on the
    cursed tree.
Sin? O, yes, we are sinners, I know—let all that be,
And read me a Bible verse of the Lord's goodwill toward men—
"Full of compassion and mercy, the Lord"—let me hear it again;
"Full of compassion and mercy—long-suffering." Yes, O, yes!
For the lawyer is born but to murder—the Saviour lives but to bless.
He 'll never put on the black cap except for the worst of the worst,
And the first may be last—I have heard it in church—and the last
    may be first.
Suffering—O, long-suffering—yes, as the Lord must know,
Year after year in the mist and the wind and the shower and the snow.

XIV
Heard, have you? what? they have told you he never repented his sin.
How do they know it? are *they* his mother? are *you* of his kin?
Heard! have you ever heard, when the storm on the downs began,
The wind that 'ill wail like a child and the sea that 'ill moan like a man?

XV

Election, Election, and Reprobation—it's all very well.
But I go to-night to my boy, and I shall not find him in hell.
For I cared so much for my boy that the Lord has look'd into
    my care,
And He means me I'm sure to be happy with Willy, I know not where.

XVI

And if *he* be lost—but to save *my* soul, that is all your desire—
Do you think that I care for *my* soul if my boy be gone to the fire?
I have been with God in the dark—go, go, you may leave me alone—
You never have borne a child—you are just as hard as a stone.

XVII

Madam, I beg your pardon! I think that you mean to be kind,
But I cannot hear what you say for my Willy's voice in the wind—
The snow and the sky so bright—he used but to call in the dark,
And he calls to me now from the church and not from the gibbet—
    for hark!
Nay—you can hear it yourself—it is coming—shaking the walls—
Willy—the moon's in a cloud—Good-night. I am going. He calls.

ALCOHOL AND DRUGS

DAN CHAON

Why did his older brother, Del, become a violent, thieving, alcohol- and drug-abusing adolescent and, finally, commit suicide? What went wrong? Years later, these are the questions Stewart ponders in this short story. He is having a rare conversation with his father on a snowy night in Nebraska, where he is paying an obligatory Christmas visit to his parents with his wife and infant son.

from "Fitting Ends," in *Fitting Ends and Other Stories*

There were no signs in our childhood, no incidents pointing the way to his eventual end. None that I could see, at least, and I thought about it quite a bit after his death. "It should have been taken care of earlier," my father said, but what was "it"? Del seemed to have been happy, at least up until high school.

Maybe things happened when they were alone together. From time to time, I remember Del coming back from helping my father in the shop with his eyes red from crying. Once I remember our father coming into our room on a Saturday morning and cuffing the top of Del's sleeping head with the back of his hand: he had stepped in dog dirt on the lawn. The dog was Del's responsibility. Del must have been about eight or nine at the time, and I remember him kneeling on our bedroom floor in his pajamas, crying bitterly as he cleaned off my father's boot. When I told that story later on, I was pleased by the ugly, almost fascist overtones it had. I remember recounting it to some college friends—handsome, suburban kids—lording this little bit of squalor from my childhood over them. Child abuse and family violence were enjoying a media vogue at the time, and I found I could mine this memory to good effect. In the version I told, I was the one cleaning the boots.

But the truth was, my father was never abusive in an especially spectacular way. He was more like a simple bully, easily eluded when he was in a short-tempered mood. He used to get so furious when we would avoid him. I recall how he used to grab us by the hair on the back of our necks, tilting our heads so we looked into his face. "You don't listen," he would hiss. "I want you to look at me when I talk to you." That was about the worst of it, until Del started getting into trouble. And by that time, my father's blows weren't enough. Del would laugh, he would strike back. It was then that my father finally decided to turn him over to the authorities. He had no other choice, he said.

He must have believed it. He wasn't, despite his temper, a bad man, a bad parent. He'd seemed so kindly, sometimes, so fatherly—especially with Del. I remember watching them from my window, some autumn mornings, watching them wade through the high weeds in the stubblefield out behind our house, walking toward the hill with their shotguns pointing at the ground, their steps slow, synchronized. Once I'd gone upstairs and heard them laughing in Del's and my bedroom. I just stood there outside the doorway, watching as my father and Del put a model ship together, sharing the job, their talk easy, happy.

This was what I thought of, that night we were talking. I thought of my own son, the innocent baby I loved so much, and it chilled me to think that things could change so much—that Del's closeness to my father could turn in on itself, transformed into the kind of closeness that thrived on their fights, on the different ways Del could push my father into a rage. That finally my father would feel he had no choices left. We looked at each other, my father and I. "What are you thinking?" I said softly, but he just shook his head.

GEORGE McGOVERN

After his daughter Terry's death as a result of alcoholism, former U.S. senator George McGovern tried even harder to understand her illness and what he might have done differently to save her life.

from *Terry: My Daughter's Life-and-Death Struggle with Alcoholism*

I believe that the key to Terry's life and death may be found around these central points: she was an alcoholic who longed desperately to be free of her alcoholism, but that disease combined with related emotional torment had so injured her mind and spirit that she was unable to live at peace without alcohol or some other drug. The one condition that was even more unbearable to Terry than intoxication was the emotional agony that seized her when she was sober. . . .

The other side . . . is the suffering of the nonalcoholics as they are caught up in the alcoholic's behavior—a behavior that produces disappointment, shattered expectations, anxiety, and anguish.

I spent many restless nights worrying about Teresa. If alcoholism produces insomnia for its victims, the family also battles this sleeplessness. I dreaded the late-night or early-morning telephone call lest it bring some new note of trouble and disappointment. I became obsessed with Terry's impact on our family gatherings, her children, her siblings, her employers, and her landlords, and her constant encounters with the police, emergency rooms, and treatment and detox centers.

It pained me to feel the resentment of my other children, who understandably wondered if a parent so obsessed with one child had any time or concern left for them. Sometimes I tried to pull away from Terry even when she may have most needed me because I wanted the others to see that I wasn't totally absorbed in their sister.

SCHIZOPHRENIA

NINA BAWDEN

*Adult and children's novelist Nina Bawden's oldest son, Niki, who
suffered from schizophrenia, committed suicide.*

from *In My Own Time: Almost an Autobiography*

A month after the funeral a letter came: he had won £50 on premium bonds.
And a friend wrote, "Now when they ask, *is it well with the child?* you can
believe that at last *it is well.*"

We went away that summer and when we came home, turning into our
street in Islington, I thought for a moment that I saw him, sitting on a bench
in the little park in Colebrooke Row and feeding the fat pigeons at his feet.
And, perhaps because I never saw him dead or dying, because the police
would not let me see photographs of his drowned body, I went on seeing
him for years. He would be on the motorbike that drew up beside me at a
traffic light; turning a street corner too far ahead for me to catch him up; on
the top deck of a passing bus.

I still see him. Several days running, a tramp sits on the seat by the canal
at the bottom of our garden. I can see him from the bathroom window. He
wears a drab, hooded, enveloping garment that he has probably slept in. He
usually has a plastic bag with a can of beer in it and a newspaper; he drinks
the beer and does the crossword and occasionally looks up at the house.

I know it cannot be Niki, but I find myself trembling. Should I get my
binoculars and make sure? Or go and walk past him? Whoever it is looks as
if he needs money. Except for the Salvation Army, I no longer give money to
charities but for Niki's sake I give on the streets, to the derelict, the homeless,
the mad. But I am too late to give this man some beer money. He gets up,
shakes the full skirt of his coat, folds his newspaper, tucks the empty can in
his pocket. The hood falls back showing a heavy-jowled face with a bulbous
nose as warty as a Jerusalem artichoke, and I find myself breathing out, a long
sigh of relief. Not just because that sad old tramp is not Niki, but because
Niki is safe now. *Is it well with the child? It is well.*

SUICIDE

GORDON LIVINGSTON

Livingston's oldest son, Andrew Lowry Livingston, hanged himself from a tree in late April of 1991 at the age of twenty-two. He suffered from bipolar illness, first manifested in his sophomore year at Swarthmore. In the eulogy Livingston delivered for Andrew, he said the disease "dominated the last three years of his life. He was forced to withdraw from college, underwent three hospitalizations, and had his moods oscillate wildly between manic disorganization and grinding depression. He struggled courageously against these disabling swings until he felt he could no longer go on. I imagine that his final desperate moments were eased with some anticipation of release from the anguish he had endured." One year later, Livingston's six-year-old son Lucas died of leukemia (see p. 53).

from *Only Spring: On Mourning the Death of My Son*

June 17, 1993

Today, Andrew's birthday, I flew to New Haven. Nina and Michael met me at the airport and dropped me off at the cemetery, where I spent a half-hour alone near the body of my first son. There is new grass on his grave and I brought some fresh flowers. Seeing his name and the dates of his life carved on the stone lent a finality to his death in the same way that I remember when I saw the names of young men I had known on my first trip to the Vietnam Memorial. Andrew was with me that day as I cried unexpected tears. Today I wept for him—and for myself. His death is a door forever slammed in our faces.

His mother joined me there. She is having trouble forgiving herself as are we all. I try to get her to see his bipolar illness as a sort of malignancy that destroyed him.

I visited the tree where he died and left a flower there. It is an oak at the top of a wooded hill with a limb suited to his purpose. When did he see this, pick it out as his hanging tree, imagine himself climbing to its first large fork, then leaning out to tie the bowline around the limb before launching himself into eternity? What was he thinking? Did he leap from this world with a final surge of control, embracing oblivion? Did his soul make a sound as it ascended, finally free, from the body that held all we loved of him?

I tried to evoke his presence today, but, though I spoke to his grave and to his dying place, I could not feel him there. His mother told me of a fire-fly coming toward her one evening, unblinking, turning away like an airplane. Andrew had gotten his pilot's license when he was eighteen and she said he had later told her that he regretted that he could no longer fly. Now perhaps, a weightless spirit, he can.

JENNIFER EGAN

Beautiful and driven to live vicariously for her depressed and then termi-nally ill father, Faith O'Conner pushed life to the limits—diving off the high dive at eleven, becoming a drug-using flower child in Haight-Ashbury in her teens after her father's death, joining a radical terrorist group in Germany—until she dived to her death on rocks off the Italian coast in 1970. Eight years later, Faith's younger sister Phoebe, the central character of this novel, thinks that if she "could string together the hours she'd spent circling this event, they would surely total years. . . . her own life falling away like a husk as she sank into the rich, bottomless well of her sis-ter's absence." Phoebe travels to Europe to retrace Faith's journey, ending up at the wall from which Faith dived, accompanied by Faith's former boyfriend, Wolf, who witnessed the suicide and explains what led up to it.

from The Invisible Circus

Phoebe looked at the wall, searching her mind for some question to draw Wolf out. But her mind was empty.

She shut her eyes and leaned her head against the church. Something un-bearable was happening inside her, a sensation like despair, only deeper, more wrenching. The wind blew dust in her face. She felt as if she were dy-ing, as if this pain were the pain of her soul being torn from her body. In fear she opened her eyes. The wind filled them with dust but it didn't matter, that pain, it was so small. It felt almost good.

Faith was gone. She was gone. Her absence felt as fresh to Phoebe as if she'd watched her sister dive from this cliff.

She tasted metal, the peculiar taste that follows a sudden sharp blow to the skull. A stunning emptiness blinked around her.

Wait, she thought. Wait.

In vain Phoebe tried to push her way clear, but her own thoughts seemed faint beside the vast finality of her sister's act. It whirled like a vortex, dragging every part of Phoebe irresistibly toward itself, swallowing her whole. She couldn't breathe.

Wait, she thought. But I always knew what happened.

Yet in all this time the reality of Faith's act, its brutal finality, had never really touched her. It was cloaked in gauze, in light, a terrific flash of light that left in its wake a soft orb.

Phoebe opened her eyes. The bright empty sky made a buzzing noise. The very air seemed full of panic, a tingling whiteness. . . .

"Come on," Faith said. Something behind that door. Faith opened every door she found, but Phoebe was afraid to.

A flash of light. Then a long glow.

Faith opened every door.

One gesture. Everything distilled.

Faith spent herself. She gave herself away. And time stopped.

She killed us both, Phoebe thought. Killed all of us.

Phoebe's limbs hurt. She wanted to move. She stood up.

The sea opened before her, wide and still. Cowed to stillness, Phoebe thought, the sea and everything else. She walked toward it.

"Stop!" Wolf cried.

Phoebe gave a violent start. Turning, she saw Wolf on his feet, poised to spring at her. She opened her mouth to speak but found she could not; her own astonishment silenced her. Wolf actually thought she would jump. Phoebe strained to imagine it—standing here, making that choice—but her mind veered away in disgust.

"I'd never do it," she said, staring at Wolf in disbelief. "Never. I would never do it." And as she spoke, Phoebe's perception of the act itself began to shift. It was a choice that appalled her.

Huddling with her mother and Barry [her brother] on the cliff near the Golden Gate Bridge, releasing Faith's ashes to the wind. Feeling so small, just the three of them together—hardly even a family. And her sister chose this.

"What about us?" Phoebe said. "What did she say about us?"

"I don't remember."

"Something, though? She said something?"

"I don't know." He looked uneasy.

"But I mean, what did she think?"

There was a long pause. "I don't think she thought," Wolf said.

Phoebe shook her head. Her ears were ringing. "Okay," she said, "that guy who died [the accidental victim of a bombing that Faith abetted] had children. But what about us?"

She looked at Wolf, who knew nothing, and was engulfed by a surge of wild anger. "I can't believe she did it," she cried. "I can't believe she stood here and did that to us!" Each word incensed her further, until she felt crazed with the need to vent her rage. "Was she out of her mind?" she shouted. "Standing here and—goddammit!" She kicked the outside of the church, hurting her foot, knocking flakes of plaster to the ground. She pounded it with her hands, raking them over its rough surface until a hot, delicious pain flashed through her. "Goddammit!" she cried. "Goddamn her!"

From behind, Wolf took Phoebe's hands, scraped and bleeding from the plaster's abrasion. He folded her in his arms, holding her still. "Stop it," he said. "You're hurting yourself."

Phoebe let her weight fall on Wolf. "I hate her," she said. "I hate her more than anything."

"Okay," Wolf said gently, holding her.

After a while Phoebe turned around, facing him. Wolf watched her a moment, as if to gauge her calm. "Phoebe, I have to say this," he said. "The last thing Faith wanted was to hurt you—any of you. In her mind it was a sacrifice. She was trying to right a balance." He paused, breathing hard. "The fact that she caused more misery is just a horrible irony. Her worst fear, all over again."

He let go of Phoebe. She moved away from him and hunched against the church, its stone warm at her back. She shut her eyes.

ROBERT LOWELL

Here Lowell recalls a conversation with Robert Frost. The son Frost refers to here is Carol, who at age thirty-eight, long bedeviled by depression, shot himself with the deer-hunting rifle he had given his wife as a wedding gift. "I took the wrong way with him," Frost later wrote a friend. "I tried many ways and every single one of them was wrong. Something in me is still asking for the chance to try once more." The daughter who "thought things" was Irma, committed to a psychiatric institution at age forty-four.

from Selected Poems

Robert Frost

Robert Frost at midnight, the audience gone
to vapor, the great act laid on the shelf in mothballs,
his voice is musical and raw—he writes in the flyleaf:
For Robert from Robert, his friend in the art.
"Sometimes I feel too full of myself," I say.
And he, misunderstanding, "When I am low,
I stray away. My son wasn't your kind. The night
we told him Merrill Moore would come to treat him,
he said, 'I'll kill him first.' One of my daughters thought things,
thought every male she met was out to make her;
the way she dressed, she couldn't make a whorehouse."
And I, "Sometimes I'm so happy I can't stand myself."
And he, "When I am too full of joy, I think
how little good my health did anyone near me."

AIDS

MARK DOTY

Mark Doty is a gay poet who aptly describes himself as "a citizen of grief's country" in his AIDS memoir, Heaven's Coast.

from *Poets for Life: Seventy-Six Poets Respond to AIDS,* edited by Michael Klein

Bill's Story

When my sister came back from Africa,
we didn't know at first how everything
had changed. After a while Anne
bought men's and boy's clothes in all sizes,
and filled her closets with little
or huge things she could never wear.

Then she took to buying out
theatrical shops, rental places on the skids,
sweeping in and saying, *I'll take everything.*
Dementia was the first sign of something

we didn't even have a name for,
in 1978. She was just becoming stranger,

all those clothes, the way she'd dress me up
when I came to visit. It was like we could go back
to playing together again and get it right.
She was a performance artist, and she did
her best work then, taking the clothes to clubs,
talking, putting them all on, talking.

It was years before she was in the hospital,
and my mother needed something
to hold on to, some way to be helpful,
so she read a book called *Deathing*
(a cheap, ugly verb if ever I heard one)
and took its advice to heart;

she'd sit by the bed and say, *Annie,
look for the light.* It was plain
that Anne did not wish to be distracted
by these instructions; she came to,
though she was nearly gone then, and looked
at our mother with what was almost certainly
annoyance. *It's a white light,*
Mom said, and this struck me
as incredibly presumptuous, as if the light
we'd all go into would be just the same.
Maybe she wanted to give herself up
to indigo, or red. If we can barely even speak

to each other, living so separately,
how can we all die the same?
I used to take the train to the hospital
and sometimes the only empty seats
would be the ones that face backwards.
I'd sit there and watch where I'd been

waver and blur out, and finally
I liked it, seeing what you've left
get more beautiful, less specific.

Maybe her light was all that gabardine
and flannel, khaki and silks
and stripes. If you take everything,

you've got to let everything go. Dying
must take more attention than I ever imagined.
Just when she'd compose herself
and seem fixed on the work before her,
Mother would fret, trying to help
just one more time— *Look for the light*—

until I took her arm
and told her wherever I was in the world
I would come back, no matter how difficult
it was to reach her, if I heard her calling.
Shut up, mother, I said, and Annie died.

MARCIE HERSHMAN

*We cannot keep our loved ones safe: this is the theme of Hershman's novel.
Joy Eichenbaum Buckland's parents, Jewish immigrants, were unable to
save their families from the Holocaust, nor their oldest son, who was
killed in World War II. A generation later, Joy is unable to save her gay
son, Hal, from AIDS. The scene is the hospital where Hal is dying.*

from Safe in America

Hal's feet, naked—that's what she was thinking about now. . . . Hal's feet,
naked, mature, and strangely beautiful. In that way too he's come to resemble her father. One memory Joy has of the years of her own early mother-
hood is how her infant son, her first son, wiggled his toes in the air while she
and her husband and her mother and father leaned over the bassinet. All of
the adults were laughing, really laughing. The tiny red heels had not yet
born any weight; they were rounded and soft. One by one she, Leo, Vera
and Evan put their lips to the baby's soles and kissed them. Hal loved it,
holding still, gazing up distantly beneath all the attention. . . .

Joy shivers now, remembering that Hal hasn't had the strength to stand
for some time. As he lies on his back in room ten-eighteen, his feet point up
under the hospital bed's single white sheet and mark his length, once his
height, like an end bracket.

Her son's fighting; he's hanging on. When she's allowed back in, she might ask if he'd like her to massage the arches. She saw how much this had helped John two years before. Hal's partner John was hospitalized back then, and it seemed that nothing could bring him comfort. Eyes swollen shut, skin blotched with Kaposi's sarcoma lesions, John was so feverish he could barely talk. The Hickman catheter, the antibiotic intravenous, the two long clear plastic tubes of the waste catheters made even his slightest movement difficult.

Joy was appalled. Though she'd read newspapers, seen some brief reports on TV, she hadn't truly known that this was what AIDS looked like. For years she and Leo hadn't really wanted to know; Hal was living in Chicago, and he was healthy and well; and it appeared that John was healthy and well; and so Joy and Leo managed for a long time not to ask much and to keep their distance. It seemed too difficult for them to have to get used to the possibility of anything this dire affecting anyone they loved; too difficult for them, especially after the jolts of loss and anger she and Leo already had felt when Hal told them back in college that he was gay. It didn't mean that Joy or Leo—he promised—had made mistakes; they were good parents, they had to know that. Yet he was who he was; was how he felt; was all right. But at the start of the process of when he came out, Joy could only think: *Hal is gay. Our son is different.*

And now, she would say to herself in those first years when news of a "new plague" began trickling into the public consciousness, *and now*—but immediately tossing the thought away as soon as she'd think it in the middle of the night, waking in the morning, when driving to go shopping or waiting in line for a movie, when climbing into bed next to Leo—*now this.*

ABRAHAM VERGHESE

The child of Indian parents, raised in Ethiopia, and trained as an M.D. in internal medicine in India and the United States, Verghese decided to settle with his wife and newborn son in Johnson City, Tennessee—"a small town in the country, a town of clean-living, good country people. AIDS was clearly a big city problem. It was something that happened in other kinds of lives." But AIDS came to Johnson City, and Verghese became the "AIDS doctor." His true account follows the lives and deaths of his AIDS patients, and the impact of this scourge on their loved ones, as well as on his own life.

from My Own Country: A Doctor's Story of a Town and Its People in the Age of AIDS

That afternoon I went over to the University Clinic at lunchtime to meet B.J. Hilton's father and to check my mail.

B.J. worked as a manager at a well-known restaurant near the mall. He was, according to Carol [clinic nurse], the handsomest man the front-office staff at our clinic had ever seen. She told me that at his first visit, they were all swooning over him. He wore his blond hair in a ponytail; he had the long limbs and muscular physique of a ballet dancer. Had you seen him on the street, you might have wondered if God was fair in blessing one person with all these attributes. He came to me when he found out he was HIV positive. He was asymptomatic with a CD4 count near a thousand.

B.J. told me on his first visit that there was no possible way he could tell anyone but his mother about his infection. His father and his brothers would never understand.

Imagine my surprise, then, when his father called and asked to see me. I telephoned B.J. at once at the restaurant where he worked. He said he had just had a wonderful heart-to-heart with his father and that I should feel free to talk to him.

B.J.'s father was a large balding man who showed up in a safari shirt and slacks. If B.J. possessed a ballet dancer's body, his father was more in the line-backer mode, a linebacker who had gone to fat. He told me how sad he was at the news that his son had HIV. And yet, he was glad that his son had come out and told him. He said, "For the first time in ten years, I hugged my son and told him how much I loved him. I would not want him to get sick without knowing that." He reached for a handkerchief and dabbed the corners of his eyes.

I told him as much about HIV infection as I thought he could digest; I told him what B.J. could expect in years to come. He seemed reluctant to leave. I asked him if this was the first he knew his son was gay.

"No, I suppose I've known for some time now. One time he got in trouble with the law. I had to go bail him out. It had to do with something in the bathroom at J.C. Penney." At this point his face hardened and he looked at me and said, "All I can tell you is it was something disgusting. Just plain disgusting."

I could imagine what it might have been and how painful it was for the father to picture it.

"Plain disgusting. I mean, I more or less knew then but I just turned away from him. Well, even before that, growing up, he was always . . . dif-ferent. And maybe I was hard on him, tried to get him to do the things his brothers were doing, but it never worked. He had his own friends, his own interests—still does."

He stared away now and was silent before he looked back at me, the tears pouring down his cheeks, the hankie quite ineffective. "Isn't it a shame for it to take a disease like this for me to be close to my boy again? The little baby boy that I carried and loved—he was the youngest—somehow got away from me. Now we're back loving again, but he's going to die, isn't he? That's the bottom line, isn't it?"

I hedged. But yes, it was the bottom line.

RICK BARRETT

A former CPA, the father in this short story always understood balance and order and "watching men chase balls up and down a field" better than he understood his own, only son, Todd. Here, Todd, twenty-eight, returns home—at his father's urging—for his first visit in ten years. He is a professional artist, gay, and ill with AIDS.

from "Running Shoes," in *Best American Gay Fiction 1996*, edited by Brian Bouldrey

When I woke up the next morning Helen [his second wife] had already gone, and the notion of filling up a day for and with Todd frightened me. It was as if one day, with my son in it, represented an expanse of land and sky that I could neither walk nor see across. I could think only of meals, of where to get ourselves fed; or of movies, of where to sit in a dark cave, facing the pulse of a screen. I heard the aluminum door slam against its jamb, and, sitting up in bed, saw, through the frosted window, Todd in his running gear, cutting through the gravel drive in his tattered shoes. Then I saw him running toward the road. Long, loping, deliberate strides, his hands in gloves.

I don't move quickly, then or now. But on that morning I came close to leaping from my bed and running for the room where Todd had slept. He had brought, in addition to his running shoes, two other pairs: black boots with heavy buckles and a pair of rubber sandals. Both were size 11, 11-D. I dressed as quickly as I could and was out of the trailer and the park before Todd came home. I was, I think, giddy with the notion that I knew what to buy my grown son for Christmas.

They were the most colorful, highly technical, expensive shoes I had ever bought or seen. The logos on the shoes reminded me of Mercury's wings and

I thought of Todd, in these shoes, running, running, running. In the three days before Christmas, I bought him books on running, running shorts, shirts, a journal. I bought him a book of runners' recipes. Running became the one thing I knew about him that was safe to ask, a thing for which doing homework brought no fear. He ran when the weather was not too bad, and on days he felt strong, days he felt his wind would not fail him. He ran around a reservoir, a battery, and a village—all in Manhattan. He had been in Vermont for October and had run through rains of falling leaves, a thing he had returned to New York to paint, the motion of falling leaves, "you and light passing through them," he said.

I see now that our zeal for his running, both his and mine, was also about fear. I feared Todd would stop running because he could run no longer, because he had fallen sick again, too sick to run. And Todd, I imagine, feared the same. I thought that to engage him in his running, to encourage him in it, might perpetuate the running, him.

I would be able to divine, perhaps because I am his father—no matter that I was inept or absent much of his life—Todd's reaction to my gift the moment the lid came off the box. Todd simply stared at the shoes, his face naked from discovery, his eyes pooling and blinking, and slowly plucked away the tissue paper.

"You got me shoes," he said.

"It looked like you needed some new ones."

"They fit," he said, pulling them on over his socks.

"I checked your others. While you were out. Running. I didn't mean to snoop. It was only your shoes."

He stood up, looked down at them on his feet, wiggled his toes in them. Helen offered that the shoes were cute, that she would love a pair like that for the hospital.

Todd looked at her. "I think the idea," he said, "is to keep them, and me, out of the hospital." Todd stared across the room at me, and said, I think, though I was never quite sure I heard him correctly, "You get it, don't you?"

"You look strong when you run," I said. "I mean, you seem to be a strong runner. Your form. Long, solid strides. As though you were built that way."

"Am," he said, just, "am." He then said thank you.

I do not remember what he gave me, only that when he handed it to me, he said, "You win. You tore the tape, crossed the line first." He looked down at his shoes. "I could never beat these." His jaw was trembling.

The looming regret I have about life is that there are stationary fronts, banks of cloud between fathers and sons, between men, between a man and himself. Because of these I had no idea how to touch him then, he in his new shoes, I sitting, staring lamely at a gift I cannot recall. Now that he is gone, I have no idea how to bear having failed at this, the knowledge of how to stand and hold on to my one son.

9

We Feel Like Aliens in the World

Allie was killed one-half mile from our home at 6:15 on a Friday evening. Neighbors knew within an hour, and the news was broadcast on radio and television. Friends rushed over, shocked and horrified, wanting to know what they could do. I am the kind of person who takes care of my business myself, and at first I wanted people to leave me alone so I could figure out what to do. But in the middle of the night I knew this was beyond anything I could possibly handle. I was completely, utterly lost.

People took over everything from driving us to the funeral parlor and the cemetery to answering the phone, arranging meals, and even ironing a shirt for Allie. We only had to make decisions about the funeral and greet the mourners. And after the funeral and mourning period, people kept us busy. It was the first time in twenty-one years that there were no children in our house. I was afraid we would go insane in the silence and emptiness. We turned down no opportunity to be with people. "Just keep moving," Peter said. And we did. A few people avoided us, but many more extended themselves. It must have been so hard for them. Grief surrounded us like a thundercloud. In a couple of months, I shrank until I looked like a Holocaust survivor. I am eternally grateful to the people who gave us their shoulders to lean on in this most terrible of times.

But in time it became clear that although friends cared deeply, they could not fathom our devastation. Well-intended things they said infuriated me. "Have a very Merry Christmas and a wonderful New Year" was a message a friend left for me on my answering machine. I wanted to call her and scream, *Are you crazy? Can you possibly believe I will ever enjoy Christmas or New Year's again?* "I guess you'll have to look at the glass half full, rather than the glass half empty," a cousin told Peter at a wedding. "Please don't try to console me with platitudes," Peter replied. "It doesn't help, and it offends me." My mother told me Allie was in a better place. "How do you know? And what about me, I'm in hell!" I wailed. "I could never bear to lose a child," some said. *Nobody asked if I could bear it. Should I kill myself?* I felt like responding. "You're coping so well" drove me mad. How did they know, and did they think I felt complimented to be told I was handling my son's death well? "It has to get better," said a social-worker friend of mine. "Who says? Allie's still dead."

I was angry at things people said, and I was also angry when they didn't say anything. We would have ordinary conversations about commonplace things. *Don't you know that we are just going through the motions of living?* I was screaming inside. *Can't you tell this is an act and that I wish I were dead?* Even when I tried to find the words to describe how I felt, I was afraid I'd overwhelm people. I could only say so many times that I missed Allie terribly and could hardly stand to be alive. What could they say? I was angry they couldn't understand my suffering, even though I knew I couldn't have understood if I were they. And, bottom line, I was angry that it was my precious Allie who was killed and I who had to bear the unbearable.

Until Allie died, we all traveled similar routes—the normal, predictable life cycle. Allie's catastrophic death brought our family to a screeching halt. Our old friends continue along the same road through predominantly green pastures and sunshine. We have detoured into the valley of the shadow of death. Our friends' children thrive. They are passing important milestones of life, and even though we have Hilary and the pleasure of sharing her journey, it is painful that Allie is missing all these wonderful experiences. When we get together with friends and talk about our children, it is hard to only talk about Hilary, as if Allie never existed. But then there's nothing new to report about someone who's dead.

For a long time, the people I felt most comfortable with after Allie died were other bereaved parents or people who had also endured severe losses. I could talk about Allie freely; I could express my pain without inhibition. Sometimes I could even laugh without feeling self-conscious, without thinking that people were either wondering how I could laugh when my son was dead or assuming that I was "over it." People who have survived losses, who share "the long mourner's bench," understand that you go on because you have to, and even laugh now and then, but the hurt, the sorrow, and the everlasting longing for the one you love and have lost are a large and permanent part of you.

In a way, it is easier to be with new friends. They distract us and help us to pass the time, but we share no history. I care deeply about our friends from our old life and would not lose them, but they highlight the contrast between then and now. And it hurts.

MARY

The pain of Jake's death does not stop with me. Like the rivulets of a tidal delta, it carries its silt into other lives too.

My sister calls from the hospital, exhausted and exuberant. She's had her baby. She does not say its sex, and when I ask, she hesitates. I hear in her voice reluctance to tell me it's a boy, and she hears in mine the anguish I can't disguise. This is not right. I've brought sadness and fear to a room which should never see those faces.

My mother, long widowed, grieves for us all. She wishes my father back to comfort her but rejoices too that he escaped the pain. "This would have killed him," she says firmly. And I wonder why it hasn't killed her. I am *her* firstborn. She bleeds for me. As I do for her.

And there are others. For years, until she died at ninety-nine, my normally upbeat grandmother began every conversation lamenting that she was still alive. "Why am I here, when poor little Jake is dead?" she'd ask, as if because she held her spot, someone made him relinquish his.

Jake had two close friends at the time of the accident, both too young to understand death. For them, Jake just disappeared. Now fourteen, one is still reluctant to ever hug friendship that tightly again. And the other, once as close as Jake's shadow, won't speak of him. Say his name and she smiles, then quickly looks away.

Grief is as self-centered as a teenager. I need to remind myself that others loved Jake too.

Eight years after Jake's death, a good friend tells me she still has trouble vacuuming under the antique desk in her living room. Around age four and a half, Jake and her daughter used to hide there. It became their game. "We're here, can't you see us?" they'd squeal, when my friend, feigning blindness, would poke the vacuum underneath. "I still hear their voices," she says softly. "Every time I go near that desk. And they're loud."

Others loved Jake too. He did not belong just to me. I need to remember that.

ANNE

WE FEEL LIKE ALIENS

IGOR KOSTIN

Kostin was the first photographer at Chernobyl in 1986, the site of the worst nuclear power plant accident in history.

from a newspaper interview

It's hard to live among normal people now. A person who has been through hell has a different attitude. He breathes the air and feels the sunshine differently.

C. S. LEWIS

Surprised by the discomfort he perceived he caused others, Lewis commented on it in the journal he kept after his wife died (see p. 61).

from *A Grief Observed*

An odd by-product of my loss is that I'm aware of being an embarrassment to everyone I meet. At work, at the club, in the street, I see people, as they approach me, trying to make up their minds whether they'll "say something about it" or not. I hate it if they do, and if they don't. Some funk it altogether. R. has been avoiding me for a week. I like best the well-brought-up young men, almost boys, who walk up to me as if I were a dentist, turn very red, get it over, and then edge away to the bar as quickly as they decently can. Perhaps the bereaved ought to be isolated in special settlements like lepers.

CAROL SHIELDS

In this novel, Daisy's alcoholic husband falls out the window on their European honeymoon and is killed. Ten years later, she still feels like a marked woman in her hometown: "Wherever she goes, her story marches ahead of her. Announces her. Declares and cancels her true self." It is only when she takes a trip by herself that she can escape the stigma.

from *The Stone Diaries*

It seemed to her that June day, as the train slid at last over the Michigan State line and entered Canada, that she had arrived at a healing kingdom.

No one here could guess at her situation. No one here knew her story. Here she was simply one more young woman wearing a linen dress and matching jacket and standing by the railing at Niagara Falls, catching a fine spray on her cheek.

C. J. HRIBAL

"Thirteen months ago she was just another divorced mother of three."
Now with her son Peter dead (see p. 82), Janie, the narrator of this short
story, feels like a magnet for bad luck.

from "The Clouds in Memphis," in *TriQuarterly,* spring/summer 1995

Some people are just singled out, it seems. Major griefs and minor inconveniences: it's only by size that you can distinguish them. In the year after Peter was killed Stevie had his truck wrecked by a couple of drunk teenagers in a car that turned out to be stolen, Nikki had her car stereo stolen, and Janie herself had backed into a light pole and sideswiped a neighbor's car while parallel parking. There'd also been a break-in at her studio and her cat had been run over right in front of the house. Renting in a block where everyone else owns she already feels singled out. Now she's becoming known as "the catastrophe lady." The people in the apartment upstairs, a history professor and his wife, talk about her. She was backing her car out of the curved driveway—she had snapped the mudflap off previously, and was now smashing in the wheelwell—when a deadfall from the pin oak in the front yard landed smack on the hood of her car. The professor's words to his wife and guests (they were having drinks on the front porch before the Memphis State-Ole Miss game) floated out to her. "Some people," the professor said, "just aren't born to luck."

WE TRY TO EXPLAIN HOW WE FEEL

WILLIAM SHAKESPEARE

Shortly after his eleven-year-old son, Hamnet, died in 1596, Shakespeare
wrote King John. *In this excerpt, Lady Constance tries to explain*
her grief over the death of her son to King Philip of France and to

Cardinal Pandolf, but she finds they do not understand or give comfort. In all of Shakespeare's plays, this passage is thought to be the most closely autobiographical.

from *King John*, in William Shakespeare: The Complete Works
(compact edition), edited by Stanley Wells, Gary Taylor,
John Jowett, and William Montgomery

PANDOLF: Lady, you utter madness, and not sorrow.

CONSTANCE: Thou art not holy to belie me so.
I am not mad: this hair I tear is mine;
My name is Constance; I was Geoffrey's wife;
Young Arthur is my son; and he is lost.
I am not mad; I would to God I were,
For then 'tis like I should forget myself.
O, if I could, what grief should I forget!
Preach some philosophy to make me mad,
And thou shalt be canonized, Cardinal.
For, being not mad, but sensible of grief,
My reasonable part produces reason
How I may be delivered of these woes,
And teaches me to kill or hang myself.
If I were mad I should forget my son,
Or madly think a babe of clouts were he.
I am not mad; too well, too well I feel
The different plague of each calamity.

  . . . .

And Father Cardinal, I have heard you say
That we shall see and know our friends in heaven.
If that be true, I shall see my boy again;
For since the birth of Cain, the first male child,
To him that did but yesterday suspire,
There was not such a gracious creature born.
But now will canker-sorrow eat my bud,
And chase the native beauty from his cheek;
And he will look as hollow as a ghost,
As dim and meagre as an ague's fit,
And so he'll die; and rising so again,
When I shall meet him in the court of heaven,

I shall not know him; therefore never, never
Must I behold my pretty Arthur more.

PANDOLF: You hold too heinous a respect of grief.

CONSTANCE: He talks to me that never had a son.

KING PHILIP: You are as fond of grief as of your child.

CONSTANCE: Grief fills the room up of my absent child,
Lies in his bed, walks up and down with me,
Puts on his pretty looks, repeats his words,
Remembers me of all his gracious parts,
Stuffs out his vacant garments with his form;
Then have I reason to be fond of grief.
Fare you well. Had you such a loss as I,
I could give better comfort than you do.

. . . .

O Lord, my boy, my Arthur, my fair son,
My life, my joy, my food, my all the world,
My widow-comfort, and my sorrow's cure!

SUE GRAFTON

In this mystery novel, a mother whose daughter's murder remains unsolved hires sleuth Kinsey Milhone to investigate.

from "K" Is for Killer

"Anyway, I know what it's like to have your heart ripped out. I probably look like an ordinary woman, but I'm a zombie, the living dead, maybe a little bit cracked. We've been going to this support group . . . somebody suggested it, and I thought it might help. I was ready to try anything to get away from the pain. Mace—that's my husband—went a few times and then quit. He couldn't stand the stories, couldn't stand all the suffering compressed in one room. He wants to shut it out, get shed of it, get clean. I don't think it's possible, but there's no arguing the point. To each his own, as they say."

"I can't even imagine what it must be like," I said.

"And I can't describe it, either. That's the hell of it. We're not regular people anymore. You have a child murdered, and from that moment on you're from some other planet. You don't speak the same language as other folks. Even in this support group, we seem to speak different dialects. Everybody hangs on to their pain like it was some special license to suffer. You can't help it. We all think ours is the worst case we ever heard. Lorna's murder hasn't been solved, so naturally we think our anguish is more acute because of it. Some other family, maybe their child's killer got caught and he served a few years. Now he's out on the street again, and that's what they have to live with—knowing some fella's walking around smoking cigarettes, drinking beers, having himself a good old time every Saturday night while their child is dead. Or the killer's still in prison and'll be there for life, but he's warm, he's safe. He gets three meals a day and the clothes on his back. He might be on death row, but he won't actually *die.* Hardly anybody does unless they *beg* to be executed. Why should they? All those soft-hearted lawyers go to work. System's set up to keep 'em all alive while our kids are dead for the rest of time."

"Painful," I said.

"Yes, it is. I can't even tell you how much that hurts. I sit downstairs in that room and I listen to all the stories, and I don't know what to do. It's not like it makes my pain any less, but at least it makes it part of *something.* Without the support group, Lorna's death just evaporates. It's like nobody cares. It's not even something people talk about anymore. We're all of us wounded, so I don't feel so cut off. I'm not separate from them. Our emotional injuries just come in different forms." Her tone throughout was nearly matter-of-fact, and the dark-eyed look she gave me then seemed all the more painful because of it. "I'm telling you all this because I don't want you to think I'm crazy . . . at least any more than I actually am. You have a child murdered and you go berserk. Sometimes you recover and sometimes you don't. What I'm saying is, I know I'm obsessed. I think about Lorna's killer way more than I should. Whoever did this, I want him *punished.* I want this laid to rest. I want to know why he did it. I want to tell him face-to-face exactly what he did to my life the day he took hers. The psychologist who runs the group, she says I need to find a way to get my power back. She says it's better to get mad than go on feeling heartsick and defenseless. So. That's why I'm here. I guess that's the long and short of it."

"Taking action," I said.

"You bet. Not just talking. I'm sick and tired of talk. It gets nowhere."

RUSSELL BANKS

Widower Billy Ansel becomes reclusive when he loses his twins (see p. 72).
Banks's novel was adapted as a film of the same name.

from *The Sweet Hereafter*

I was unable to take the comfort offered me. Something metallic in me refused to yield, and when one by one my sisters phoned and offered to come up to Sam Dent, an old compulsion took over; the same thing happened when various local people—Reverend Dreiser, Dorothy Coburn, even the men from the garage—called or came by to see how I was or to ask if there was anything they could do for me. It's something I have done since childhood, practically. When a person tries to comfort me, I respond by reassuring him or her—it's usually a her—and in that way I shut her down, smothering all her good intentions by denying my need.

I can't help it, and I'm not sorry for it; I'm even a little proud. People think I'm cold and unfeeling, but that's a price I've always been willing to pay. The truth is that I'm beyond help; most people are; and it only angers me to see my sisters or my friends here in town wasting their time. To forestall or cover my anger, I jump in front of them, and suddenly I myself have turned into the person come to provide comfort, reassurance, help, whatever it is they originally desired to provide me with. I take their occasion and make it my own. I never know this at the time, of course; only afterwards, when I'm alone again, sitting in my living room with a glass of whiskey in my hand, brooding over my solitude, trying to generate a little feeling, even if it's only self-pity.

TALKING ABOUT IT IS AWKWARD FOR US AND THEM

SHELLY WAGNER

Wagner left her five-year-old son Andrew alone for mere moments to go into the kitchen for something. When she returned, he was gone, drowned in the river behind their house. In this poem, an acrostic of her sons' names, Wagner poses a simple question that is a source of enormous angst for all bereaved parents.

from *The Andrew Poems*

Andrew and Thomas

A simple question,
Never a problem before.
"Do you have any children?"
Really a simple question.
Easy. I say, "Yes," but
What do I say to "How many?"

"Two," my hard-headed
Heart always says.
One is dead.
Must I say only one?
Absolutely not—I have two
Sons.

ANNE TYLER

This scene from Anne Tyler's novel takes place when Macon, whose twelve-year-old son Ethan was murdered a year before (see p. 80), takes his girlfriend's son to buy clothes.

from *The Accidental Tourist*

Someone said, "Macon?"

He turned and found a woman in a trim blond pageboy, her wrap skirt printed with little blue whales. "Yes," he said.

"Laurel Canfield. Scott's mother, remember?"

"Of course," Macon said, shaking her hand. Now he caught sight of Scott, who had been in Ethan's class at school—an unexpectedly tall, gawky boy lurking at his mother's elbow with an armload of athletic socks. "Why, Scott. Nice to see you," Macon said.

Scott flushed and said nothing. Laurel Canfield said, "It's nice to see *you*. Are you doing your spring shopping?"

"Oh, well, ah—"

He looked toward the stall. Now Alexander's trousers were slumped around his ankles. "I'm helping the son of a friend," he explained.

"We've just been buying out the sock department."

"Yes, I see you have."

"Seems every other week I find Scott's run through his socks again; you know how they are at this age—"

She stopped herself. She looked horrified. She said, "Or, rather . . ."

"Yes, certainly!" Macon said. "Amazing, isn't it?" He felt so embarrassed for her.

WILLIAM STYRON

Stingo, the character who narrates Styron's novel, has quit his mundane job at McGraw-Hill to devote himself exclusively to writing. In the evening, after packing up his office, he says good-bye to his boss, Farrell, a senior editor.

from *Sophie's Choice*

"You remind me very much of my son, you know."

"I didn't know you had a son," I said with some surprise. I had heard Farrell once allude casually and wryly to his "childless state" and had simply assumed that he had not, as the phrase goes, been blessed with issue. But my curiosity had ceased there. . . .

"Oh, I *had* a son all right!" His voice was suddenly a cry, startling me with its mingled tone of rage and lament. . . . He rose to his feet and wandered to the window, gazing through the twilight at the incomprehensible mirage of Manhattan, set afire by the descending sun. "Oh, I *had* a son!" he said again. "Edward Christian Farrell. He was just your age, he was just twenty-two, and he wanted to be a writer. He was . . . he was a *prince* with language, my son was. He had a gift that would have charmed the devil himself, and some of the letters he wrote—some of those long, knowing, funny, intelligent letters—were the loveliest that ever were written. Oh, he was a *prince* with language, that boy!"

Tears came to his eyes. For me it was a paralyzingly awkward moment, one that appears now and then throughout life, though with merciful infrequency. In grieving tones a near-stranger speaks of some beloved person in the past tense, throwing his listener into a quandary. Certainly he means the departed is dead. But hold! Mightn't he simply have run off, victim of amnesia, or become a fleeing culprit? Or was now pathetically languishing in a lunatic asylum, so that use of the past tense is merely sorrowfully euphemistic? When Farrell resumed talking, still offering me no clue to his son's fate, I turned away in embarrassment and continued to sort out my belongings.

"Maybe I could have taken it better if he hadn't been my only kid. But Mary and I could have no more children after Eddie was born." He stopped suddenly. "Ah, you don't want to hear . . ."

I turned back to him. "No, go ahead," I said, "please." He seemed to be suffering from an urgent need to talk, and since he was a kindly man whom I liked and, furthermore, one who in some fashion had indeed identified me with his son, I felt it would have been indecent for me not to encourage him to unburden himself. "Please go ahead," I said again.

Farrell poured himself another huge shot of rye. He had become quite drunk and his speech was a little slurred, the freckled indoor face sad and haggard in the waning light. "Oh, it's true that a man can live out his own aspirations through the life of his child. Eddie went to Columbia, and one of the things that thrilled me was the way he took to books, his gift for words. At nineteen— *nineteen,* mind you—he had had a sketch published in *The New Yorker,* and Whit Burnett had taken a story for *Story.* One of the youngest contributors, I believe, in the history of the magazine. It was his eye, you see, his *eye.*" Farrell jabbed his forefinger at his eye. "He *saw* things, you understand, saw things that the rest of us don't see and made them fresh and alive. Mark Van Doren wrote me a lovely note—the loveliest note, really—saying that Eddie had one of the greatest natural writing gifts of any student he'd ever had. Mark Van Doren, imagine! Quite a tribute, wouldn't you say?" He eyed me as if in search for some corroboration.

"Quite a tribute," I agreed.

"And then—and then in 1943 he joined the Marine Corps. Said he'd rather join up than be drafted. He honestly loved the glamour of the marines, although basically he was too sensitive to have any illusions about war. *War!*" He spoke the word with revulsion, like a seldom-used obscenity, and paused for an instant to shut his eyes and nod in pain. Then he looked at me and said, "The war took him to the Pacific and he was in some of the worst of the fighting. You should read his letters, marvelous, jolly, eloquent letters, without a trace of self-pity. He never once doubted that he'd come home and go back to Columbia and finish up and then become the writer he was meant to be. And then two years ago he was on Okinawa and got hit by a sniper. In the head. It was July and they were mopping up. I think he must have been one of the last marines to die in the war. He'd been made corporal. He won the Bronze Star. I don't know why it happened. *God,* I don't know *why* it happened! God, *why?*"

Farrell was weeping, not obtrusively but with the sparkling, honest tears welling up at the edge of his eyelids, and I turned away with such a feeling of shame and humiliation that years later I am able to recapture the slightly fevered, faintly nauseous sensation that swept over me.

JOHN TITTENSOR

Tittensor lost both his son and daughter in a house fire (see p. 67). His ex-wife and the children's mother, Sheila, tells him about visiting Jonathan and Emma's school one day and seeing women there she knew.

from Year One: A Record

December 3

. . . And what right have I to criticize the reactions of others? The memory of my own response to this kind of loss before I became an initiate myself, leaves me burning with shame and embarrassment. The friend I had not seen for years whose seven-year-old son was knocked down by a car and killed. The fellow-teacher whose twin daughters died shortly after they were born. The cousin whose child simply died, inexplicably, in its cot. Did I say anything, send any message of consolation? Did I go to the funerals—as that cousin came to Jonathan and Emma's? I look back at the me of those days—not very long ago at all—with contempt and disgust and bafflement. So busy with my own preoccupations while knowing nothing of these most basic realities. I seem blind and without feeling; hardly human.

Yet there is a comfort: I have learnt something about what Martin Buber calls "living on the hard earth" and can at least hope that I am the better for it. And one day I am going to be able to face some poor, shattered human being and say, "You can talk to me about it because I know *exactly* how you feel." And thus make up in some small way for the self-centeredness, the inexcusable insensitivity of that earlier, uninitiated me.

March 21

. . . They wouldn't (couldn't?) speak to her. Muttered something and made their escape. As Sheila said, it makes you feel as though you're carrying a disease.

In one frame of mind I can understand and forgive those people; in another I despise them for their weakness and unwitting cruelty.

PEOPLE TRY, BUT THEY JUST DON'T UNDERSTAND

STEPHEN KING

This passage prefaces Stephen King's novella about a thirteen-year-old boy's loss of innocence the summer his older brother is killed in boot camp. It was made into the movie Stand by Me.

from "The Body," in *Different Seasons*

The most important things are the hardest things to say. They are the things you get ashamed of, because words diminish them—words shrink things that seemed limitless when they were in your head to no more than living size when they're brought out. But it's more than that, isn't it? The most important things lie too close to wherever your secret heart is buried, like landmarks to a treasure your enemies would love to steal away. And you may make revelations that cost you dearly only to have people look at you in a funny way, not understanding what you've said at all, or why you thought it was so important that you almost cried while you were saying it. That's the worst, I think. When the secret stays locked within not for want of a teller but for want of an understanding ear.

JAMES RUSSELL LOWELL

Three of James Russell Lowell's children died in childhood. Lowell wrote this poem in 1850 after the death of his second child, Rose. He is responding to a friend who attempts to console him with talk of faith and immortality.

from *The Complete Poetical Works of James Russell Lowell,*
edited by Horace E. Scudder

After the Burial

Yes, faith is a goodly anchor;
    When skies are sweet as a psalm,
At the bows it lolls so stalwart,
    In its bluff, broad-shouldered calm.

And when over breakers to leeward
    The tattered surges are hurled,

It may keep our head to the tempest,
    With its grip on the base of the world.

But, after the shipwreck, tell me
    What help in its iron thews,
Still true to the broken hawser,
    Deep down among sea-weed and ooze ?

In the breaking gulfs of sorrow,
    When the helpless feet stretch out
And find in the deeps of darkness
    No footing so solid as doubt,

Then better one spar of Memory,
    One broken plank of the Past,
That our human heart may cling to,
    Though hopeless of shore at last !

To the spirit its splendid conjectures,
    To the flesh its sweet despair,
Its tears o'er the thin-worn locket
    With its anguish of deathless hair !

Immortal ? I feel it and know it,
    Who doubts it of such as she ?
But that is the pang's very secret, —
    Immortal away from me.

There 's a narrow ridge in the graveyard
    Would scarce stay a child in his race,
But to me and my thought it is wider
    Than the star-sown vague of Space.

Your logic, my friend, is perfect,
    Your moral most drearily true;
But, since the earth clashed on *her* coffin,
    I keep hearing that, and not you.

Console if you will, I can bear it;
    'T is a well-meant alms of breath;
But not all the preaching since Adam
    Has made Death other than Death.

It is pagan; but wait till you feel it, —
　　That jar of our earth, that dull shock
When the ploughshare of deeper passion
　　Tears down to our primitive rock.

Communion in spirit ! Forgive me,
　　But I, who am earthly and weak,
Would give all my incomes from dreamland
　　For a touch of her hand on my cheek.

That little shoe in the corner,
　　So worn and wrinkled and brown,
With its emptiness confutes you,
　　And argues your wisdom down.

GAIL GODWIN

In Godwin's novel, Lily's adult son Theo has killed himself. "If Lily had learned anything these past ten days," writes Godwin, "it was the foolishness of presuming you could dictate someone else's feelings."

from A Southern Family

The things people had said, the letters she had received . . . Why were some just right and others all wrong? That woman who had actually followed her into the kitchen to say, "But at least we know it was God's will." "Do we know that?" Lily had answered coldly. And that poem Peggy Smith from Altar Guild had written out in her elaborate italic script and sent:

Do not stand at my grave and weep.
I am not there, I do not sleep.
I am a thousand winds that blow.
I am the diamond glints on snow . . .

and on and on about how the dead person wasn't really dead, because he was the sunlight on ripened grain and the gentle autumn rain. Peggy Smith had lost a daughter—the girl was driving home from college and skidded off the road—and this poem, Peggy had said in her letter of sympathy, had been a lot of help to her. But it's no help at all to me, Lily had thought. I want Theo to go on being Theo forever, not subsumed into snow and sunshine.

VICTOR HUGO

Three years after his daughter Leopoldine drowned in 1843 (see p. 15), worried friends urged Hugo to get back to his work.

from "Three Years After," in The Poems of Victor Hugo

The humble child God snatched away,
   By her mere loving helped me well;
It was my happiness each day,
   To see her eyes upon me dwell.

Leave me! rest is my sole desire.
   I've ended!—Fate is conqueror.
Why strive you to re-light the fire
   In my sad heart, grief-shadowed o'er?

Still you solicit, and you say,
   I must, for duty, reason, right,
Show the blind multitude the way
   Towards the horizon's waking light.

. . . .

You see the tears run down my cheek,
   And still you urge and hold me wrong,
As by the arm you shake, and seek
   To rouse a man who sleeps too long.

But think what 'tis you do. Ah, woe!
   That angel fair, with locks of gold,
When to your feast you bid me go,
   May in her silent grave be cold.

Wan, pallid, livid, it may be,
   She asks, in her straight bed and still,
"Can Father have forgotten me?
   No longer here?—I am so chill."

What? When I now can scarcely bear
   The memory of my vacant home—
When, wounded, wearied, I despair,
   And seem to hear her saying, "Come."

What? You can wish me to desire,
  Though bowed by blow of sudden fate,
The fame which greets the poet's lyre,
  The shouts which on the champion wait.

TOM CRIDER

When his daughter, Gretchen, a student at Lafayette College, died (see p. 59), Crider found some people's attempts to help beyond comprehension.

from *Give Sorrow Words: A Father's Passage through Grief*

His friend Alan suggests he try something called a Body Harmony treatment. It is supposed to relieve stress and provide other psychological and even spiritual benefits. While he lies on a table, the therapist lifts and holds his arm. Moving the arm slowly in a circle, the therapist asks, "Do you feel Gretchen's presence?" He says, "No." The therapist says, "I do. She's here."

A stranger feels her presence, when her father does not!

On his way out, after an hour or so of this, the therapist follows him to the door, whispering, "It's OK to be happy. It's OK to be happy." . . .

In the health club sauna, Leo is sitting on the upper bench as he comes in. When Leo asks how he's doing, he says, "It's hard, Leo, if you want the truth."

They talk about Leo's new career training people how to love. After a while, Leo gets up to leave, and says, "Gretchen had done what she came here to do, Tom."

"I wish I believed that, but I don't," he says.

"Know this, Tom," Leo says, shaking a finger at him, "It was her time. Her time had come."

He should have told Leo to stuff it.

He doesn't understand how people believe such things. Her time had come? Is there something he lacks, some facility that enables other people to understand what he can't?

REV. WILLIAM SLOANE COFFIN

Ten days after his son Alex died in a car accident, Rev. William Sloane Coffin delivered a provocative sermon on grieving and condolence-giving before his congregation at Riverside Church in New York City. A former chaplain at Williams College and Yale University, as well as a prominent activist for social justice, Coffin is no stranger to the beauty and wisdom of the Bible. But in this excerpt from his sermon, he dares to point out that biblical quoting is not what many parents want or need in their early grief.

from "Alex's Death," in *The Book of Eulogies: A Collection of Memorial Tributes, Poetry, Essays, and Letters of Condolence*, edited by Phyllis Theroux

I mentioned the healing flood of letters. Some of the very best, and easily the worse, came from fellow reverends, a few of whom proved they knew their Bibles better than the human condition. I know all the "right" biblical passages, including "Blessed are those who mourn," and my faith is no house of cards; these passages are true, I know. But the point is this. While the words of the Bible are true, grief renders them unreal. The reality of grief is the absence of God—"My God, my God, why hast thou forsaken me?" The reality of grief is the solitude of pain, the feeling that your heart is in pieces, your mind's a blank, that "there is no joy the world can give like that it takes away" (Lord Byron).

That's why immediately after such a tragedy people must come to your rescue, people who only want to hold your hand, not to quote anybody or even say anything, people who simply bring food and flowers—the basics of beauty and life—people who sign letters simply, "Your brokenhearted sister." In other words, in my intense grief I felt some of my fellow reverends—not many, and none of you, thank God—were using comforting words of Scripture for self-protection, to pretty up a situation whose bleakness they simply couldn't face. But like God herself, Scripture is not around for anyone's protection, just for everyone's unending support.

And that's what hundreds of you understood so beautifully. You gave me what God gives all of us—minimum protection, maximum support. I swear to you, I wouldn't be standing here were I not upheld.

PEOPLE WHO UNDERSTAND ARE TREASURES

ISADORA DUNCAN

In 1913, dancer Isadora Duncan's two young children drowned when a car they were in rolled down an embankment into the Seine. She found refuge with actress Eleanora Duse in Italy.

from *Isadora: The Autobiography of Isadora Duncan*

From then on I lived at Viareggio, finding courage from the radiance of Eleanora's eyes. She used to rock me in her arms, consoling my pain, but not only consoling, for she seemed to take my sorrow to her own breast, and I realised that if I had not been able to bear the society of other people, it was because they all played the comedy of trying to cheer me with forgetfulness. Whereas Eleanora said:

"Tell me about Deirdre and Patrick," and made me repeat to her all their little sayings and ways, and show her their photos, which she kissed and cried over. She never said, "Cease to grieve," but she grieved with me, and, for the first time since their death, I felt I was not alone.

BRET LOTT

"How are you doing?" Ted, a neighbor-friend, courageously asks Hugh not long after his seven-year-old son, Michael, is killed (see p. 20). Hugh, the main character in this novel, answers, but then has a question for Ted.

from *Reed's Beach*

He said, "Do you remember when we took the Staten Island Ferry over?" He paused. "We four. You, me, Gerry and Michael."

He'd said his son's name, let it out in conversation, as slight and unmeasured as any other word that existed.

Ted looked up, silent, and Hugh believed he had broken this moment. . . .

But then Ted seemed to smile, somehow the moon giving in this moment just enough light to illuminate the lines of his face, his mouth moving into a smile.

"We froze our butts off," Ted said, and Hugh saw him slowly shake his head. "And the boys—" He stopped, looked at Hugh.

He said, "Go on."

. . . "The boys were fighting the whole time we were on the ferry." He paused, looked up at Hugh. "You remember that?"

"No," Hugh said, the answer true. He said, "All I remember is waiting at the terminal. On Staten Island.". . .

He said, "What were they fighting about?"

"Nothing," Ted said right away. He was still smiling and shrugged. "Something about hot chocolate, I think. But nothing." He paused. "Kids," he said.

Hugh smiled. He said, "Kids."

"But we froze, all of us," Ted went on, and now his words, Hugh could hear, were speaking their own truth, speaking what he saw: "We froze our butts off walking around South Street Seaport, and then we went over to that Chinese place at Pier 17." He stopped again, and the quiet that came after the warmth of his words seemed too heavy, the silence a weight on them both.

"You don't remember this?" Ted said. "I feel like I'm blabbing."

"You're not," Hugh said and looked at him. "You're not talking too much at all." He paused. He saw them now on the boardwalk at South Street, saw them now hunched in the cold wind, saw the boys bumping into each other on purpose as they walked. They weren't fighting now, he saw, but were just kids, freezing cold on a big adventure. And he saw them, too, at the Chinese place, the four of them sitting at a table near the window, so that they were still cold, and he saw, too, deep bowls of hot and sour soup brought to them, smelled the fragrant steam up off the soup, saw the four of them eating with wide white plastic spoons. All four of them—Michael one of them, Michael alive and breathing and perhaps kicking Gerry's legs beneath the table, Gerry kicking right back, two boys with conspiratorial grins on their faces as they lifted spoon after spoon of soup to their lips, and ate.

But that was as far as he could go, ushered here by Ted's words. He'd been there, could now recall this all, but needed Ted to lead him through this story, through this memory. . . .

He looked at Ted again, said, "I guess I wanted to know one thing. About that day."

"Go ahead," Ted said.

He swallowed. He said, "Did we make it to your office? I mean, did we get up to the Trade Center?"

"Oh, did we," Ted said, and here he was, slowly shaking his head again in the moonlight. "We could see everything, it was so clear. Perfect day, cold and clear. It was like we could just bend down and touch the Statue of Liberty, it was so clear." He stopped, let out a low whistle, astonished, Hugh could see, at what he himself could remember. "Brooklyn, Staten Island. We could see Sandy Hook out past the Verrazano." He paused and gave a small laugh, a sound sharp and foreign and good in the dark. "I think we could see all the way to Asbury Park that day."

Hugh saw it, saw the blue-green water, the deep blue sky and sunlight, the Statue of Liberty close enough to touch. He saw red brick buildings in Brooklyn Heights, saw Fort Jay out on Governor's Island, saw the expanse of steel of the Verrazano Narrows. He saw Jersey, too, the spit of land curling up that was Sandy Hook.

And he saw himself kneeling beside his son, saw himself pointing out each landmark he knew and naming it for the boy, his son smiling and pointing to one landmark after another and asking for more names, Hugh sometimes shrugging, sometimes knowing, Michael nodding and pointing and asking yet again.

He saw his son's eyes taking in the world, saw the way sunlight played into his brown irises to make them glisten like polished stones, and the way sunlight made the whites of his eyes so white there was no word to capture that color.

"I remember," Hugh said.

Ted was quiet, took his hands from his pockets, crossed his arms. He said, "That's good. Because it was a good day."

ANTONYA NELSON

In this short story, Lois receives a phone call from her daughter Gwen's college friend. He was with Gwen just before she died (see p. 119).

from "Mud Season," in *Prairie Schooner* (1989)

"I saw her at the Union," he chose to say. "She was getting a salad and paying a parking ticket." And then he was silent again. "I don't really know why I called," he said after a moment.

"Thank you, anyway," Lois said. "Even if you don't know, I appreciate it." She was crying, but she thought she could sit for a long time saying nothing with this man.

"It's useless," he finally said, "but what I feel like is that if I could take some of your pain, I would."

"You probably have enough already," she said. "Thank you, though."

MARY ANN TAYLOR-HALL

This scene from Taylor-Hall's novel takes place when, almost immobilized by grief after her five-year-old daughter Molly dies (see p. 48), Carrie Marie Mullins calls her mother on the phone. She has "mixed feelings" about her mother's response.

from *Come and Go, Molly Snow*

There's a moment of silence, Mama poised on the brink of some drama, debating with herself. Then she announces, in a breathless rush, like she can't help herself: "Molly's all right, Carrie."

In spite of me, my heavy heart gives a dumb clumsy lurch. It knocks the breath out of me; I lean against the table.

"I was getting ready to call you about it." She takes another gulp of air. "I had a dream," she announces.

I hold on tight to the receiver, so as not to scream at her. "Oh, Christ, Mom!" My eyes sting with tears. I could kill her.

"I came home from work tonight," she goes on, unnoticing, relishing her story, taking her time. "I was just beat, and I sat down on the sofa to watch the news and fell right to sleep and there was little old Molly walking along a beautiful, beautiful path—it went through woods, and then there was a meadow on one side, full of wildflowers. It wasn't like a regular dream—I felt like I was looking through a window at something that was really happening. She was having a wonderful time, Carrie. Looking at everything—strolling, you might say."

Her voice is rushed, but light and elated. It's the elation in it that terrifies me. "She was by herself, but there were lights flitting all around her. It reminded me of Snow White—do you remember when she wakes up and the bluebirds are flying all around her, singing away?" I clench my teeth and roll my eyes upward, for my own benefit. "I *think* it was Snow White," she chatters on. "Anyway, I figured out after a while that the lights were angels, keeping her company and helping her. Oh, I'm glad you called. You must have just felt it, that I had something to tell you."

I hear a kind of low growl coming from the back of my throat.

"I think it was a true vision, Carrie," she confides shyly. "It was so real it woke me up. I wanted to go right back to sleep and see if I could talk to her, but I was too stirred up. That's why I was praying. Saying thank you. She wasn't lonely or sad or lost or anything. She was full of—delight. And busy.

I think she has a crowd of angels *all around* her to watch over her and teach her and help her."

"I hope so, Mom." She's waiting for me to be overjoyed, but I'm thinking, *You idiot.* "It'll probably *take* a crowd," I say in a snappish voice. "And they better be hard as nails. I don't think bluebirds are going to get the job done."

"Oh, don't, Carrie. Don't be sarcastic. It's like throwing my wonderful dream back in my face."

"I'm sorry, Janette. I don't mean to be mean to you. But I think we just dream what we have to." I know I'm cruel, but you have to watch this one. She told me, when it rained the day after the accident, that God had turned on his sprinklers for Molly to play in. She's one-third gloom and one-third unbelievable hokum. It's that other one-third that keeps me hanging on, her generous nature.

"Oh, maybe it *was* a true vision," I say, relenting. "Who am I to say it wasn't? I've had enough visions of my own like that. I just wish they could have spared a couple of those angels to come down here while she was alive. They should have seen she was too much for her mama. If they've got so many that they're swarming around her now. One good, full-time guardian angel, that's all I would have asked." . . .

"Oh, they *all* need one, Carrie!" This is the one-third I like of Mama, the one who goes right on to the next thing and doesn't hold a grudge, except against Daddy. "It's a miracle any child makes it to the age of six. I sure don't know how you did. I thought if a rattler didn't get you, you'd drown. I found you on the fifth step of a ladder when you were eight months old. Just grinning away. Connie and Dexter didn't give me anything like the trouble you did. You took after your father—daring. Some children *are* daring, and if they make it, they usually turn out good. But a lot *don't* make it. And she wasn't too much for you. You were right on top of things."

"Not quite, it looks like," I say, my jaw clenched so it won't tremble. "I feel like she'd still be here if I hadn't been neglectful." I'm surprised by how I can't keep myself from saying this out loud, to *Janette,* of all people, can't keep my voice from choking up when I say it.

"You *weren't* neglectful," she cries, taking up for me—I need it so bad. "You were never neglectful, you were a good mother! You watched her like a hawk. It only took a second, Carrie."

STEPHEN DOBYNS

Both a poet and a novelist, Dobyns makes clear just how unsettling our stories of tragedy can be to the untouched.

from The Bread Loaf Anthology of Contemporary American Poetry,
edited by Robert Pack, Sydney Lea, and Jay Parini

Spider Web

There are stories that unwind themselves as simply
as a ball of string. A man is on a plane between
New York and Denver. He sees his life
as moving along a straight line. Today here,
tomorrow there. The destination is not so
important as the progression itself. During lunch
he talks to the woman seated beside him.
She is from Baltimore, perhaps twenty years older.
It turns out she has had two children killed
by drunk drivers, two incidents fifteen
years apart. At first I wanted to die everyday,
she says, now I only want to die now and then.
Again and again, she tries to make her life
move forward in a straight line but it keeps
curving back to those two deaths, curves back
like a fishhook stuck through her gut. I guess
I'm lucky, she says, I have other children left.
They discuss books, horses; they talk about
different cities but each conversation keeps
returning to the fact of those deaths, as if
each conversation were a fall from a roof
and those two deaths were the ground itself—
a son and daughter, one five, one fourteen.
The plane lands, they separate. The man goes off
to his various meetings, but for several days
whenever he's at dinner or sitting around
in the evening, he says to whomever he is with,
You know, I met the saddest woman on the plane.
But he can't get it right, can't decide whether

she is sad or brave or what, can't describe
how the woman herself fought to keep the subject
straight, keep it from bending back to the fact
of the dead children, and then how she would
collapse and weep, then curse herself and
go at it again. After a week or so, the man
completes his work and returns home. Once more
he gathers up the threads of his life.
It's spring. The man works in his garden,
repairs all that is broken around his house.
He thinks of how a spider makes its web,
how the web is torn by people with brooms,
insects, rapacious birds; how the spider
rebuilds and rebuilds, until the wind
takes the web and breaks it and flicks it
into heaven's blue and innocent immensity.

ALEXANDER WOOLLCOTT

Attractive, intelligent, and wealthy, Gerald and Sara Murphy were the golden couple of the Jazz Age. They counted among their close friends many of the great writers of their time. F. Scott Fitzgerald even modeled the glamorous Dick and Nicole Diver after them in Tender is the Night. *Years later, the Murphys again became literary models. But ironically, tragedy, not glamour, proved the inspiration this time. The Murphys' loss of both sons prompted their friend Archibald MacLeish to write* J.B., *a modern retelling of the biblical book of Job (see p. 121). This letter from Alexander Woollcott, well-known radio broadcaster, theater critic, and columnist for* The New Yorker, *was written two days after young Patrick Muphy's death from tuberculosis.*

from *Letters from the Lost Generation:*
Gerald and Sara Murphy and Friends, edited by Linda Patterson Miller

Alexander Woollcott to Sara Murphy,
New York, 1 February [1937]

Dear Sara
When I was talking to Saranac on Saturday—was it only Saturday?—
Alice Lee [Myers] gave me your message to the effect that you were glad I

had come up. Sara, I have no words emphatic enough to tell you how glad *I* am, how thankful I am, that I made that trip to Saranac early in December. It scares me—it makes me seasick—when I think how easily I might have postponed that week-end, how casually I might have gone off instead to some flossy engagement I thought important.

I count it one of the great privileges of my life to have known Patrick— just as I am thankful I knew Father Duffy and Mrs. Fiske and that I know and can sometimes go to see Edward Sheldon. I hoard every memory I have of Patrick. I suppose that really, in some confused, unconfessed, frightened way, I am counting on him to put in a good word for me on Judgment Day, or—if thats asking too much—I'm planning myself to put forth in my defence before the throne of grace the fact that anyway Patrick thought well of me. It ought to count. I think it ought to count.

Sara, among the few things I'm sure of is this—as long as I live, as long as I remember anything at all, I shall remember Patrick—not hazily, no perfume growing fainter and fainter with time, no mere formless glow like the setting sun shining on the snow, but sharp and clear forever, like some precise and perfect masterpiece, a Vermeer, changeless as long as paint and canvas last. And years from now, Sara, when you are old and I am so feeble I can just about walk and chance brings us together in some town, you will be glad to see me and wont even have to talk to me because you'll know without any word from me that I'm still thinking of Patrick with undiminished respect—indeed that I cannot, cannot forget him.

A.W.

OLD FRIENDS CAN BE PAINFUL REMINDERS

JUDITH GUEST

Conrad, unlike his brother Buck, survives a boating accident in Guest's novel (see p. 99). He is taken off guard when Lazenby, a friend of both boys, confronts him after school.

from *Ordinary People*

"What is it with you, man? We've been friends for a long time—"

"Laze," he says, "we're still friends."

"Are we?" Lazenby's voice is flat, strained. "Look, I don't know why you want to be alone in this, but I wouldn't shit you, man. I miss him, too."

A blow he is not expecting at all. He concentrates on the cold bunching of metal, his car keys under his hand, against his thigh. He looks out at the bare, black-limbed trees.

"I can't help it," he says. "It hurts too much to be around you."

10

A Fire in the Mind: Memories, Dreams, Fantasies

For months after Allie was killed, I had inertia as far as housekeeping was concerned. The house was like a tomb without Allie, so why bother?

I felt like Miss Havisham in Charles Dickens's *Great Expectations.* Her bridegroom jilted her on her wedding day and life stopped. The wedding feast remained on the table covered with spiderwebs and dust. Mice inhabited the remains of the wedding cake. Miss Havisham grew withered and old, still wearing her wedding gown and veil. Inside, I was Miss Havisham!

Then, about a year and a half after he died, a brilliant fall day with snap in the air came along. Fall always meant the beginning of school to me—the promise of a fresh start. Allie should have been starting college that fall. I read in the paper that Vice President Dan Quayle's son was entering Lehigh and another wave of grief crashed over me. Allie and I visited Lehigh on our only college trip.

Although Allie wasn't too interested in Lehigh (he said the hills were too steep), in my imaginary script for the rest of his life, I had him going to Lehigh. I could see us loading the car, unloading and helping him settle in to his dorm, kissing him on a certain soft spot near his ear, and leaving him, all of us filled with pride and high hopes. *Dan Quayle, do you have any idea how lucky you are that you got to go through this with your son? What I wouldn't give for the pleasure of seeing my son through this exciting phase of life!*

In spite of this, the fall weather stirred some ancient sap in me, and I felt the urge to clean and set my house in order. I did not realize what an ordeal it would turn out to be.

I sorted out a pile of old magazines in the den and found the June 1991 issue of *Guitar.* Allie bought it. He was killed May 31—he never even lived in June. How unbelievable! How could he have done such a mundane thing as buy this magazine when catastrophe loomed before us? How could we all have been so oblivious? Did Allie ever read this magazine? How can I throw it out when he will never bring another issue of *Guitar* into our home? Back on the rack it went. Better to live like Miss Havisham!

Finishing my bedroom, I recalled that this was the day of the Princeton Sports Store Ski Swap. I planned to bring over some old ski equipment of mine and Allie's. I had already decided that I would not part with the new boots I bought for his last Christmas (*damn it, Allie, you* promised *you'd wear them for years*), but I needed to clean out the basement and some other boy might want his previous boots. I could handle giving them away.

I put on my sunglasses, threw the stuff in the car, and headed down to Princeton. As usual, it was hot and crowded at the Swap. Parents and kids were milling around buying and selling. Everyone was sweaty. Thermal clothing and heavy boots were ludicrous. Sonny, the owner, bustled about. He nodded recognition. I'd been there so many times before with Allie.

Maybe, if I moved fast and kept my sunglasses on, I could avoid the pain. But I couldn't fool my own mind. The scene and Allie's gray Caber boots triggered image after image. Allie and I buying the boots from a cute salesman; lugging the boots with all the other equipment through parking lots of ski areas; Allie and Ben racing down the slopes; Peter grumbling about the boots cluttering our motel room. The boots were stained on the top where Allie's sweat-soaked red ski socks ran when we skied in Vermont during a freak heat wave.

By the time I got home, I was immobilized by pain. I longed for Allie so ferociously I could do nothing but sit in my living room and stare into space the rest of the afternoon. Another piece of my heart was hacked off with the ski boots. Downstairs was a basement full of toys, clothes, and books to sort and dispose of. And down the hall, Allie's room. I couldn't let someone else clean them out. I coveted the memories too much. But how would I bear the pain?

MARY

From the start, I knew that Jake, who had already left me, would drift even farther away, so that like a boat in mist, all I'd see would be his outline. I'd learned this after my father died. So important in my life, my dad, and shockingly early his face went out of focus; like there was Vaseline on the camera lens. How can this be? Faces I've studied as intently as any portrait artist—my father's and my son's—how is it that I can no longer see them clearly? In the end it may be a blessing, but not one I asked for.

And the *voices* of the dead: they don't fade, they disappear. I can *see* Jake at five and a half, clip-on bow tie askew, his chest puffed out, his thumbs jauntily pulling at his suspenders, smirking and surprising us with a TV replay: "Hi. I'm George Bush." Or at the beach, uncharacteristically crawling into the porch hammock midafternoon and explaining, "I'm one tired old moose." I can see him, but I can't hear him. And why this should bother me, since I no longer *have* him, I can't tell you. But it does.

Jake was smitten with Peter Pan; the book first, then the filmed version of the Broadway hit with Mary Martin. A friend gave it to us, and he watched it dozens of times. The day before he was killed, we were winding up a summer visit with his grandmother in Virginia. We went to a lake in a nearby state park. It was a weekday and only a few people, mainly mothers and young children, were on the beach. Later in the afternoon, though, two male college-age camp counselors arrived with a pack of boisterous high school boys; boys with special behavioral problems, it turned out. But they were sweet with Jake, playing ball and Frisbee before fleeing to the deep water. Taking no offense, Jake grabbed his inner tube and went back in himself.

On the beach, his grandmother, his sister, Hollis, and I sat savoring the bittersweet taste of this late August day, watching skinny Jake in the goofy red Speedo cap he had to wear to protect ear shunts. Suddenly he burst out of the water, joyfully singing, "Oh, my mysterious lady, from whence have you come?" The high school boys and their counselors stopped dead, clearly unversed in Captain Hook's lines. Astonished, they laughed and shook their heads. Crazy kid. Jake beamed. He couldn't have been happier.

I love that memory.

And I love it for several reasons. I love it because it's so funny, I can bear it. I love it because it epitomizes the all-boy, mischievous performer that Jake was at almost six years old. But mostly I love it because he's happy.

He's not a little boy wondering what's happened to him and where are we and when is he going to see us again? He's happy.

My brain sternly tells me that Jake lives on only in memory—mine, Tom's, Hollis's, and a few others'. All else is wishful thinking. But my heart is dismissive of such talk and long ago took Jake to Neverland, where he gleefully runs with other Lost Boys who never grew up. It's terribly sentimental, I know, but it's damn comforting.

In the movie Jake watched so often, Captain Hook tries to engage his archenemy in a ship duel, and Peter Pan just laughs and flies away. *What art thou? What sort of being are you?* Hook asks in exasperation. *I am youth,* answers Peter. *I am joy. I am freedom.* I like to think of our little Peter Pan as that high-spirited and happy. Desperate, infantile drivel? Yes, certainly. But why not? If I can call back some of my childish wonder, if I can pretend that *believing,* as Tinkerbell once told us, is all it takes, then who is hurt? Jake in Neverland comforts me, when comfort is in short supply.

Still, lose a child and you will find even your own fantasies fail you. They can turn as bittersweet as that late August afternoon by the lake. Neverland is the best place I've found for Jake. But sometimes, not always, I hear echoes at my window: *You won't forget me, Peter, will you?* Wendy called to him. Peter promised, and then he flew away.

ANNE

OUR MINDS CAN'T GRASP THAT OUR CHILDREN ARE GONE

WILLIAM STAFFORD

William Stafford spent most of his adult life teaching at Lewis and Clark College in Oregon and was poet laureate of that state for several years. His poetry awards are numerous. He also lost a son, Bret.

from Passwords: A Program of Words

For a Lost Child

What happens is, the kind of snow that sweeps
Wyoming comes down while I'm asleep. Dawn
finds our sleeping bag but you are gone.
Nowhere now, you call through every storm,
a voice that wanders without a home.

Across bridges that used to find a shore
you pass, and along shadows of trees that fell
before you were born. You are a memory
too strong to leave this world that slips away
even as its precious time goes on.

I glimpse you often, faithful to every country
we ever found, a bright shadow the sun
forgot one day. On a map of Spain
I find your note left from a trip that year
our family traveled: "Daddy, we could meet here."

Going On

On the hollow night a small hand
taps just once. It is our child,
whose eyes reflected me, a tiny mote
but in those eyes a giant man.
A heart beats, and all the world
surges in my breast. Then, the stillest
way a hand can be and still be,
it lies there in mine.

Easy world, you gave it once—
please quietly welcome it back,
that hand.

OSCAR HIJUELOS

From the author of The Mambo Kings Play Songs of Love *comes this most unsentimental of Christmas stories. "No warm, fuzzy epiphany," Hijuelos admits. "There is an element of darkness and pain, of darkness lurching toward the light." The darkness comes with the murder of Mr. Ives' seventeen-year-old son, Robert, by a teenage street thug.*

from Mr. Ives' Christmas

That had all happened long ago, and a few weeks before another Christmas Ives awoke in the bedroom of his apartment on Ninety-third Street as a much older man and recalled how for years he would get up for work at seven in the morning, and swear that he could hear his son, Robert, whistling the theme to *The Andy Griffith Show* in the hallway, as he used to in the days when he delivered newspapers. Ives would dress, half expecting to find the boy in the hall, ready to start his morning's work regardless of the weather; or he would hear Bach sung faintly through his door, or find one of the books his son had been reading in the living room, left casually open on the couch as if he had just been reading it again. And although he would think, "Caroline [his daughter]," another part of him imagined his boy, nostalgic for the habits of this life, materializing from the hereafter.

WE CHERISH MEMORIES

RANDALL JARRELL

Jarrell's sister died in infancy before he was born. The motif of a lost sibling, particularly a sister, frequently appears in his poetry. This poem was inspired by a dream his wife had about her adult daughter and a girl who had died.

from *Selected Poems*, edited by William H. Pritchard

The Lost Children

Two little girls, one fair, one dark,
One alive, one dead, are running hand in hand
Through a sunny house. The two are dressed
In red and white gingham, with puffed sleeves and sashes.
They run away from me . . . But I am happy;
When I wake I feel no sadness, only delight.
I've seen them again, and I am comforted
That, somewhere, they still are.

It is strange
To carry inside you someone else's body;
To know it before it's born;
To see at last that it's a boy or girl, and perfect;
To bathe it and dress it; to watch it
Nurse at your breast, till you almost know it
Better than you know yourself—better than it knows itself.
You own it as you made it.
You are the authority upon it.

But as the child learns
To take care of herself, you know her less.
Her accidents, adventures are her own,
You lose track of them. Still, you know more
About her than anyone *except* her.

Little by little the child in her dies.
You say, "I have lost a child, but gained a friend."
You feel yourself gradually discarded.

She argues with you or ignores you
Or is kind to you. She who begged to follow you
Anywhere, just so long as it was you,
Finds follow the leader no more fun.
She makes few demands; you are grateful for the few.

The young person who writes once a week
Is the authority upon herself.
She sits in my living room and shows her husband
My albums of her as a child. He enjoys them
And makes fun of them. I look too
And I realize the girl in the matching blue
Mother-and-daughter dress, the fair one carrying
The tin lunch box with the half-pint thermos bottle
Or training her pet duck to go down the slide
Is lost just as the dark one, who is dead, is lost.
But the world in which the two wear their flared coats
And the hats that match, exists so uncannily
That, after I've seen its pictures for an hour,
I believe in it: the bandage coming loose
One has in the picture of the other's birthday,
The castles they are building, at the beach for asthma.
I look at them and all the old sure knowledge
Floods over me, when I put the album down
I keep saying inside: "I *did* know those children.
I braided those braids. I was driving the car
The day that she stepped in the can of grease
We were taking to the butcher for our ration points.
I *know* those children. I know all about them.
Where are they?"

I stare at her and try to see some sign
Of the child she was. I can't believe there isn't any.
I tell her foolishly, pointing at the picture,
That I keep wondering where she is.
She tells me, "Here I am."
                                        Yes, and the other
Isn't dead, but has everlasting life . . .

The girl from next door, the borrowed child,
Said to me the other day, "You like children so much,
Don't you want to have some of your own?"
I couldn't believe that she could say it.
I thought: "Surely you can look at me and see them."

When I see them in my dreams I feel such joy.
If I could dream of them every night!

When I think of my dream of the little girls
It's as if we were playing hide-and-seek.
The dark one
Looks at me longingly, and disappears;
The fair one stays in sight, just out of reach
No matter where I reach. I am tired
As a mother who's played all day, some rainy day.
I don't want to play it any more, I don't want to,
But the child keeps on playing, so I play.

ANNE TYLER

In Tyler's novel, Macon's sister and brothers want him to give away his unmanageable dog, Edward, but Macon resists. He can't explain that he is attached to the dog because the dog is a link to his dead son, Ethan (see pp. 80 and 208).

from The Accidental Tourist

"Rose?" Macon said. "It seems Edward's given me a little sort of nip."

She turned, and Charles and Porter stopped work to examine the hand he held out. It was hurting him by now—a deep, stinging pain. "Oh, Macon!" Rose cried. She came down off the stepstool. "How did it happen?"

"It was an accident, that's all. But I think I need an antiseptic."

"You need a tetanus shot, too," Charles told him.

"You need to get rid of that dog," Porter said.

They looked at Edward. He grinned up at them nervously.

"He didn't mean any harm," Macon said.

"Takes off your hand at the elbow and he means no harm? You should get rid of him, I tell you."

"See, I can't," Macon said.

"Why not?"

"Well, see . . ."

They waited.

"You know I don't mind the cat," Rose said. "But Edward is so disrup-
tive, Macon. Every day he gets more and more out of control."

"Maybe you could give him to someone who wants a guard dog,"
Charles said.

"A service station," Rose suggested. She took a roll of gauze from
a drawer.

"Oh, never," Macon said. He sat where she pointed, in a chair at the
kitchen table. He propped his crutches in the corner. "Edward alone in some
Exxon? He'd be wretched."

Rose swabbed Mercurochrome on his hand. It looked bruised; each
puncture mark was puffing and turning blue.

"He's used to sleeping with me," Macon told her. "He's never been alone
in his life."

Besides, Edward wasn't a bad dog at heart—only a little unruly. He was
sympathetic and he cared about Macon and plodded after him wherever he
went. There was a furrowed W on his forehead that gave him a look of concern. His large, pointed, velvety ears seemed more expressive than other
dogs' ears; when he was happy they stuck straight out at either side of his
head like airplane wings. His smell was unexpectedly pleasant—the sweet-
ish smell a favorite sweater takes on when it's been folded away in a drawer
unwashed.

And he'd been Ethan's.

Once upon a time Ethan had brushed him, bathed him, wrestled on the
floor with him; and when Edward stopped to paw at one ear Ethan would
ask, with the soberest courtesy, "Oh, may I scratch that for you?" The two
of them watched daily at the window for the afternoon paper, and the instant it arrived Ethan sent Edward bounding out to fetch it—hind legs meeting front legs, heels kicking up joyfully. Edward would pause after he got the
paper in his mouth and look around him, as if hoping to be noticed, and
then he'd swagger back all bustling and self-important and pause again at the
front hall mirror to admire the figure he cut. "Conceited," Ethan would say
fondly. Ethan picked up a tennis ball to throw and Edward grew so excited
that he wagged his whole hind end. Ethan took Edward outside with a soccer ball and when Edward got carried away—tearing about and shouldering

the ball into a hedge and growling ferociously—Ethan's laugh rang out so high and clear, such a buoyant sound floating through the air on a summer evening.

"I just can't," Macon said.

There was a silence.

**BUT MEMORIES ARE POOR SUBSTITUTES—
AND THEY DO FADE**

SHELLY WAGNER

Keeping memories and souvenirs of Andrew vivid is a losing battle for bereaved mother Shelly Wagner (see p. 207).

from *The Andrew Poems*

Faded

After the funeral
I went to the cemetery
and pulled each blossom off its stem
the way you picked flowers,
bringing me a bouquet
cupped in the palm of your hand.
I left at the grave
wreaths of barren stems,
then buried the dining room table
with petals,
trying to dry them, preserve them.
I still have them
but they are faded.

Your uncle framed six of your drawings,
the smiling clowns with your trademark eyelashes:
straight lines with tiny circles on each tip.
You used every magic marker,
each eyelash was a different hue.
They were vibrant, but he hung your pictures

near a window. The lashes and smiles
disappeared in the sunlight.

Your brother and I noticed
every blond little boy.
It was a game we played:
looking for hair like yours,
a head shaped like yours,
anything like yours
but I knew the game was over
when he asked,
"Mom, when you close your eyes,
can you still see him?"

Someone offering comfort said,
"This will pass."
I recoiled like a slapped child,
fearing if the grief were to fade,
I would be left with nothing.

NORMAN MACLEAN

On August 5, 1949, fifteen Smokejumpers—an elite group of young fire-
fighters in the United States Forest Service—dropped by parachute into
Mann Gulch, Montana, to fight a small forest fire. A catastrophic collision
of fire, clouds, and wind caused a "blow up," surrounding the firefighters
in flames. Less than an hour after they were dropped, all except three were
dead or mortally wounded. Norman Maclean was haunted by this event.
He himself worked for the U.S. Forest Service in his youth and also suffered
the death of his brother, which he wrote about in A River Runs Through
It *(see p. 287). In 1977, at the age of seventy-four, Maclean began work on*
a book about the fire which was published posthumously in 1992. Here
Maclean reflects upon the families' silence in the aftermath of the fire.

from *Young Men and Fire*

The reasons why parents, relatives, and close friends hoped for silence are
naturally very different from the government's. The Forest Service sought
silence; the parents were reduced to it, although in sad ways they may also
have sought it. On the whole, they were not people of means and could not

afford to appeal their case. . . . Most important of all probably is the secrecy of the grief and moral bewilderment suffered at the death of one of ourselves who was young, had a special flair, a special daring, a special disregard for death, who seemed, both to himself and to us, to be spared from death, especially from death leaving behind no explanation of itself either as a sequence of events or as a moral occurrence in what-kind-of-a-universe-is-this-anyway. It is the frightened and recessive grief suffered for one whom you hoped neither death nor anything evil would dare touch. Afterwards, you live in fear that something might alter your memory of him and of all other things. I should know.

ROBB FORMAN DEW

This excerpt from Dew's novel about the impact of the death of a child on a family (see pp. 10 and 131) illustrates the tension most bereaved parents feel between the desire to hold on to the lost child and the inevitability of letting go.

from *Fortunate Lives*

His son's death would be an event that crossed Martin Howell's mind at least once every day of his life. On this mild June day, Martin walked along the crest of Bell's Hill and looked down at the village that lay across the valley and spread up the first rise of the opposing mountains, and felt a curious sense of homesickness for West Bradford, even though he was within it. He often experienced this unquenched yearning, and he had learned to hold it at bay, not to investigate it too carefully. It was a familiar state of mind that, in its vague manifestation, was really no more than a longing still to be held innocently within the years before his son died. . . .

. . . The notion of only *remembering* his second child was horrible to Martin. It would be as painful to him as looking though old photographs, which only emphasized the loss of the tangible person each time he held before him a flat, brittle approximation of the image of the boy his son had been.

Martin had never let go of the idea of a continuing association with Toby. . . . He recognized that he had at last relinquished it. Martin was forty-five years old, and he felt terrifyingly disburdened. His father was dead, and his mother was failing. His oldest son was an adult, his daughter was growing increasingly aloof, and he and Dinah would soon be all that the other had left. It was too much weight to lose, all that.

He was afraid to be stripped so lean, to be attenuated, thinned, and chilled in the encroaching solitude. Martin sagged back against the chair, exhausted, as the determined tension of holding on to Toby dissipated. There was nothing left at the moment but sorrow and ashy regret.

JILL KER CONWAY

Having already lost her father, Conway knew immediately what she was facing when she was told her older brother had been killed (see p. 139).

from The Road from Coorain

This time I knew no effort at committing a loved face or voice to memory could arrest the passage of time. There would be a time when I couldn't recall his voice and his laugh at will. I might live out a large part of my life without the laughter and the joy he brought into it. As I took in the facts and imagined the battered thatch of golden hair, I felt a sharp physical loss, as though my own body were mutilated.

TOO YOUNG FOR MEMORIES

THOMAS LYNCH

"Every year I bury a couple hundred of my townspeople" is how Lynch, a poet and funeral director, begins his book. Understandably, spending a lifetime between "the living and the living who have died" has both informed and shaped his life.

from The Undertaking: Life Studies from the Dismal Trade

I would sit with the moms and dads of these [sudden infant death syndrome] babies—dead of no discernible cause—they simply forgot to breathe, trying to make some sense of all of it. The fathers, used to protecting and paying, felt helpless. The mothers seemed to carry a pain in their innards that made them appear breakable. The overwhelming message on their faces was that nothing mattered anymore, nothing. We would arrange little wakes and graveside services, order in the tiny caskets with the reversible interiors of pink and blue, dust off the "baby bier" on which the casket would rest during the visitation, and shrink all the customs and accouterments to fit this hurt.

When we bury the old, we bury the known past, the past we imagine sometimes better than it was, but the past all the same, a portion of which we inhabited. Memory is the overwhelming theme, the eventual comfort.

But burying infants, we bury the future, unwieldy and unknown, full of promise and possibilities, outcomes punctuated by our rosy hopes. The grief has no borders, no limits, no known ends, and the little infant graves that edge the corners and fencerows of every cemetery are never quite enough to contain that grief. Some sadnesses are permanent. Dead babies do not give us memories. They give us dreams.

ALWAYS THE PRESENCE OF AN ABSENCE

LAURA KALPAKIAN

In this short story, all three of Mrs. Manila Dance's sons left St. Elmo, California, to serve their country in World War II. Only two came home. Her youngest, Ben, was killed in the battle for the Philippines, ironically in Manila itself. As the decades pass, Manila comes to be known as the "crazy lady of Guadalupe Street," where she isolates herself, clinging to her memories and dreams of the son who did not return.

from "The Battle of Manila," in *Dark Continent and Other Stories*

It's a new dream. Not real new, but since Christmas, maybe, or some holiday like that. Before, I only dreamed of Ben little, running up these steps and falling and hurting his knee and his little arms around my neck while I carry him into the house and wash the blood and mud off him, my lips against his sweet cheek. Or little Ben in the bathwater taking the suds from his hair and putting them on his chin and saying to me, ho ho ho, like he was Santy Claus. Or little Ben all dressed up to be a pirate on Halloween and coming into the kitchen where I am making popcorn balls, coming up behind me and saying "Boo!" and scaring me out of my wits. But in this new dream, I am in the middle of the amphibious assault on Manila Bay. The fighting is going on all around me, but it don't notice me and I don't pay no mind to the shocks and shells, the blast and shriek all around while I am looking for my son. I am in my old dress like the one I got on now and my old green checked apron that's wore through here and there and I kneel in the mud beside a body I know is Ben. I pull him into my lap and turn him over slowly. The first few times I have this dream, that's all I do: just kneel and turn him over, glad to see his face is only muddy, no blood or nothing. I am glad they have not shot up his face. But lately in my dream I find fresh water from somewheres and I bathe that mud from his face and I am so happy that with the mud washed off, it is still perfect.

Maybe Ben didn't die in the mud, but that's the way I dream it, so that's how it is, even if that ain't how it was. I rock on this porch and suck on the ice and wait for the dream to come get me, even though I can hear the dog snuffling and kids' voices somewheres, kids up to no good, no doubt, and the foxtails rasping against one another and the weight of this honeysuckle vine sagging down on the porch and pretty soon I don't hear no kids or dog, nor nothing but the fighting going on all around me in Manila Bay and I scrape the mud from my son's beautiful young face, his nice tanned skin and fine mouth, his sandy colored hair and I bathe his closed eyes with fresh water. I kiss his eyes.

After a time the sun squints under the tin roof and lights up my eyelids bright and I know it's time to quit the dream and go in and get supper for me and this old dog. I heave my bones out of the rocker and the dog follows me to the kitchen. I don't worry about losing the dream. It will come back and it don't scare me in the least because I know it means I have accepted Ben's death and God's will and I am not fighting God any longer.

Ben's death near killed me. They said I was wild with grief. They said they couldn't figure it because I had took Hank's [her husband] death so well. Well, of course I did. Hank and me, we had our good times, we had our family and our laughs and our cries and a few beers after the boys were abed, our days on this porch, our nights in that old bed for nearly twenty-five years and always, even in the worst of the Depression, Hank always had work with the railroad and our boys never knew the cramp of hunger in the gut. Me and Hank, we had all of that, but Ben was only twenty-two. Ben had nothing unless you count that slut Connie, which I don't.

I didn't always think she was a slut. I used to like her. A pretty girl. Plump and pink and blue-eyed and mad for Ben. She set her cap for him and she went after him and if Connie Frett had been my daughter, I'd have tanned her hide before I'd let her run after a boy like that, but she got him. They was in love and they couldn't keep their eyes off one another—or their hands neither is my guess. After Ben died I kept watch on Connie Frett, hoping I'd see her sprout a big belly, but I told myself it wouldn't be Ben's baby anyway. He had been gone too long. But Connie was a good girl in her way and after Ben died, she couldn't do enough for me. She was over here all the time, like we had to be together because we was the only ones who loved Ben that much. I shared her grief, but I couldn't let her share mine. She and me, we'd come out on this porch in the evenings and sit on the steps together and I'd say, thank you for cooking supper, Connie, and for cleaning up, or thank you for sweeping the porch and dusting up the place, Connie. And then she'd put her head in my lap and weep and I'd pat her back. We'd stay that way for a long time, but I couldn't let her share my grief. That was all my very own. . . .

. . . Will and Archie [her older sons] are getting old! I wonder why I never noticed it in the flesh. Then I say to myself: Manila, it's because you never much look at them in the flesh. But I think on them now, think on them hard, on what they look like now. Will's hair is all pepper and salt and he's got one more chin than God gave him. Archie's hair clings alongside his ears, but it has deserted the top of his head and Archie has a paunch. Will and Archie never was no beauties (and their children ditto and their wives the same), but I had never before noticed that they are getting old.

I reach down and pick up Ben's pictures and set them on the piano, first the football one and then high school graduation and then Ben in his uniform. I touch his beautiful young face. Ben will never grow old, Ben will never be bald or have a paunch or gray hair. Everyone else will change, but not Ben. I pick up the uniform picture and press it to me, but I have to sit down at the piano bench because I get dizzy when I think how it's been ten years since Roosevelt died, since all the boys come home. I get weak when I think how pretty soon everyone will forget all about the boys that didn't come home. No one will remember them. They won't have children to look like them. The dead don't have no law offices with their names on shingles, don't have their pictures in the paper cutting ribbons for new stores. The boys that didn't come home don't have friends and families and boys of their own who will go to high school and court girls in yellow cotton dresses with gardenias in their hair. Ben won't have none of that. Ever. I hold Ben's picture but I won't cry because I have accepted his death and God's will. I hear a voice come into my ear, steady as the drone of a gnat. *Ben has you, Manila. You're all Ben's got, Manila. Ben and you will live in this house till you die.* I start to cry then and the dog comes over and rubs against my bandaged leg. He thinks I am crying for Ben's death, but I have accepted Ben's death. I am crying because Ben won't have no life. I am crying because I am all the life Ben has and he deserves better than me. I am crying because I know when I die, Ben will die too. He will stay forever young and beautiful and die when

I do and no one will ever know he once lived. No one will remember how he filled my arms with his baby body, how he said ho ho ho in the bathwater and Boo at Halloween, that he brought in the newspaper or teased me for the cherries on my hat, that he grinned at Connie Frett while he sat on this piano bench. I slide to the floor with the dog. I cry into his dog smell and promise Ben that when I die they'll put Ben's name on the stone too. Ben don't have no stone in St. Elmo. Ben's buried in the Philippines, but he won't die till I do. Ben Dance 1923–1945, Manila Dance, 1898 to whenever she dies. Ben and Manila, they died together, knee deep in the mud and blood and smoke and stink of battle, the last battle of Manila, the one they fought in St. Elmo, California.

LOUISA MAY ALCOTT

When she wrote Little Women, *Alcott drew heavily on her own family. Her sister Elizabeth died in late childhood, as does Beth in the novel. The following scene occurs the first time the March family is together after Beth's death. Amy has just returned from Europe with Laurie, her new husband, a close friend of the girls.*

from *Little Women*

"We must have our sing, in the good old way, for we are all together again once more," said Jo, feeling that a good shout would be a safe and pleasant vent for the jubilant emotions of her soul.

They were not *all* there. But no one found the words thoughtless or un-true; for Beth still seemed among them, a peaceful presence, invisible, but dearer than ever, since death could not break the household league that love made indissoluble. The little chair stood in its old place; the tidy basket, with the bit of work she left unfinished when the needle grew "so heavy," was still on its accustomed shelf; the beloved instrument, seldom touched now, had not been moved; and above it Beth's face, serene and smiling, as in the early days, looked down upon them, seeming to say, "Be happy. I am here."

"Play something, Amy. Let them hear how much you have improved," said Laurie, with pardonable pride in his promising pupil.

But Amy whispered, with full eyes, as she twirled the faded stool,—

"Not to-night, dear. I can't show off to-night."

But she did show something better than brilliancy or skill; for she sung Beth's songs with a tender music in her voice which the best master could

---

not have taught, and touched the listeners' hearts with a sweeter power than any other inspiration could have given her. The room was very still, when the clear voice failed suddenly at the last line of Beth's favorite hymn. It was hard to say,—

> "Earth hath no sorrow that heaven cannot heal;"

and Amy leaned against her husband, who stood behind her, feeling that her welcome home was not quite perfect without Beth's kiss.

DREAMS AND FANTASIES BRING THEM TO LIFE

RABINDRANATH TAGORE

In 1913, Indian poet, philosopher, and novelist Rabindranath Tagore was the first Asian to receive the Nobel Prize for literature. His life was marked by numerous untimely deaths: his mother, sister-in-law, and devoted wife, Nalini, all died young women. Nine months after Nalini died, Rani, their thirteen-year-old daughter, died. Five years later Tagore's youngest son, Samindranath, died of cholera.

from Collected Poems and Plays of Rabindranath Tagore

The Recall

The night was dark when she went away, and they slept.

The night is dark now, and I call for her, "Come back, my darling; the world is asleep; and no one would know, if you came for a moment while stars are gazing at stars."

She went away when the trees were in bud and the spring was young.

Now the flowers are in high bloom and I call, "Come back, my darling. The children gather and scatter flowers in reckless sport. And if you come and take one little blossom no one will miss it."

Those that used to play are playing still, so spendthrift is life.

I listen to their chatter and call, "Come back, my darling, for mother's heart is full to the brim with love, and if you come to snatch only one little kiss from her no one will grudge it."

C Y N T H I A   O Z I C K

For many, the Holocaust is the ultimate reference point for measuring human suffering and horror. No one knows for sure how many of the eleven million Jews and non-Jews exterminated by the Nazis were children, but there were millions. Ozick's novella The Shawl *is about one such child. Conceived when her mother, Rosa, was raped by a Nazi and born in a concentration camp, Magda survives while hidden in her mother's shawl. As long as she has the shawl, Magda will keep quiet and still, and therefore safe. When Rosa's niece, Stella, filches the shawl, Magda toddles into the camp yard and is murdered by a guard. More than thirty years later, alone and half-crazed in Miami, Rosa still revolves her life around Magda. Visions of Magda are conjured up when Stella sends the shawl to Rosa from New York City.*

from *The Shawl*

Magda sprang to life. Rosa took the shawl and put it over the knob of the receiver: it was like a little doll's head then. She kissed it. . . . The whole room was full of Magda: she was like a butterfly, in this corner and in that corner, all at once. Rosa waited to see what age Magda was going to be: how nice, a girl of sixteen; girls in their bloom move so swiftly that their blouses and skirts balloon; they are always butterflies at sixteen. There was Magda, all in flower. She was wearing one of Rosa's dresses from high school. Rosa was glad: it was the sky-colored dress, a middling blue with black buttons seemingly made of round chips of coal, like the unlit shards of stars. Persky [a retired button manufacturer courting Rosa] could never have been acquainted with buttons like that, they were so black and so sparkling; original, with irregular facets like bits of true coal from a vein in the earth or some other planet. Magda's hair was still as yellow as buttercups, and so slippery and fine that her two barrettes, in the shape of cornets, kept sliding down toward the sides of her chin—that chin which was the marvel of her face; with a different kind of chin it would have been a much less explicit face. The jaw was ever so slightly too long, a deepened oval, so that her mouth, especially the lower lip, was not crowded but rather made a definite mark in the middle of spaciousness. Consequently the mouth seemed as significant as a body arrested in orbit, and Magda's sky-filled eyes, nearly rectangular at the corners, were like two obeisant satellites. Magda could be seen with great clarity. She had begun to resemble Rosa's father, who had also had a long oval face anchored by a positive mouth. Rosa was enraptured by Magda's healthy forearms. She would have given everything to set her before an easel, to see whether she could paint in watercolors; or to have her seize a violin, or a chess queen; she knew little about Magda's mind at this age, or whether she had any talents; even what her intelligence tended toward. And also she was always a little suspicious of Magda, because of the other strain, whatever it was, that ran in her. Rosa herself was not truly suspicious, but Stella was, and that induced perplexity in Rosa. The other strain was ghostly, even danger-ous. It was as if the peril hummed out from the filaments of Magda's hair, those narrow bright wires.

My Gold, my Wealth, my Treasure, my Hidden Sesame, my Paradise, my Yellow Flower, my Magda! Queen of Bloom and Blossom!

ANNE MORROW LINDBERGH

Lindbergh found dreams were more vivid than memories as she struggled to hold on to her murdered baby, the victim of a bungled kidnapping (see pp. 64 and 108).

from *Hour of Gold, Hour of Lead:*
Diaries and Letters of Anne Morrow Lindbergh 1929-1932

Hopewell, Friday, May 20, 1932

Last night I sat a long time with my eyes closed and tried to see and feel, re-live that last weekend, to reconstruct the baby. It was good to do. I found my fingers could reconstruct better than anything else. My sense of touch. But I've always, since the early train game as a child, been able to re-create sensation of touch, at least in my right hand. I can put my hand across the top of his curls and feel his hand in mine when I said, "Shall we go upstairs, Charlie?" and his weight when I pulled him out of bed and took him to the bathroom at night. It was so lovely. I went to bed eagerly to be alone and quiet to think about him, as one waits to be alone when one is in love so that one can remember all He said and did and warm oneself with the memory. . . .

Englewood, Wednesday, May 25, 1932
. . . In the afternoon the baby was so far away, I could not bear it—that he is growing further and further away, the faded daguerreotype of a little boy who died, a long time ago.

Englewood, Sunday, May 29, 1932
Mother's birthday
. . . Terribly vivid dream about the baby, condemned to die—saw him running, hair all curly and tangled, and I (not realizing what I know awake and yet conscious he had been away) said, "Betty, I cannot remember how you combed his hair." Then I was raging, raging like an animal, against the people who were going to take his life. The dream—a certain reality in memory as though I'd just seen him—stayed with me all day, warm and delicious like a remembered tune.

Englewood, Thursday, June 9, 1932
. . . I wake each morning (even when I do not dream) with the vague feeling that I have been close to the baby all night. I go to bed thinking of him—so vividly I almost see him—and then continue unconsciously in sleep. It is good, for by day he is getting further and further away—even the clothes, now I have looked at them three or four times, have lost his presence.

Englewood, Friday, June 24, 1932
. . . Night—so long to live forgetting that baby—with the picture getting dimmer and dimmer. The ghost of a little boy whom I can't even see in my waking mind. Then, as though something in me denied this, I dreamed heavily about him. Under the crust of consciousness lay another consciousness that held the image of him securely. Only I could not bring it back with me when I woke early in the morning and cursed the birds and could not get to sleep again.

MARK TWAIN

When Mark Twain's daughter Susy was thirteen, she secretly began writing a biography of her famous father. Eventually Twain read it and swelled with fatherly pride. "I had had compliments before," he wrote, "but none that touched me like this; none that could approach it for value in my eyes." After Susy's death at age twenty-four (see pp. 4 and 37), Twain reread the biography and added his personal commentary, which ends with this quote.

from *Papa: An Intimate Biography of Mark Twain* by Susy Clemens, edited by Charles Neider

So ends the loving task of that innocent sweet spirit—like her own life, unfinished, broken off in the midst. Interruptions came, her days became increasingly busy with studies and work, and she never resumed the biography, though from time to time she gathered materials for it. When I look at the arrested sentence that ends the little book, it seems as if the hand that traced it cannot be far—is gone for a moment only, and will come again and finish it. But that is a dream; a creature of the heart, not of the mind—a feeling, a longing, not a mental product: the same that lured Aaron Burr, old, gray, forlorn, forsaken, to the pier, day after day, week after week, there to stand in the gloom and the chill of the dawn gazing seaward through veiling mists and sleet and snow for the ship which he knew was gone down—the ship that bore all his treasure, his daughter.

HOPE OF REUNITING

RICHARD HOFFMAN

Two brothers of writer and poet Richard Hoffman died of muscular dystrophy after years of suffering. This is taken from his memoir.

from *Half the House: A Memoir*

For many years my mother's hair was lacquered blacker than it was when she was young. Once she was embarrassed when I came home from college a couple of days early and she hadn't gotten to the salon and her roots were showing. Shame, that goes to the roots: my mother bore two congenitally ill, doomed sons. For her, muscular dystrophy was a mythic curse: only males are afflicted by it, and only females carry it. A genetic defect. I can imagine my mother washing her face in the morning, looking at herself in the mirror, protecting herself, vigilant against the gray or silk-white roots that prove the past, that say that time is once, once, once. For so many years she knew her sons would die before her that she had to deny time every day to be there for them, to feed them, wash them, bring them books, papers and pencils, change the channel, bring the pisspot. Michael screamed in the night most every night for five or six years, waking everyone. She slept in a chair downstairs so she could wake him faster from his nightmares. How could she possibly believe one lifetime is all there is? She went to the cemetery, often. She had kept them alive inside her once before. "We'll be together again someday," she would insist, holding up her index finger. "Nobody can say it's not true."

CHARLES DICKENS

Dickens's sister-in-law Mary Hogarth, whom he adored and who lived with him and his wife, got sick at the theater one evening and died the next day at the age of seventeen. He admittedly relived his grief over Mary's loss when writing the death of Little Nell in The Old Curiosity Shop. *The novel was published in weekly installments. Readers in England and the United States were enthralled by Nell's story. In New York, crowds gathered at the waterfront waiting to discover her fate. The old man in this excerpt is Nell's grandfather, who raised her.*

from *The Old Curiosity Shop*

If there be any who have never known the blank that follows death—the weary void—the sense of desolation that will come upon the strongest minds, when something familiar and beloved is missed at every turn—the connexion between inanimate and senseless things, and the object of recollection, when every household god becomes a monument and every room a grave—if there be any who have not known this, and proved it by their own experience, they can never faintly guess how, for many days, the old man pined and moped away the time, and wandered here and there as seeking something, and had no comfort.

Whatever power of thought or memory he retained, was all bound up in her. . . .

On that one theme, which was in his and all their minds, it was impossible to touch. Dead! He could not hear or bear the word. The slightest hint of it would throw him into a paroxysm, like that he had had when it was first spoken. In what hope he lived, no man could tell; but that he had some hope of finding her again—some faint and shadowy hope, deferred from day to day, and making him from day to day more sick and sore at heart—was plain to all. . . .

At length they found one day that he had risen early, and, with his knapsack on his back, his staff in hand, her own straw hat, and little basket full of such things as she had been used to carry, was gone. As they were making ready to pursue him far and wide, a frightened schoolboy came who had seen him, but a moment before, sitting in the church—upon her grave, he said.

They hastened there, and going softly to the door, espied him in the attitude of one who waited patiently. They did not disturb him then, but kept a watch upon him all that day. When it grew quite dark, he rose and returned home, and went to bed, murmuring to himself, "She will come to-morrow!"

Upon the morrow he was there again from sunrise until night; and still at night he laid him down to rest, and muttered, "She will come to-morrow!"

And thenceforth, every day, and all day long, he waited at her grave for her. How many pictures of new journeys over pleasant country, of resting-places under the free broad sky, of rambles in the fields and woods, and paths not often trod—how many tones of that one well-remembered voice—how many glimpses of the form, the fluttering dress, the hair that waved so gaily in the wind—how many visions of what had been, and what he hoped was yet to be—rose up before him, in the old, dull, silent church! He never told them what he thought, or where he went. He would sit with them at night, pondering with a secret satisfaction, they could see, upon the flight that he and she would take before night came again; and still they would hear him whisper in his prayers, "Oh! Let her come to-morrow!"

The last time was on a genial day in spring. He did not return at the usual hour, and they went to seek him. He was lying dead upon the stone.

They laid him by the side of her whom he had loved so well; and, in the church where they had often prayed and mused, and lingered hand in hand, the child and the old man slept together.

11

Time Moves Differently Now

STOP THE CLOCKS

SYDNEY LEA

This is the beginning of a long poem from a poet known for his storytelling.

from "After Labor Day," in *The Bread Loaf Anthology of Contemporary American Poetry*, edited by Robert Pack, Sydney Lea, and Jay Parini

Your son is seven years dead.
"But it seems," I said, seeing your face
buckle in mid-conversation
as over the fields came winging the trebles
of children at holiday play—
I said, "But it seems like yesterday."

"No," you said,
"Like today."

JOHN EDGAR WIDEMAN

A two-time PEN/Faulkner Award–winner, Wideman (see pp. 94 and 170) writes here from the perspective of a mother who is trying to adjust to the death of her young daughter Njeri.

from "Welcome," in *The Stories of John Edgar Wideman*

You could lose a child in an instant . . . and for a long time after feel each lurch forward of the hands of the clock, as if you were stuck there like a naked chicken turning on a spit but you didn't turn you ticked one click at a time so time didn't change night into day one hour into the next one minute passing to another minute, time stopped then had to start up again, again and again. You wondered why anybody wanted to continue, how others could pretend to keep going. Your children. Why were they such noisy survivors? As if only she could remember. Till their eyes, their demands shocked her into speeding up again, matching herself to the business around her so she can step again into the frantic pace of those who were not skewered as she was, who were not clicking as she was, miles between clicks, lifetimes between each tiny lunge forward.

You could lose a child like that, once and for always in an instant and walk around forever with a lump in your throat, with the question of *what might have been* weighing you down every time you measure the happiness in someone else's face.

NORMAN MACLEAN

Sometimes someone else's tragedy grabs and marks us forever. For Maclean, who lost his brother early and who briefly worked for the U.S. Forest Service, it was a wilderness fire in 1949 that lingered a lifetime in his thoughts. In it, twelve young firefighters died. At seventy-four, Maclean finally surrendered his full attention to the tragedy and began a book.

from Young Men and Fire

A few summers ago, thirty years after the fire, I sent what I hoped was gentle word through a common friend to a mother of one of the Mann Gulch dead asking if I could talk to her, and she returned through the common friend gentle word saying that even after all these years she was unable to talk about her son's death. I thought next I would try a father, and he came in dignity, feeling no doubt it was a challenge to him that he must meet as a man, and he talked in dignity until I began to tell him about his son's death. I had assumed that he knew some of the details of that death and, as a scientist, would care for other details that would help him participate in his son's last decisions, very thoughtful ones though tragic. As I mistakenly went on talking, his hands began to shake as if he had Parkinson's disease. He could not stop them, so there is no story, certainly no ending to a story, that can be found by communicating with the living who loved the young who are dead, at least none that I am qualified to pursue. A story at a minimum requires movement, and, with those who loved those who died, nothing has moved. It all stopped on August 5, 1949.

JOHN IRVING

Sometimes, as in this one line from Irving's novel (see pp. 39 and 127), amazingly few words say it all.

from The World According to Garp

"Ever since Walt died," wrote T. S. Garp, "my life has felt like an epilogue."

AND IF IT DOESN'T ACTUALLY STOP, TIME CERTAINLY DRAGS LIKE NEVER BEFORE

THE MOTHER OF THE COMMANDER MICHITSUNA

This long-ago night took place sometime in the middle of the tenth century.

from One Hundred Poems from the Japanese, translated by Kenneth Rexroth

Have you any idea
How long a night can last, spent
Lying alone and sobbing?

JUDITH GUEST

In the novel Ordinary People, *Cal, on the second Christmas since his firstborn son died, is suddenly reminded of a secret trivia game they used to play at extended family gatherings like this one. He looks over at his surviving son, who exchanges a knowing glance, then looks away.*

from Ordinary People

A blessing. That you do not know at the moment of impact how far-reaching the shock waves will be. He is at once achingly aware of the force of Jordan's absence. Only a year and a half. Still, it is a long time to discover that you are still in shock, still in the infant stages of recovery.

UNDO IT, TAKE IT BACK

NESSA RAPOPORT

Even as she makes it, Rapoport knows that her plea is as futile as a child's on a playground after someone has been ugly and hurtful.

from A Woman's Book of Grieving

Undo it, take it back, make every day the previous one until I am returned to the day before the one that made you gone. Or set me on an airplane traveling west, crossing the date line again and again, losing this day, then that, until the day of loss still lies ahead, and you are here instead of sorrow.

LIKE LOST VOICES IN THE MOUNTAINS LONG AGO

W. D. EHRHART

Although he writes about a friend, not a child, Ehrhart expresses here the bewilderment so commonly felt by bereaved parents when they lose daughters and sons young. As neurosurgeon Harvey Cushing observed, grieving his comrades killed in World War I, they are "doubly dead in that they died so young."

from Out of Season: An Anthology of Work by and about Young People Who Died, edited by Paula Trachtman

". . . the light that cannot fade . . ."
for Carolyn Sue Brenner, 1948–1966

Suzie, you picked a hell of a time
to teach me about mortality.
I was in North Carolina then,
talking tough, eating from cans,
wearing my helmet John Wayne style—
and you were suddenly dead:
a crushed skull on a pre-dawn road
just two weeks shy of college,
and me about to leave for Vietnam.

I wanted you and me alive;
I wanted out.
That night I cried till dawn.

Funny, how I managed to survive
that war, how the years have passed,
how I'm thirty-four and getting on
and how your death
bestowed upon my life a permanence
I never would have had
if you had lived:

you'd have gone to college,
married some good man from Illinois,
and disappeared like all the other
friends I had back then who meant
so much and whom I haven't
thought about in years.

But as it is, I think of you
whenever dancers flow across a stage
or graceful gymnasts balance on the beam.
And every time I think of you,
you're young.

THOMAS WOLFE

*Closely autobiographical, Thomas Wolfe's "The Lost Boy" is about a
child's death, its impact on his family—and time. The youngest of seven
children, Wolfe was four when his mother took the children from their
home in Asheville, North Carolina, to St. Louis, Missouri, to run a
boardinghouse for visitors to the 1904 World's Fair. Once there, eleven-
year-old Grover, who had a job at the fairgrounds, caught typhoid fever
and died. Grover's death, Wolfe wrote, was "the most terrible wound" of
his mother's life. "Thirty-four years later, when she was told that Tom
himself was going to die," writes biographer Elizabeth Nowell, "she re-
verted to the death of Grover and described it almost word for word as
Wolfe had quoted her in his story 'The Lost Boy.'"*

*Written in four parts, the story begins with Grover in Asheville and is
picked up years later by his mother, sister Helen, and finally Eugene, the*

character who represents Wolfe. Still struggling with Grover's death, mother, sister, and brother are caught in the crosscurrents of then and now, where they try to reconcile what has been lost in between.

from "The Lost Boy," in *Literature: Structure, Sound, and Sense,*
edited by Laurence Perrine

2

THE MOTHER

[She describes how Grover looked when they used to travel on the train together to St. Louis]

. . . And I can still remember how he looked that morning, with his black eyes, his black hair, and with the birthmark on his neck—so grave, so serious, so earnest-like—as he sat by the train window and watched the apple trees, the farms, the barns, the houses, and the orchards, taking it all in, I reckon, because it was strange and new to him.

It was so long ago, but when I think of it, it all comes back, as if it happened yesterday. Now all of you have either died or grown up and gone away, and nothing is the same as it was then. But all of you were there with me that morning and I guess I should remember how the others looked, but somehow I don't. Yet I can still see Grover just the way he was, the way he looked that morning when we went down through Indiana, by the river, to the Fair.

3

THE SISTER

[She reflects on her first great loss, the death of Grover, and asks brother Eugene to explain the unexplainable.]

. . . I got to thinking of the afternoon we sneaked away from home. Mama had gone out somewhere. And Grover and I got on the street car and went downtown. And my Lord, we thought that we were going Somewhere. In those days, that was what we called a *trip*. A ride in the street car was something to write home about in those days . . . I hear that it's all built up around there now. . . .

. . . [Back home] Mama was waiting for us. She looked at us—you know how "Miss Eliza" looks at you when she thinks you've been doing something that you shouldn't. Mama said, "Why, where on earth have you two children been?" I guess she was all set to lay us out. Then she took one look at Grover's face. That was enough for her. She said, "Why, child, what in the

world!" She was white as a sheet herself . . . And all that Grover said was—
"Mama, I feel sick."

He was sick as a dog. He fell over on the bed, and we undressed him and
mama put her hand upon his forehead and came out in the hall—she was so
white you could have made a black mark on her face with chalk—and whispered to me, "Go get the doctor quick, he's burning up."

And I went chasing up the street, my pigtails flying, to Dr. Packer's
house. I brought him back with me. When he came out of Grover's room he
told mama what to do but I don't know if she even heard him.

Her face was white as a sheet. She looked at me and looked right through
me. She never saw me. And oh, my Lord, I'll never forget the way she
looked, the way my heart stopped and came up in my throat. I was only a
skinny little kid of fourteen. But she looked as if she was dying right before
my eyes. And I knew that if anything happened to him, she'd never get over
it if she lived to be a hundred.

Poor old mama. You know, he always was her eyeballs—you know that,
don't you?—not the rest of us!—no, sir! I know what I'm talking about. It
always has been Grover—she always thought more of him than she did of
any of the others. And—poor kid!—he was a sweet kid. I can still see him
lying there, and remember how sick he was, and how scared I was! I don't
know why I was so scared. All we'd done had been to sneak away from
home and go into a lunchroom—but I felt guilty about the whole thing, as
if it was my fault. . . .

. . . Sometimes I lie awake at night and think of all the people who have
come and gone, and how everything is different from the way we thought
that it would be. Then I go out on the street next day and see the faces of the
people that I pass . . . Don't they look strange to you? Don't you see something funny in people's eyes, as if all of them were puzzled about something?
As if they were wondering what had happened to them since they were kids?
Wondering what it is that they have lost? . . . Now am I crazy, or do you
know what I mean? You've been to college, Gene, and I want you to tell me
if you know the answer. Now do they look that way to you? I never noticed
that look in people's eyes when I was a kid—did you?

My God, I wish I knew the answer to these things. I'd like to find out
what is wrong—what has changed since then—and if we have the same
queer look in our eyes, too. Does it happen to us all, to everyone? . . .

How is it that nothing turns out the way we thought it would be? It all
gets lost until it seems that it has never happened—that it is something we

dreamed somewhere . . . You see what I mean? . . . It seems that it must be something we heard somewhere—that it happened to someone else. And then it all comes back again.

And suddenly you remember just how it was, and see again those two funny, frightened, skinny little kids with their noses pressed against the dirty window of that lunchroom thirty years ago. You remember the way it felt, the way it smelled, even the strange smell in the old pantry in that house we lived in then. And the steps before the house, the way the rooms looked. And those two little boys in sailor suits who used to ride up and down before the house on tricycles . . . And the birthmark on Grover's neck . . . The Inside Inn . . . St. Louis and the Fair.

It all comes back as if it happened yesterday. And then it goes away again, and seems farther off and stranger than if it happened in a dream.

4

THE BROTHER

[Eugene, grown-up now, goes to St. Louis to find the house where Grover died. Here he speaks with the current owner.]

. . . "Won't you come in? I don't believe it's changed much. Would you like to see?"

He thanked her and said he would, and he went up the steps. She opened the screen door to let him in.

Inside it was just the same—the stairs, the hallway, the sliding doors, the window of stained glass upon the stairs. And all of it was just the same, except for absence, the stained light of absence in the afternoon, and the child who once had sat there, waiting on the stairs.

It was all the same except that as a child he had sat there feeling things were *Somewhere*—and now he *knew*. He had sat there feeling that a vast and sultry river was somewhere—and now he knew! He had sat there wondering what King's Highway was, where it began, and where it ended—now he knew! He had sat there haunted by the magic word "downtown"—now he knew!—and by the street car, after it had gone—and by all things that came and went and came again, like the cloud shadows passing in a wood, that never could be captured.

And he felt that if he could only sit there on the stairs once more, in solitude and absence in the afternoon, he would be able to get it back again. Then would he be able to remember all that he had seen and been—the brief sum of himself, the universe of his four years, with all the light of Time upon it—that universe which was so short to measure, and yet so far, so endless, to remember. Then would he be able to see his own small face again, pooled in the dark mirror of the hall, and peer once more into the grave eyes of the child that he had been, and discover there in his quiet three-years' self the lone integrity of "I," knowing: "Here is the House, and here House listening; here is Absence, Absence in the afternoon; and here in this House, this Absence, is my core, my kernel—here am I!"

But as he thought it, he knew that even if he could sit here alone and get it back again, it would be gone as soon as seized, just as it had been then—first coming like the vast and drowsy rumors of the distant and enchanted Fair, then fading like cloud shadows on a hill, going like faces in a dream—coming, going, coming, possessed and held but never captured, like lost voices in the mountains long ago—and like the dark eyes and quiet face of the dark, lost boy, his brother, who, in the mysterious rhythms of his life and work, used to come into this house, then go, and return again. . . .

The years dropped off like fallen leaves: the face came back again—the soft dark oval, the dark eyes, the soft brown berry on the neck, the raven hair, all bending down, approaching—the whole appearing to him ghost-wise, intent and instant.

"Now say it—*Grover!*"

"Gova."

"No—not Gova. —*Grover*! . . . Say it!"

"Gova."

"Ah-h— you didn't say it. You said Gova. *Grover*—now say it!"

"Gova."

"Look, I tell you what I'll do if you say it right. Would you like to go down to King's Highway? Would you like Grover to set you up? All right, then. If you say Grover and say it right, I'll take you to King's Highway and set you up to ice cream. Now say it right—*Grover!*"

"Gova."

"Ah-h, you-u. You're the craziest little old boy I ever did see. Can't you even say Grover?"

"Gova."

"Ah-h, you-u. Old Tongue-Tie, that's what you are . . . Well, come on, then, I'll set you up anyway."

It all came back, and faded, and was lost again. Eugene turned to go, and thanked the woman and said good-by.

"Well, then, good-by," the woman said, and they shook hands. "I'm glad if I could show you. I'm glad if—" She did not finish, and at length she said: "Well, then, that was a long time ago. You'll find everything changed now, I guess. It's all built up around here now—and way out beyond here, out beyond where the Fair Grounds used to be. I guess you'll find it changed."

They had nothing more to say. They just stood there for a moment on the steps, and then shook hands once more.

"Well, good-by."

And again he was in the street, and found the place where the corners met, and for the last time turned to see where Time had gone.

And he knew that he would never come again, and that lost magic would not come again. Lost now was all of it—the street, the heat, King's Highway, and Tom the Piper's son, all mixed in with the vast and drowsy murmur of the Fair, and with the sense of absence in the afternoon, and the house that waited, and the child that dreamed. And out of the enchanted wood, that thicket of man's memory, Eugene knew that the dark eye and the quiet face of his friend and brother—poor child, life's stranger, and life's exile, lost like all of us, a cipher in blind mazes, long ago—the lost boy was gone forever, and would not return.

12

The Legacy of Loss

I am a clinical social worker, so, shortly after Allie died, I did what I was trained to do. I consulted my *Diagnostic and Statistical Manual,* the bible of mental disorders. I wanted to see how the death of a child was rated on the Severity of Psychosocial Stressors Scale. Of course I already knew it was the worst thing that could happen, but there was something about seeing "death of a child" in the most severe category—catastrophic—that brought it home. This time the bomb had dropped on me.

So how does someone, skilled at helping others to cope, cope when the worst of the worst has happened? What helped me and what have I learned?

I learned that when people described their feelings as "painful" it was not a metaphor. I felt pain beyond anything I could possibly have imagined: pain so searing it raised goose bumps on my arms, made me nauseous, left me panting and wondering how soon I could die so I wouldn't have to feel it anymore. I learned that I could live, work, and love in spite of excruciating pain. And what's more, a lot of very ordinary-looking people are out there, more than I ever suspected, who also live with extraordinary wounds. Time and care do temper the pain. It is not always as sharp, but it is always there.

I found that certain words people used to console me—words that implied this would end, words like "healing," "recovery," "resolving my grief," and "bringing closure"—infuriated me. Once I wailed to a kindly therapist that I had lost the entire meaning of my life. When she responded that I would find new meaning, I was aghast. Clearly she did not understand the miracle of Allie, how utterly irreplaceable he was, nor the crater he had left in our family. I knew from the first moment that I would never get over Allie's death, that I would hurt for him forever, that our family would never be whole again. That was precisely *why* I was in such agony.

Although I know that some people find hope and inspiration in the notions of recovery and healing, I think these notions can sometimes be harmful. Giving bereaved parents the message that there is a time when we should have "worked through" our loss can be interpreted as suggesting that we have failed somewhere if we continue to mourn. Bereaved parents do not need to be made to feel worse about *anything*. We are doing well when we get out of bed and put one foot in front of the other. The most truthful and helpful words along these lines that anyone ever said to me were, "It will not always be this bad."

Some things did help. Perhaps the one advantage to being a therapist was that I did not hesitate to look for support from other people. I found that the pain did subside when I talked about it in Compassionate Friends meetings, bereavement groups, and with other compassionate souls (often people who had sustained great loss themselves). Also, I could not insist that I could not bear to live in such pain while in the same room with others who were managing it. If they could stand it, so could I.

I looked for things I could do that would bring relief, knowing full well it would be short lived, maybe lasting only an hour at a time. When I found something that worked, I indulged myself as much as I could. I thought of myself as finding stepping-stones across a river of pain. Some of the things I tried were aerobics, swimming, yoga, tennis, writing, and above all, good books. This led to my search for literature about the death of children. Then I met Anne, who was searching too, and we began to share the stones we found, and to cross the river together. That, of course, brought us to this book. Now we offer our stepping-stones to you, in the hope that they will help you across your river.

I had no idea when I began my literary search that it would end in a published book. I was simply looking for the solace of contact with other wounded souls. I had no idea that a book was in me, and in fact, I don't think there was one before Allie was killed. Something else I have discovered is that, in my opinion, grief often inspires creativity. When everything is hunky-dory, you just don't have the same compelling need to express yourself creatively, nor to do all the hard work it requires. That is probably why so much of the world's great literature is about grief and loss.

Channeling my grief into this book has been the most helpful thing I have done for myself since Allie died. And it is something I have done for Allie too. Obviously, the book is dedicated to his memory, but that is not all. The last year of Allie's life he became quite a reader (inspired, I suspect, by a beautiful blond English teacher who would raise the sap of any young man's creativity). That spring, when I told him how pleased I was that he was discovering the joy of reading, he grinned and said, "I come from a reading family." After he died, we discovered some beautiful and sophisticated po-etry he had written and kept to himself. I never knew he had it in him. So, in reading and writing for this book, I feel as if I am advancing Allie's life a little further for him. Of course, I would much rather use my creativity to make pancakes for him on a cozy Sunday morning and have him here fac-ing the challenge of *his* book. Since that is not to be, this is the best I can do for both of us.

MARY

When my great-grandfather was sixteen, one of the battles of the Franco-German War of 1870 was fought near his town in Alsace. After the slaugh-ter, the boys and old men of the town, my great-grandfather included, went to bury the dead. The horror he saw turned his hair white.

I sometimes wish that great loss would mark sorrowful parents this clearly. People could see, without our having to explain, that we too have known horror. That grief has left behind its giant paw prints. As it is, noth-ing shows when our hearts break, but indeed, we *are* changed.

Friends say we're brave, we're strong. They mean it as a compliment, and I take it as that. But the truth is we have few options. We can stay bitter. We can put guns to our heads. Or we can struggle to find reasons to live—mine was my surviving child. Heaven help those who don't have that. They do go on, I see them, and my admiration is huge.

Always before, I'd linked courage and strength to great heroics. But now I see their quieter sides. There's courage on the battlefield, yes, but it's no greater than that shown on the children's cancer floor of any hospital. As many parents know firsthand, those children with their little bald heads set high standards. We can learn from them.

True courage, I now know, shows itself in our daily struggles to get back some semblance of the lives we once enjoyed. Journalist Linda Ellerbee was staring at her own mortality, fighting breast cancer, when she said it for all of us: "I think laughter may be a form of courage. . . . As humans we some-times stand tall and look into the sun and laugh, and I think we are never more brave than when we do that."

It sounds so simplistic to say that with great loss our perspective changes, but it does. When I could look up from my suffering, I noticed the obvious: My heartache was a mere dot on the landscape of pain. All-consuming to me, but still a dot. And to heal at all, I had to make myself see it that way.

We all have salves that work for us. On my worst days, early on, I used to think of a little plaque left anonymously by a mother at Verdun, France, where 420,000 died in battle in 1916. On it, she inscribed: *To my son / Since your eyes / were closed mine / have / never ceased to weep.* All those young men. Each as precious to his mother as Jake was to me. It served as good reminder that I was by no means alone in my pain.

And the pain does lessen; our eyes do stop weeping. Like a watercolor wash, time does soften our suffering. We laugh again. We enjoy our work, our family, our friends. We move on, but there's no great resolution—at least none for me. Divorced couples can remember the good years, minimize the bad, and, feeling wiser, hold out hope for even better. But there's no happy chapter, drawing on our newfound wisdom, just ahead for bereaved parents.

Instead, we move on because we know we must. Otherwise, our time here is wasted. And not that I'm living for them, but I do think of those young men at Verdun, who, like Jake, would have given anything for more years. That bugle call, I can't ignore.

Still, it is a struggle, and nothing short of mythologist Joseph Campbell's hard dictum: "You have to give up the life you planned to find the life that is waiting for you." We've been ripped away from the land we loved, a place where children outlive their parents, and thrown down on heartless, arid soil. We can't go home, and we can't give up. We have to stay and make the best of it.

Thankfully, we do so with a few new tools: gifts from loss. One is strength. Let's admit it, we feel tougher for the wear. The paradox here, for many of us, is that our great fears of change and the unknown, once so inhibiting, died with our children. As Eleanor Roosevelt, who by age ten had lost both parents and a brother, and later, her own baby, well understood: "You are able to say to yourself, 'I lived through this horror. I can take the next thing that comes along.' "

It is also liberating to know what real tragedy is. Losing a promotion, even a job, is not tragic. Losing a house to fire, if everyone escapes, is not tragic. We know real tragedy, and it gave us a new yardstick. Use it well, and surely we can benefit. We have cried enough tears. We need not waste any.

In the car accident that killed Jake, I was badly cut by the shattered windshield. Cosmetic surgeons worked hard on my face. They thought they got everything. But nine years later, little slivers of glass, small as grains of sand, occasionally still poke through my skin. Everyone else seems amazed by this. But I like the symbolism in it.

After all, most wounds heal, even deep ones, but not the death of a child. It seems fitting then that glass from that accident keeps emerging as though from the depths of my early pain. Over the years, time and sunny beach days have faded my red raw scars. Though they're still visible, even I don't always notice them. But when I'm old, if glass still pushes through those scars, I won't be surprised. Or sorry. That glass is my hair turned white.

ANNE

WE SURVIVE SOMEHOW

SHELLY WAGNER

Like an ancient Greek storyteller, Wagner spins a tale of how she has survived a tragedy she never thought she could and of the hard-earned wisdom she has gained (see pp. 207 and 236).

from The Andrew Poems

Your Questions

I'll tell you;
I'll be bold.
You cannot know what this is like.
I don't want you to know
firsthand. But do not dare surmise
or worse, pass judgment—
you'll hear a different poem from me.
Not the poem that tries
with constricted throat
to speak the unspeakable,
recapture in foolish, shallow syllables
the trauma of loss
so you might
know for a moment
grief that gives life,
transcends,

blesses with wisdom.
It's my choice to share these lessons.
It's your choice to not listen
if you cannot bear
what I also thought
I could not survive.
I will understand
and wait
until you need this lesson
like a lifeline
when you are drowning.
You will die, too, you know.
There's nothing I can do about it
but have you drown in my poem
for only a moment,
then come gulping to the surface
looking into my eyes
smiling because you are not dead
but happier than you were before
to shake the water off your head,
go home and kiss your children,
tuck them in bed,
sleep yourself unsettled
but wake somehow refreshed.
So I keep telling my story,
what I know to be true.

I am different.
I felt it right away.
I wanted to die to be
with Andrew.
Others knew;
some forced themselves to touch me
as though my flesh *had* fallen away,
leaving my skull
to remind everyone of death.
It has taken me years
to recognize my face in the mirror,

to know who I am,
but I tell you
my face shines like Moses' face
and I refuse to hide it anymore,
cover it with makeup
or put on a smile
to make it easier for you.
Do not avoid my eyes.
Do not walk away from me.
I am a mother.
Come close, sit down
and listen.

We'll begin with your questions.
Ask me, for example,
why you never received a thank-you note
for flowers, food
or charity contributions
because I need to tell you.
After the funeral, I threw away
the funeral home's inadequate
thank-you notes given to me in a box.
I intended to write all of you,
but years went by,
and I never thanked you
for salvation in flowers,
nourishment of fried chicken,
poetry in "Given in memory of. . . ."
One day I hope to see
the Jerusalem pine a friend planted in Israel,
Andrew's oak pew in a new chapel by the beach,
a music room full of children singing
where his memorial plaque proclaims:
"Make a joyful noise."
When my knees buckled,
I fell backward
onto your gifts like pillows
and like a person convalescing

propped them around me.
Now that I am better I can
write a long note to say thank you
and I love you
and I'm sorry it all happened.

For words of comfort even now,
you might say and some did say,
"You still have another son."
Now I ask you,
"Do you hear
your logic?
When your mother died
did your living father make it easier?"
What saved you, you ask?
Unconditional love.
I was lucky with Andrew.
We were happy.
Nothing left undone.
Our last moments together were filled
with laughter. Pushing him in his tire swing
by the river,
he was curled inside the circle
like a baby in the womb,
giggling
because he knew at random
I would catch him,
hold him close to my heart,
unwilling to let go,
and cover his face with kisses.
Fill your relationships
with all the photos in your mind
until they are so good
you will be afraid of losing them, and you will.
But that will not kill you,
you'll survive and live on.
It's regret that destroys you,
anything left undone.

You see I tell you
what you already know.
Don't shake your head
and dismiss this because it is simple.

Let's pretend you have climbed
a dangerous mountain,
reached the summit to see
the wise old woman who lives on the peak.
Your bruised knuckles knock on her door.
It opens. She's standing there—
you can't believe it—
wearing shorts,
her hair pulled back in a rubber band.
You've come all this way,
it's not what you expected
and worse yet
she goes to her desk,
gives you a paper,
one of hundreds, all typed,
"Live each day as though it were your last."

You see our problem,
you already have this at home
in a needlework picture.
Because it is nothing new
you may turn away,
but I won't worry about you.
You are a climber,
an asker of questions
with answers
cross-stitched on your walls at home,
hung in old frames on a nail,
hiding a flaw in the plaster.

I'll ask the next question for you
because you may not think to wonder,
"Is there anything you would have done differently?"
Yes, I'd bring his body home,

put his blue casket in my living room,
group all the flowers around him.
Imagine all the flowers.
Think of two more days
for me to look at my child,
discover the bruise
on his forehead that wasn't there
when we were playing.
I learned of his injury
weeks later
when the funeral director told me,
"He was so beautiful.
We did nothing but cover the blow."
For two more days
I could have spoken to my child face to face
before forced to speak
only to darkness or you.
There were not enough chances
to touch him,
put my cheek next to his.
I wouldn't have been afraid
of my child's body;
but I left him at the funeral home
in the corner room
on the second floor
and visited whenever I could
because I did not want to scare you.

Next time will be different.
I'll put my loved one in the house
like my mother's family used to do,
and we'll all gather around
like sitting by a fire.
At the cemetery, like a rabbi
I'll take the shovel
and heap the dirt back in the hole,
do the raking and sodding myself.

Let me tell you.
You would not know to ask

about the day they set his tombstone.
I watched them stand the small granite cross
in a footing of wet cement.
When the workers left,
I touched the stone
carved with his name in full
because that's the way he said it,
written in all capitals
because that's the way he wrote it:
ANDREW CAMERON MINTON.
I broke a branch
so I could write to my child
in the margin of wet cement,
"I love you. I miss you.
Thank God I will see you again."
You see I have learned
chances don't come again.
I listen when they say,
"Opportunity is brief.
Remember cement gets hard.
Yesterday is set concrete
unable to record your words."

Shall we go on? I have seven years to tell you.
I read the next question in your eyes:
"How have you managed to go on?"
You'll hate my answer:
more needlework,
perhaps a needlepoint pillow?
Let me paint
the canvas for you.
Now go home with your fists
full of rainbows of wool,
thread the needle yourself,
strain to see
through your tears,
pull each thread through the holes,
in and out like a pulse.
Nail your finished canvas on a frame,

stretch it square,
bind it with cord
braided of your hair.
Put it on your sofa, show it to your friends,
teach them *One Day At a Time.*

No more questions, but you are concerned.
You suggest I get out and get some exercise.
Exercise!? Exercise!?
Grief is isometric.
Are you looking at my face?
I have the face of a sprinter.
I grimace and strain
like the runners I saw
in the New York marathon.
Those toward the end were suffering,
dying, though more alive than most of us
cheering for people we didn't know,
"Don't give up! Keep going!"
Some were passing them water.
The runners ran on, some fell skinning their knees.
If you pass me a cup of water
you will see
what I see up the road—
a rugged uphill course I'm determined to finish.
I'll make it
if I pace myself,
forgive myself when I fall,
and stop long enough to accept the water you offer.

LUCILLE CLIFTON

This poem by Lucille Clifton, a former poet laureate of Maryland, honors black women whose sons so frequently and tragically die young.

from Good Woman: Poems and a Memoir 1969-1980

For deLawd

people say they have a hard time
understanding how I
go on about my business
playing my Ray Charles
hollering at the kids—
seems like my Afro
cut off in some old image
would show I got a long memory
and I come from a line
of black and going on women
who got used to making it through murdered sons
and who grief kept on pushing
who fried chicken
ironed
swept off the back steps
who grief kept
for their still alive sons
for their sons coming
for their sons gone
just pushing

ALBERT CAMUS

In this quote, which has inspired so many, Camus (see p. 41) uses imagery of the seasons to explain how he learned to "meet both joy and sorrow with equanimity."

from "Return to Tipasa," in Lyrical and Critical Essays,
translated by Ellen Conroy Kennedy, edited by Philip Thody

In the depths of winter, I finally learned that within me there lay an invincible summer.

THEIR LIVES MADE A DIFFERENCE

ROBERT FROST

At age sixty-eight, Frost won a Pulitzer Prize for his poetry collection,
A Witness Tree, *making him the only poet ever to receive the coveted
award four times. "The book seemed to herald a new way of life—
a breaking out of the prison of his loneliness," wrote biographer Natalie
Bober. "'Never Again Would Birds' Song Be the Same' evoked the memory of Marjorie [his daughter who had died from septicemia after childbirth eight years prior; see p. 111] and showed how, as he had often said,
'each poem was a surmounting of something in life.' It was, in large measure, the lyric reflection of his tragic losses." And more specifically, it was
Frost's way of expressing the yearning, common to bereaved parents, that
his daughter made a difference for having been here.*

from The Poetry of Robert Frost: The Collected Poems, Complete and Unabridged,
edited by Edward Connery Lathem

Never Again Would Birds' Song Be the Same

He would declare and could himself believe
That the birds there in all the garden round
From having heard the daylong voice of Eve
Had added to their own an oversound,
Her tone of meaning but without the words.
Admittedly an eloquence so soft
Could only have had an influence on birds
When call or laughter carried it aloft.
Be that as may be, she was in their song.
Moreover her voice upon their voices crossed
Had now persisted in the woods so long
That probably it never would be lost.
Never again would birds' song be the same.
And to do that to birds was why she came.

JOHN TITTENSOR

*Entering his second year of bereavement (see pp. 67 and 211), Tittensor
had come to some important conclusions.*

from *Year One: A Record*

25 July

. . . The important thing seems to me to be that my children were *of this
world:* they were born, they lived, they found and gave happiness in the
world they shared with me and their fellow human beings. And so their
meaning—if that is the word—is to be sought here. That search, in a positive and un-morbid way, will be my life from now on—although I do not
expect ever to be united with them again, except in mutual non-being.

And I have to confess that in many ways I yearn for this non-being—but
only in due course. To hark back to something I have already said, their loss
never really made me want death for myself. What it *has* done is to remove
completely any fear of death I had; I can now accept calmly . . . that one day
I will lie, as they do, "with the unborn." And while I am here, "living on the
hard earth" but freed by my children from the fear of death, I find life opening to me: those things I spoke of as inherently, self-evidently good—friendship, love, the life of the mind and the senses—seem now to be beginning to
offer themselves to me in a new, more intense way; a *cleansed* way; as if, for
the first time in my life, I see them and appreciate them clearly—as if at last
I am learning something of their true value and complexity. As if in a
strange, secular way, I've begun to find an authentic spiritual life.

Is being done with death the key to this growing joy, this sense of liber-
ation? I think of Rilke's remark in *The Notebook of Malte Laurids Brigge* that
to approach any one book seriously you must be prepared to read them all.
And that is the way I feel about my life now: that I want to give myself to it
whole-heartedly, loving all the people I love as well as I can, and reading all
the books; and doing it in a truly *informed* way, as Bruno Bettelheim puts it.
I would like to live to be a hundred because loving and being loved are so
good and there are so many books; but were I to learn now that I had only
a week left, I would finish today's spell of writing, have the cup of coffee I
crave and go on with the one book I'm reading. And so I feel that my children's death has empowered me in some way within the life which I still have
and they do not.

"Sorrow is knowledge," Byron declaims in *Manfred.* This is a terrible over-simplification; but sorrow can be a pathway to knowledge. I was lucky: there was something in me that enabled me to face my loss and see at least part of what could be got from it. Not that I am a person suddenly, magically rendered wise by adverse circumstance; but I see myself now as willingly, joyfully in search of a wisdom that will embrace all the things I have seen and known—and above everything else the death of the two people dearest to me in all the world.

That search can have no end. But—an honourable cliché this—it is the journey and not the arrival that matters, that journey on which the death of Jonathan and Emma so abruptly launched me. And so, surviving for me in the love that passed between us, in the beauty to which they gave me access, they enrich me in death as they did in life. In this sense I am united with them; in this sense I can never be separated from them. Perhaps this is a kind of immortality for the three of us. And I don't mind that at all.

WE ARE DEFINED FOREVER BY OUR LOSS

ANNA QUINDLEN

In a column inspired by writing an obituary for her sister-in-law, Sherry Quindlen, who died of cancer at forty-one, novelist and former New York Times *columnist Anna Quindlen describes what survivng a major loss has been like for her. Twenty-two years earlier, Quindlen's mother died of cancer when Quindlen was still a teenager. Of all the columns Quindlen wrote, this elicited the greatest response, perhaps because she openly acknowledges what bereaved parents have always known—there are some losses you don't get over.*

from "Life After Death," in the *New York Times*, May 4, 1994

Grief remains one of the few things that has the power to silence us. It is a whisper in the world and a clamor within. More than sex, more than faith, even more than its usher death, grief is unspoken, publicly ignored except for those moments at the funeral that are over too quickly, or the conversations among the cognoscenti, those of us who recognize in one another a kindred chasm deep in the center of who we are.

Maybe we do not speak of it because death will mark all of us, sooner or later. Or maybe it is unspoken because grief is only the first part of it. After a time it becomes something less sharp but larger, too, a more enduring thing called loss.

Perhaps that is why this is the least explored passage: because it has no end. The world loves closure, loves a thing that can, as they say, be gotten through. This is why it comes as a great surprise to find that loss is forever, that two decades after the event there are those occasions when something in you cries out at the continual presence of an absence.

"An awful leisure," Emily Dickinson once called what the living have after death. . . .

The landscapes of all our lives become as full of craters as the surface of the moon. . . . And I write my obituaries carefully and think about how little the facts suffice, not only to describe the dead but to tell what they will mean to the living all the rest of our lives. We are defined by who we have lost.

HOPE EDELMAN

Motherless Daughters *was published thirteen years after Edelman's mother died of breast cancer at the age of forty-two, leaving Edelman, then seventeen, and two younger siblings. It quickly became a* New York Times *best-seller. Like Anna Quindlen, Edelman does not attempt to "soft pedal" the fact that loss changed her indelibly.*

from Motherless Daughters: The Legacy of Loss

Most often, I'm a woman looking for an answer, or at least for a clue, still trying to understand how such a tragic loss could have happened, exactly how it's molded me, and how I can prevent it from happening to me again.

I didn't plan to be this person, for whom loss always hovers at the edge of my awareness like next month's bills, but there you have it. I've carried the remote ache of longing with me long enough to understand it's part of who I am now. . . . This is a part of my identity that I can never change. . . .

. . . Our lives are shaped as much by those who leave us as they are by those who stay. Loss is our legacy. Insight is our gift. Memory is our guide.

JEWISH PRAYER FOR HIGH HOLYDAYS

This prayer, or some variation of it, is said on Yom Kippur, when Jews take special time to remember the dead.

from a memorial service prayer sheet

It is hard to sing of oneness when our world is not complete, when those who once brought wholeness to our life have gone, and naught but memory can fill the emptiness their passing leaves behind.

But memory can tell us only what we were, in company with those we loved; it cannot help us find what each of us, alone, must now become. Yet no one is really alone; those who live no more, echo still within our thoughts and words, and what they did is part of what we have become.

We do best homage to our dead when we live our lives most fully, even in the shadow of our loss.

TO OUR CREDIT, WE DO MORE THAN ENDURE

EDNA ST. VINCENT MILLAY

Literary critic Edmund Wilson wrote of Edna St. Vincent Millay: "In giving supreme expression to profoundly felt personal experience, she was able to identify herself with more general experience and stand forth as a spokesman for the human spirit."

from *Collected Poems*, edited by Norma Millay

Read history: thus learn how small a space

Read history: thus learn how small a space
You may inhabit, nor inhabit long
In crowding Cosmos—in that confined place
Work boldly; build your flimsy barriers strong;
Turn round and round, make warm your nest; among
The other hunting beasts, keep heart and face,—
Not to betray the doomed and splendid race
You are so proud of, to which you belong.
For trouble comes to all of us: the rat
Has courage, in adversity, to fight;

But what a shining animal is man,
Who knows, when pain subsides, that is not that,
For worse than that must follow—yet can write
Music; can laugh; play tennis; even plan.

BARBARA KINGSOLVER

A poet and novelist, Barbara Kingsolver counts among her own losses the death of an unborn child. In her novel Animal Dreams *(see p. 161), Codi, a young woman, reflects on her own miscarriage years before: "All told, probably more women have lost a child from this world than haven't. Most don't mention it, and they go on from day to day as if it hadn't happened, and so people imagine that a woman in this situation never really knew or loved what she had. But ask her sometime: how old would your child be now? And she'll know." The following excerpt is from a collection of her essays.*

from "High Tide in Tucson," in *High Tide in Tucson: Essays from Now or Never*

In my own worst seasons I've come back from the colorless world of despair by forcing myself to look hard, for a long time, at a single glorious thing: a flame of red geranium outside my bedroom window. And then another: my daughter in a yellow dress. And another: the perfect outline of a full, dark sphere behind the crescent moon. Until I learned to be in love with my life again. Like a stroke victim retraining new parts of the brain to grasp lost skills, I have taught myself joy, over and over again.

It's not such a wide gulf to cross, then, from survival to poetry. We hold fast to the old passions of endurance that buckle and creak beneath us, dovetailed, tight as a good wooden boat to carry us onward. And onward full tilt we go, pitched and wrecked and absurdly resolute, driven in spite of everything to make good on a new shore. To be hopeful, to embrace one possibility after another—that is surely the basic instinct. Baser even than hate, the thing with teeth, which can be stilled with a tone of voice or stunned by beauty. If the whole world of the living has to turn on the single point of remaining alive, that pointed endurance is the poetry of hope. The thing with feathers.

What a stroke of luck. What a singular brute feat of outrageous fortune: to be born to citizenship in the Animal Kingdom. We love and we lose, go back to the start and do it right over again. For every heavy forebrain solemnly cataloging the facts of a harsh landscape, there's a rush of intuition behind it crying out: High tide! Time to move out into the glorious debris. Time to take this life for what it is.

COMING TO TERMS WITH GOD

TOM CRIDER

As his rage over his daughter's death (see pp. 59 and 216) diminished, Crider became more open minded.

from *Give Sorrow Words: A Father's Passage through Grief*

I accept them all now, God the Father, Yahweh, Odin, Zeus, falcon-headed Horus, Vishnu, and all the lesser gods and goddesses, the lordly faces, the flowing robes, the golden elephants, the multiarmed whirlers. I see them and embrace them as images shaped by humans afraid of chaos and dazzled by the light. All the myths, gospels, and theologies, I accept as pointing toward something having more to do with hope than reason.

Saint Thomas Aquinas said, "The divine essence by its immensity surpasses every form to which our intellect reaches; and thus we cannot apprehend it by knowing what it is." But we try because not knowing is hard on us. Months ago I was angry at what I thought was the sheeplike stupidity of people who believed in a God who cared about them. Enraged by Gretchen's death, I could not understand how people, especially those whose children had died, could believe they were loved by God. Having myself grown up with that image of the fatherly taskmaster, I needed something to blame, something to hate for what had happened; and there He was, still present in my memory, somehow alive under layers of consciousness. Shortly after Gretchen died I saw a woman driving a car with a bumpersticker saying GOD LOVES YOU, and I felt like running her off the road. I saw the same message the other day and shrugged.

Now that my anger is subsiding, I see Him and all the other gods as not unlike my own "pathetic fallacies," the fantasies of minds and hearts unhinged by grief. I may not believe what others do, but I have experienced the desperate longing to understand, and I know I, too, am one of the sheep. So I don't begrudge anyone a belief that can help them through the day.

TOM ROBBINS

A former student of religion, Robbins philosophizes here through one of fiction's most unlikely wise women: the belly dancer Salome. At a packed bar, swathed in gauzy purple scarves, she performs the Dance of the Seven Veils. One by one, Salome's silk scarves drop, and so do her audience's illusions about life.

from *Skinny Legs and All*

The illusion of the seventh veil was the illusion that you could get somebody else to do it for you. To think for you. To hang on your cross. The priest, the rabbi, the imam, the swami, the philosophical novelist were traffic cops, at best. They might direct you through a busy intersection, but they wouldn't follow you home and park your car.

Was there a more difficult lesson for a human being to learn, a paradox harder to accept? Even though the great emotions, the great truths, were universal; even though the mind of humanity was ultimately one mind, still, each and every single individual had to establish his or her own special, personal, particular, unique, direct, one-on-one, hands-on relationship with reality, with the universe, with the Divine. It might be complicated, it might be a pain in the ass, it might be, most of all, lonely—but it was the bottom line.

It was as different for everybody as it was the same, so everybody had to take control of their own life, define their own death, and construct their own salvation. And when you finished, you didn't call the Messiah. He'd call you.

WE HEAL BY DOING

ROSE FITZGERALD KENNEDY

After Joe Jr. was killed in World War II, his grieving father, Joseph P. Kennedy, asked the family for ideas on what should be done to best perpetuate Joe's memory. Since Rosemary, one of the surviving eight Kennedy siblings, was retarded, and federal efforts in the field of mental retardation were then practically nonexistent, the Kennedys decided to establish a foundation in Joe's name to fund special schools. Over a span of fifteen months, Joseph Sr. started schools in the various cities in which each of his sons and daughters lived, and he encouraged all to take part in the schools' development. In this excerpt, Rose Kennedy, who later lost three more of her children—daughter Kathleen in a plane crash and sons John and Robert in assassinations—reminisces.

from *Times to Remember*

How can one endure in the face of tragedy? People have asked me. And surely I have often had reason to ask myself.

Joe [Sr.] was right in his words: "Carry on . . . take care of the living . . . there is a lot of work to be done." And right in his instinctive and immediate recognition that in sorrow we must look outward rather than inward, and thus can come peace of mind and peace of spirit.

JOHN ANDREW HOLMES

from *The Book of Positive Quotations*, edited by John Cook

There is no better exercise for the heart than reaching down and lifting people up.

ANDRÉ GREGORY

When his wife was dying, film director and actor André Gregory, known for My Dinner with André, *assembled a group of actor friends to perform Chekov's* Uncle Vanya. *This project, begun for his own benefit, eventually became the movie* Vanya on 42nd Street. *Gregory spoke about the therapeutic value of the experience at a conference for therapists in Washington, D.C.*

from "Around the Network" by Katy Butler,
in *The Family Therapy Networker*, May/June 1995

"We were looking for a place where we could channel our despair, anger and hopelessness," he told the audience, saying that when rehearsals began, his own wife was terminally ill with breast cancer, actor Wallace Shawn was having a nervous collapse, another actor was dying of cancer and a third had just lost a son in a freak accident in India. So they chose to work on Chekov's play about people who speak of unrequited love, lost ambitions and bitter regrets. . . .

... "In the process of working on this play, the ... question arose: what could we hope for? We kept working even in the most desperate of times. We worked with passion and love. We didn't do it really for each other. We did it for ourselves, so that it could reach others.

"When my wife was very ill, a close friend said this must be so difficult. Obviously, it was horrible. But the real art of poker, I told my friend, isn't winning with a winning hand—anybody can win with a full house. It's winning with a losing hand. We had a losing hand, all of us. And in some way we won."

SUSE LOWENSTEIN

Alexander Lowenstein, a twenty-one-year-old senior at Syracuse University, was flying home from London for the holidays when the plane, Pan Am 103, exploded over Lockerbie, Scotland. His mother, Suse, has sculpted herself and other bereaved mothers, grandmothers, and widows in poses recreating their shocked grief when they learned of the crash. That work is called Dark Elegy.

from *No Voice Is Ever Wholly Lost*, edited by Louise J. Kaplan

When I work ... I think of all the children who were lost. Their photographs hang on the wall at the entrance to my studio. Alexander is there, too, on the other wall. I speak to him every day. I think about him all the time, even when I am thinking about something else. Funny, I think about him more now than I ever did when he was alive. His spirit is somewhere, maybe right here, in this room, right now, listening to us talk about *Dark Elegy.* Alexander wants me to hold up and carry on. Perhaps he is the spirit inside the Other Suse, the one that picks me up evey time I am feeling like I can't go on.

TAKE LIFE FOR WHAT IT IS

RITA DOVE

In this sonnet from her collection based on the myth of Persephone (see p. 63), Rita Dove exhorts us not "to deny this world."

from *Mother Love: Poems*

Lamentations

Throw open the shutters
to your darkened residences:
can you hear the pipes playing,
their hunger shaking the olive branches?
To hear them sighing and not answer
is to deny this world, descend rung
by rung into no loss and no desire.
Listen: empty yet full, silken
air and brute tongue,
they are saying:
To refuse to be born is one thing—
but once you are here,
you'd do well to stop crying
and suck the good milk in.

AN EXQUISITE PARADOX:
FROM LOSS AND SUFFERING WE CAN MORE DEEPLY
APPRECIATE LOVE, COMPASSION,
AND THE CYCLE OF LIFE AND DEATH

FRANCES GUNTHER

Frances Gunther shared the wisdom she gained from the death of her son (see p. 97) in the endnote of her former husband's memoir.

from "A Word From Frances," in Death Be Not Proud: A Memoir by John Gunther

Today, when I see parents impatient or tired or bored with their children, I wish I could say to them, But they are alive, think of the wonder of that! They may be a care and a burden, but think, they are alive! You can touch them—what a miracle! You don't have to hold back sudden tears when you see just a headline about the Yale-Harvard game because you know your boy will never see the Yale-Harvard game, never see the house in Paris he was born in, never bring home his girl, and you will not hand down your jewels to his bride and will have no grandchildren to play with and spoil. Your sons and daughters are alive. Think of that—not dead but alive! Exult and sing.

All parents who have lost a child will feel what I mean. Others, luckily, cannot. But I hope they will embrace them with a little added rapture and a keener awareness of joy.

I wish we had loved Johnny more when he was alive. Of course we loved Johnny very much. Johnny knew that. Everybody knew it. Loving Johnny more. What does it mean? What can it mean, now?

Parents all over the earth who lost sons in the war have felt this kind of question, and sought an answer. To me, it means loving life more, being more aware of life, of one's fellow human beings, of the earth.

It means obliterating, in a curious but real way, the ideas of evil and hate and the enemy, and transmuting them, with the alchemy of suffering, into ideas of clarity and charity.

It means caring more and more about other people, at home and abroad, all over the earth. It means caring more about God.

I hope we can love Johnny more and more till we too die, and leave behind us, as he did, the love of love, the love of life.

PETER DE VRIES

De Vries's autobiographical novel (see p. 42) ends with these lines.

from *The Blood of the Lamb*

Time heals nothing—which should make us the better able to minister. There may be griefs beyond the reach of solace, but none worthy of the name that does not set free the springs of sympathy. Blessed are they that comfort, for they too have mourned, may be more likely the human truth. "You had a dozen years of perfection. That's a dozen more than most people get," a man had rather sharply told me one morning on the train. He was the father of one of Carol's classmates, a lumpish girl of no wiles and no ways, whose Boston mother had long since begun to embalm her dreams in alcohol. I asked him to join me sometime in a few beers and a game or two at the bowling alleys, where one often saw him hanging about alone. He agreed. Once I ran into Carol's teacher, Miss Halsey. "Some poems are long, some are short. She was a short one," Miss Halsey had summed up, smiling, with the late-Gothic horse face which guarantees that she will never read any poems, long or short, to any children of her own. Again the throb of compassion rather than the breath of consolation: the recognition of how long,

how long is the mourners' bench upon which we sit, arms linked in unde-
luded friendship, all of us, brief links, ourselves, in the eternal pity.

HOMER

*Superwarrior Achilleus, grieving the death of his friend Patroklos, kills
his enemy, the Trojan hero Hektor. But Hektor's death does not assuage
Achilleus' sorrow. His furious grief is so unrelenting that he repeatedly
drags Hektor's corpse behind a chariot, finally throwing him facedown in
the dust. Finally, even the gods turn on the immortal Achilleus, one of
their own, for his lack of compassion. Achilleus, says Apollo, is "like a lion
who when he has given way to his own great strength and his haughty
spirit, goes among the flocks of men, to devour them. So Achilleus has destroyed pity, and there is not in him any shame." Aided by the gods,
Priam, Hektor's grieving father, makes his way to Achilleus to beg for his
son's body so that he may bury it. Achilleus, who understands only
strength, marvels at the sudden appearance before him of the impressive,
godlike Priam. Ironically, it is from this father's grief that self-centered
Achilleus finally learns compassion, as the two sit on the long "mourners'
bench" together.*

from The Iliad of Homer, translated by Richmond Lattimore

But now Priam spoke to him in the words of a suppliant:
"Achilleus like the gods, remember your father, one who
is of years like mine, and on the door-sill of sorrowful old age.
And they who dwell nearby encompass him and afflict him,
nor is there any to defend him against the wrath, the destruction.
Yet surely he, when he hears of you and that you are still living,
is gladdened within his heart and all his days he is hopeful
that he will see his beloved son come home from the Troad.
But for me, my destiny was evil. I have had the noblest
of sons in Troy, but I say not one of them is left to me.
. . . .
Honour then the gods, Achilleus, and take pity upon me
remembering your father, yet I am still more pitiful;
I have gone through what no other mortal on earth has gone through;
I put my lips to the hands of the man who has killed my children."
So he spoke, and stirred in the other a passion of grieving

for his own father. He took the old man's hand and pushed him
gently away, and the two remembered, as Priam sat huddled
at the feet of Achilleus and wept close for manslaughtering Hektor
and Achilleus wept now for his own father, now again
for Patroklos. The sound of their mourning moved in the house. Then
when great Achilleus had taken full satisfaction in sorrow
and the passion for it had gone from his mind and body, thereafter
he rose from his chair, and took the old man by the hand, and set him
on his feet again, in pity for the grey head and the grey beard,
and spoke to him and addressed him in winged words: "Ah, unlucky,
surely you have had much evil to endure in your spirit.
How could you dare to come alone to the ships of the Achaians
and before my eyes, when I am one who have killed in such numbers
such brave sons of yours? The heart in you is iron. Come, then,
and sit down upon this chair, and you and I will even let
our sorrows lie still in the heart for all our grieving. There is not
any advantage to be won from grim lamentation.
Such is the way the gods spun life for unfortunate mortals,
that we live in unhappiness, but the gods themselves have no sorrows."

NORMAN MACLEAN

Norman Maclean and his brother grew up in Montana, sons of a Protestant minister. Not much given to talking, father and sons were closest when they were fly-fishing together in the Montana wilderness. Maclean's brother was high spirited. He lived recklessly and died young. Maclean went on to become a scholar of Shakespeare and the romantic poets and to teach English at the University of Chicago. But the problem of how to understand the death of someone young and promising obviously troubled Maclean all his life. His autobiographical novella A River Runs Through It *was published after he retired from teaching. The novella was made into a movie, which Robert Redford directed and narrated. Maclean worked on* Young Men and Fire *(see pp. 237 and 252) until he was overcome by a terminal illness.*

from *Young Men and Fire*

In a journey of compassion what we have ultimately as our guide is whatever understanding we may have gained along the way of ourselves and others, chiefly those close to us, so close to us that we have lived daily in their sufferings. From here on, then, in the blinding smoke it is no longer a "seeing world" but a "feeling world"—the pain of others and our compassion for them.

from *A River Runs Through It*

Now nearly all those I loved and did not understand when I was young are dead, but I still reach out to them.

Of course, now I am too old to be much of a fisherman, and now of course I usually fish the big waters alone, although some friends think I shouldn't. Like many fly fisherman in western Montana where the summer days are almost Arctic in length, I often do not start fishing until the cool of evening. Then in the Arctic half-light of the canyon, all existence fades to a being with my soul and memories and the sounds of the Big Blackfoot River and a four-count rhythm and the hope that a fish will rise.

Eventually, all things merge into one, and a river runs through it. The river was cut by the world's great flood and runs over rocks from the basement of time. On some of the rocks are timeless raindrops. Under the rocks are the words, and some of the words are theirs.

I am haunted by waters.

STEPHEN LEVINE

Levine brings a background of study and collaboration with spiritualist Ram Dass and psychiatrist Elisabeth Kübler-Ross to his books on pain, dying, and grief.

from *Who Dies?: An Investigation of Conscious Living and Conscious Dying*

The death of a child is a fire in the mind. The mind burns with alternatives that never come to pass, with fantasies of remarkable recuperations, with dreams of adult accomplishment. If we let this fire burn compassionately within us, the grief of the mind, the fantasies, the burning of the spirit, begin slowly to melt away and the child comes more into our heart. Our anguish can be used to open more fully, to enter as completely as we can into this final sharing. And then, as Rabindranath Tagore wrote in the final lines of his poem, *The End,* "Dear Auntie will come with presents and will ask,

'Where is our baby, Sister?' and Mother, you will tell her softly, 'He is in the pupils of my eyes. He is in my bones and in my soul.'"

RABINDRANATH TAGORE

Having lost two children, his wife, and his father within five years (see p. 244), the Indian poet and spiritual leader knew grief as well as anyone. In the "allness of the universe," Tagore sought the "lost sweet touch" we all try to feel again. The "overspreading pain" of separation, he wrote, "deepens into loves and desires, into sufferings and joys in human homes; and this it is that ever melts and flows in songs throughout my poet's heart."

from *Collected Poems and Plays of Rabindranath Tagore*

The End

It is time for me to go, mother; I am going.

When in the paling darkness of the lonely dawn you stretch out your arms for your baby in the bed, I shall say, "Baby is not there!"—mother, I am going.

I shall become a delicate draught of air and caress you; and I shall be ripples in the water when you bathe, and kiss you and kiss you again.

In the gusty night when the rain patters on the leaves you will hear my whisper in your bed, and my laughter will flash with the lightning through the open window into your room.

If you lie awake, thinking of your baby till late into the night, I shall sing to you from the stars, "Sleep, mother, sleep."

On the straying moonbeams I shall steal over your bed, and lie upon your bosom while you sleep.

I shall become a dream, and through the little opening of your eyelids I shall slip into the depths of your sleep; and when you wake up and look round startled, like a twinkling firefly I shall flit out into the darkness.

When, on the great festival of *puja,* the neighbours' children come and play about the house, I shall melt into the music of the flute and throb in your heart all day.

Dear auntie will come with *puja*-presents and will ask, "Where is our baby, sister?" Mother, you will tell her softly, "He is in the pupils of my eyes, he is in my body and my soul."

WILLIAM STAFFORD

William Stafford (see p. 230) introduces this poetry collection with the words, "Here is a package, / a program of passwords. / It is to bring strangers together." Ordinarily, "passwords" are secret words or phrases that open doors when spoken. But offered up by a bereaved parent like Stafford, "passwords" take on new meaning. Secret? Unknowable? Yes, to many. But to the already initiated—the grieving—these poems have a familiar sound, the sound of hard-earned wisdom that can only come from great loss.

from *Passwords: A Program of Words*

Consolations

"The broken part heals even stronger than the rest,"
they say. But that takes awhile.
And, "Hurry up," the whole world says.
They tap their feet. And it still hurts on rainy
afternoons when the same absent sun
gives no sign it will ever come back.

"What difference in a hundred years?"
The barn where Agnes hanged her child
will fall by then, and the scrawled words
erase themselves on the floor where rats' feet
run. Boards curl up. Whole new trees
drink what the rivers bring. Things die.

"No good thing is easy." They told us that,
while we dug our fingers into the stones
and looked beseechingly into their eyes.
They say the hurt is good for you. It makes
what comes later a gift all the more
precious in your bleeding hands.

Yes

It could happen any time, tornado,
earthquake, Armageddon. It could happen.

Or sunshine, love, salvation.
It could, you know. That's why we wake
and look out—no guarantees
in this life.

But some bonuses, like morning,
like right now, like noon,
like evening.

References

CHAPTER 1

p. 8   Anne Morrow Lindbergh, *Hour of Gold, Hour of Lead: Diaries and Letters of Anne Morrow Lindbergh 1929–1932* (New York: Harcourt Brace Jovanovich, 1973), 274.

p. 15   Andre Maurois, *Olympio: The Life of Victor Hugo* (New York: Harper and Brothers, 1956), 236.

p. 27   Margot Hornblower, "Grief and Rebirth," *Time,* 10 July 1995, 65.

CHAPTER 2

p. 31   Stephen Mitchell, *The Book of Job* (New York: HarperCollins, 1987), xvii.

p. 35   Robert Payne, *Dostoevsky: A Human Portrait* (New York: Alfred A. Knopf, 1960), 242.

p. 38   Don Auchin, "William Maxwell's Paper Tale," *The Baltimore Sun,* 8 June 1997, 4E.

p. 39   Gabriel Miller, *John Irving: Portrait of an Artist* (New York: Frederick Unger Publishing, 1982), 92.

p. 40   Piers Brendon, *Ike: His Life and Times* (New York: Harper and Row, 1986), 51.

p. 41   Albert Camus, *Resistance, Rebellion and Death,* trans. Justin O'Brien (New York: Alfred A. Knopf, 1960), 71.

CHAPTER 3

p. 60   Michael Schumacher, *Crossroads: The Life and Music of Eric Clapton* (New York: Disney Book Publishing, Hyperion, 1996), 299.

p. 77   Margaret Ferguson, Mary Jo Salter, and Jon Stallworthy, eds., *The Norton Anthology of Poetry,* 4th ed. (New York: W. W. Norton & Company, 1996), 1367–68.

CHAPTER 4

p. 92   Lord Birkenhead, *Rudyard Kipling* (New York: Random House, 1978), 277.

CHAPTER 5

p. 111   Jeffrey Meyers, *Robert Frost: A Biography* (Boston: Houghton Mifflin, 1996), 346.

p. 122   Linda Patterson Miller, ed., *Letters from the Lost Generation: Gerald and Sara Murphy and Friends* (New Brunswick and London: Rutgers University Press, 1991), 272.

p. 122 Harold S. Kushner, *When Bad Things Happen to Good People* (New York: Avon Books, 1981), 146.

p. 126 Emily W. Sunstein, *Mary Shelley: Romance and Reality* (Boston: Little, Brown and Company, 1989), 168–69.

CHAPTER 8

p. 179 Laurence Lerner, *Angels and Absences: Child Deaths in the Nineteenth Century* (Nashville and London: Vanderbilt University Press, 1997), 189.

p. 186 Gordon Livingston, "A Eulogy for Andrew," *Bereavement Magazine,* July/August 1996, 36.

p. 189 Natalie S. Bober, *A Restless Spirit: The Story of Robert Frost* (New York: Henry Holt and Company, 1991), 174.

p. 190 Jim Marks, "In the Country of Grief," *Book World,* 7 April 1996, 11.

CHAPTER 10

p. 231 Laura Lippman, "Touched by Magic," *The Baltimore Sun,* 25 November 1995, 1D.

p. 247 Charles Neider, ed., *The Autobiography of Mark Twain* (New York: Harper and Row, 1959), 219–20.

CHAPTER 11

p. 254 Sherwin B. Nuland, *How We Die: Reflections on Life's Final Chapter* (New York: Alfred A. Knopf, 1993), 201.

p. 255 Elizabeth Nowell, *Thomas Wolfe: A Biography* (Garden City, N.Y.: Doubleday, 1960), 26.

CHAPTER 12

p. 274 Natalie S. Bober, *A Restless Spirit: The Story of Robert Frost* (New York: Henry Holt and Company, 1991), 178.

p. 278 Edna St. Vincent Millay, *Collected Sonnets* (New York: Washington Square Press, 1959), xii.

p. 279 Barbara Kingsolver, *Animal Dreams* (New York: HarperCollins Publishers, 1990), 52–53.

About the Editors

MARY SEMEL is a psychotherapist in Baltimore, Maryland, where she lives with her husband, Peter. Her son, Alexander, was killed in an automobile accident in 1991. Her daughter, Hilary, practices maritime law in New York City.

A former newspaper reporter and feature writer, ANNE McCRACKEN lives in Baltimore with her husband, Tom, and their daughter, Hollis. She lost her son, Jake, in 1989.